ENTREPRENEURIAL FAMILY FIRMS

Frank Hoy

Worcester Polytechnic Institute
Worcester, Massachusetts

Pramodita Sharma

John Molson School of Business
Concordia University
Montreal

Prentice Hall

Boston • Columbus • Indianapolis • New York • San Francisco • Upper Saddle River • Amsterdam
Cape Town • Dubai • London • Madrid • Milan • Munich • Paris • Montreal • Toronto • Delhi
Mexico City • Sao Paulo • Sydney • Hong Kong • Seoul • Singapore • Taipei • Tokyo

Editorial Director: Sally Yagan
Editor in Chief: Eric Svendsen
Acquisitions Editor: Kim Norbuta
Editorial Project Manager: Claudia Fernandes
Director of Marketing: Patrice Lumumba Jones
Marketing Manager: Nikki Jones
Marketing Assistant: Ian Gold
Project Manager: Holly Shufeldt
Art Director: Jayne Conte

Manager, Rights and Permissions:
 Charles Morris
Full-Service Project Management:
 Sudip Sinha, Aptara®, Inc.
Composition: Aptara®, Inc.
Printer/Binder: Bind-Rite
Cover Printer: Bind-Rite
Text Font: Times Ten Roman

Credits and acknowledgments borrowed from other sources and reproduced, with permission, in this textbook appear on appropriate page within text.

Many of the designations by manufacturers and seller to distinguish their products are claimed as trademarks. Where those designations appear in this book, and the publisher was aware of a trademark claim, the designations have been printed in initial caps or all caps.

Library of Congress Cataloging-in-Publication Data
Hoy, Frank.
 Entrepreneurial family firms / Frank Hoy, Pramodita Sharma.
  p. cm.
 ISBN-13: 978-0-13-157711-4
 ISBN-10: 0-13-157711-5
 1. Family-owned business enterprises—Management. 2. Entrepreneurship.
  I. Sharma, Pramodita. II. Title.
 HD62.25.H69 2010
 658.4'21—dc22

2009018777

10 9 8 7 6 5 4 3 2 1

Prentice Hall
is an imprint of

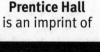

www.pearsonhighered.com

ISBN 10:   0-13-157711-5
ISBN 13: 978-0-13-157711-4

Dedication

To our families of origin and of attachment
As we cycle with them through life stages

Hoy, Stowe, and Echegaray families
(for Frank Hoy)

Dada, Joshi, and Sharma families
(for Pramodita Sharma)

BRIEF CONTENTS

CONTENTS

PREFACE

FAMILY BUSINESSES—THEY'RE EVERYWHERE!

Family business management is finally getting the recognition it deserves. Family-owned and managed firms dominate the economies in most nations in terms of the number of enterprises. Many institutions of higher education have organized executive education programs for the leaders of family-owned enterprises and have introduced courses on the subject into their degree programs. Why would they do this? Isn't running a family business just like running any other business? Obviously, the authors and publisher of this book think there is more to family business management than what is taught in the traditional business curriculum. It comes down to this: The family cannot be divorced from the business. If you ignore the influence of the family, you are missing the nuances of how the firm was organized, how its strategy was formulated, and how long it will survive. In this book, we use the cliché of "unscrambling eggs." We believe that the family and business become intertwined in subtle and not-so-subtle ways that need to be understood both by the family owners and by the nonfamily managers and employees who join the firm. And be assured, you will be involved with family businesses. If it is not your family that is directly involved, you may be working for one or have one as a customer or supplier or creditor or borrower. They are everywhere.

OBJECTIVES OF THE BOOK

The primary purpose of this book is to help you, the reader, launch or join and lead entrepreneurial ventures in which your family is involved. We call them entrepreneurial family firms—entities that progress across life-cycle stages of individuals, families, their businesses, industry, and economic environment. For creators of entrepreneurial family firms, your relatives may be partners, lenders, employees, or just supporters. The book is written to assist you to understand the intricate dynamics of handling the interactions and overlaps between the family and business systems. For those who may expect to join a family-owned firm, the book assists you by letting you know what to expect and how to prepare for it.

This book is directed at both college students, entrepreneurs, and their family members. We have drawn from the most recent empirical studies of family businesses as well as classic studies in the business and family literatures to give readers the foundation for making their companies and families function successfully.

As we focus on entrepreneurial family firms that create value across generations of leaders, this is not a book for the stereotypical "mom and pop" business that has little or no potential for growth. We are not writing for families who see their businesses as substitutes for working for someone else. Our aim is to help families prosper in their ventures, survive through generational transitions, and innovate and grow in the dynamic global economy. For many families, this includes helping relatives spin off new enterprises from the base business. The book is intended for those who want to go beyond mere administration, but who see themselves as creative opportunity seekers.

DISTINGUISHING FEATURES

What sets this book apart from others that address entrepreneurship or family business management? There are five features that make this book stand out.

COMBINING FAMILY BUSINESS AND ENTREPRENEURSHIP

The entrepreneurship literature stresses creation, and the family business literature stresses management. In this book, the two perspectives are brought together with a focus on innovation. What role does the family play in forming a venture out of an idea? How can the family govern a company in such a way to foster an innovative culture? And how can that culture be sustained across generations?

PROVIDING REAL LIFE EXAMPLES

This book represents a collaboration with *Family Business* magazine. The introductory stories for each chapter come directly from *Family Business* articles. In this way, we share the stories of real people who have faced situations similar to those that the reader may be facing or will face.

DRAWING FROM BOTH CLASSIC LITERATURE AND THE LATEST RESEARCH FINDINGS

As you read the book, you will discover that some of our references are from books and articles written 20, 30, or more years ago. Why include these "old" citations? Because these are the seminal pieces that formed how we look at the management and ownership of family firms. They contributed to directing the attention of researchers toward the critical issues that family business owners deal with. From this foundation, we add the most recent knowledge that scholars have published to give you the best information currently available for making your business a success.

BUILDING ON LIFE-CYCLE MODELS

Many authors have used life-cycle models to help us understand businesses generally and family businesses specifically. We draw from their contributions but add the interplay among life-cycle stages. We point out that life-cycle models have been applied not only to people and organizations, but also to products, technologies, industries, and families themselves. The stages of these cycles do not line up in convenient manners. We show how you can anticipate conflicts and formulate strategies based on how the cycles interrelate.

INTRODUCING PRACTICAL TOOLS

Although we introduce dominant entrepreneurship and family business theories, this book is intended to give you practical advice on making your business successful. We offer a variety of tools that entrepreneurial family businesses have found effective in fostering innovative behavior and keeping their ventures prosperous.

SUPPLEMENTS

At www.pearsonhighered.com/irc, the following supplements are available to adopting instructors for download (for detailed descriptions, please visit www.pearsonhighered.com/irc). Registration is simple and gives you immediate access to new titles and new editions. If you ever need assistance, our dedicated technical support team is ready to help with the media supplements that accompany this text. Visit http://247.pearsoned.com/ for answers to frequently asked questions and toll-free user support phone numbers.

- Instructor's Manual
- PowerPoint Slides

COMPANION WEB SITE   A useful companion Web site, www.prenhall.com/ entrepreneurship, offers free access to teaching resources for all books in the Prentice Hall Entrepreneurship Series including additional activities, links to latest research, sample entrepreneurship curriculum and syllabi, teaching tips, and web resource links.

COURSESMART TEXTBOOKS ONLINE   CourseSmart textbooks online is an exciting new choice for students looking to save money. As an alternative to purchasing the print textbook, students can subscribe to the same content online and save up to 50 percent off the suggested list price of the print text. With a CourseSmart etextbook, students can search the text, make notes online, print out reading assignments that incorporate lecture notes, and bookmark important passages for later review. For more information, visit www.coursesmart.com.

ACKNOWLEDGMENTS

The authors are especially indebted to Barbara Spector, Editor-in-Chief, and Caro Rock, Publisher, of *Family Business* Magazine. The opening stories for each chapter of this book were drawn from various issues of *Family Business*. We believe these stories bring to life the triumphs and tragedies of families in business, and that they will help readers see how they can keep their firms entrepreneurial. We are grateful to Barbara for guiding us in selecting and editing stories that fit the themes of our chapters.

This book has been in the making for over 18 months. For any extended project such as this, there are several individuals who work behind the scenes. Series editors Duane Ireland and Michael Morris tirelessly went through earlier versions of our chapters guiding us and challenging us to think in this virgin intellectual territory of the interface between entrepreneurship and family business studies. While their comments triggered us to start over in many instances, the final product is significantly superior because of their dedicated encouragement.

Our special gratitude goes to many of our colleagues who generously shared their experiences with us and continued to encourage us with this project. Of special note are – Jim Chrisman, Jess Chua, Pat Cole, Pat Frishkoff, John Hadjimarcou, Santiago Ibarreche, Kit Johnson, Ernesto Poza, Reg Litz, Justin Craig, and Mattias Nordqvist.

Without accepting support of our families' patience, we could not have devoted the countless weekends and long nights that went into the writing of this book. We acknowledge their generosity to letting us explore the world of entrepreneurial family firms. Our own experiences in such firms enabled us to bring insights that are sometimes only visible to those who work in family firms rather than those who view them from outside.

ABOUT THE AUTHORS

FRANK HOY is the Paul Beswick Professor of Entrepreneurship and Director of the Collaborative for Entrepreneurship & Innovation at Worcester Polytechnic Institute. He received his Ph.D. in Management from Texas A&M University. From 1991 to 2001, Dr. Hoy served as dean of the College of Business Administration at UTEP, where he launched UTEP's Family & Closely Held Business Forum. Prior to that appointment, he was at Georgia State University as the Carl R. Zwerner Professor of Family-Owned Businesses.

Dr. Hoy's research concentrations are family business, franchising and technology entrepreneurship. He is a former editor of *Entrepreneurship Theory and Practice*, and was the editor for Latin America for the *Journal of World Business*. Most recently, he edited a special issue of the *European Journal of International Management* on entrepreneurship in Europe. Hoy is a Fellow of the Family Firm Institute and of the International Family Enterprise Research Academy.

PRAMODITA SHARMA is a professor at the John Molson School of Business, Concordia University, in Canada, and serves as the editor of *Family Business Review*, the leading scientific journal devoted to publishing interdisciplinary research on family firms.

Her research on the dynamics underlying family firms has been honored with several international awards, including the NFIB Best Dissertation award from the entrepreneurship division of the Academy of Management. Supported by various private and government agencies, her research is well received both in academic and practitioner outlets.

Sharma takes an active leadership and advisory role in a number of professional associations such as FFI and the International Family Enterprise Research Academy (ifera). In 2005, she cofounded the annual *Family Enterprise Research Conference,* which provides a venue for family business scholars from around the globe to share their research and build professional networks.

Sharma maintains close links with the business community through her research and teaching activities in support of various international family business associations. She is a frequent speaker at gatherings of family business leaders around the world. These valuable experiences enable her to ground her research on issues of significant importance to the family business community.

CHAPTER 1

ENTREPRENEURIAL FAMILY FIRMS
POACHED OR SCRAMBLED EGGS?

In 2009, *Family Business* published a list of America's 100 largest family companies. Compiling such a list is a significant challenge by any measure. This list includes firms in which a single family controls the company's owner-ship, controlling family members are active in management (not necessarily holding the top management position though), and the family has been involved in the company for at least two generations. In other words, these are firms in which members of a family have the potential to exert significant influence on the strategic direction of a firm. This list was compiled in 2008 and used the most recent figures of revenues and numbers of employees available at that time. The five largest American family firms from 2009 are listed below:

1. * WAL-MART STORES, INC.

Walton family
Discount retail chain/Bentonville, AR
Founded: 1945
Revenues: $378.79 billion
Employees: 2.1 million
www.walmartstores.com

From a single store in Arkansas in 1962, founder Sam Walton (d. 1992) and younger brother James L. (Bud) Walton built Wal-Mart into the world's largest

---

* Denotes company whose stock is publicly traded.

retailer. It now has about 7,250 stores. Sam's descendants own about 40%. Sam's son, S. Robson Walton, 63, is the chairman.

2. * FORD MOTOR COMPANY

Ford family
Auto manufacturer/Dearborn, MI
Founded: 1903
Revenues: $172.45 billion
Employees: 246,000
www.ford.com

Pioneering auto firm now in fourth generation. Henry Ford (1863–1947) introduced mass production and dominated early auto market with Model T. His grandson Henry II (1917–1987) rebuilt the company as CEO, 1960–1980, with younger brother William (retired 1995) as finance committee chairman. William's son William Clay (Bill) Ford Jr., 51, now the executive chairman of the board of directors, served as president, CEO, and COO until naming Alan Mulally as his replacement in 2006. The Ford family owns about 40% of the voting stock.

3. KOCH INDUSTRIES, INC.

Koch family
Holding company/Wichita, KS
Founded: 1928
Revenues: $98 billion
Employees: 80,000
www.kochind.com

Fred C. Koch, who invented a crude oil refining process, founded a vast empire of oil and gas services, cattle ranches, coal mines, real estate ventures, and manufacturing facilities. In 1983, dissident sons Frederick and William filed suit contesting the $1.1 billion price that Charles and David (William's twin) paid for their brothers' share. The dissidents lost after 13 years; Charles, 73, and David, 68, control the company.

4. CARGILL, INC.

Cargill/MacMillan families
Commodities/Wayzata, MN
Founded: 1865
Revenues: $88.26 billion
Employees: 158,000
www.cargill.com

The company buys and sells grain, poultry, beef, steel, seeds, salt, and other commodities on six continents. Founder William Cargill and brothers provided grain elevators to store wheat after the Civil War. His Cargill and MacMillan descendants, now in the fourth and fifth generations, have run the firm ever since (with nonfamily CEOs). The company created one of the first management training programs in the 1930s. Whitney MacMillan, who retired in 1995 after 18 years as CEO, was the last family leader, although family members own about 90% of the company and several remain on the board.

5. CARLSON COS., INC

Carlson family
Travel, hotels, restaurants/Minnetonka, MN
Founded: 1938
Revenues: $37.1 billion
Employees: 176,000
www.carlson.com

Grocer's son Curtis Carlson (1914–1999) created Gold Bond Stamp Company with a $55 loan and built it into a conglomerate. Today, the company owns 972 hotels, including Radisson and Regent hotels. Carlson Company acquired business travel firm Navigant International in 2006. Ownership is shared by Curtis Carlson's two daughters, Marilyn Carlson Nelson, 68, and Barbara Gage, 65. The founder's son-in-law, Skip Gage, formerly president, left the company in 1991 with a piece of his own when the founder resumed control after successful bypass heart surgery. Carlson Wagonlit President and CEO Hubert Joly succeeded Marilyn Carlson Nelson as CEO of Carlson Companies in 2008; Nelson remains chairman. Nelson's son Curtis Nelson, former heir apparent, was fired by his mother; a legal battle ensued.

Source: America's largest family businesses, *Family Business.* www.familybusinessmagazine.com/largest_u.s.html, accessed January 4, 2009.

Questions

1. Name some other large corporations that are still owned and managed by members of the founding family. When were the companies formed? Which generation is running them today? (HINT: You may find this information by tracking the history of the firm and through the membership of the board of directors)
2. Does anyone in your family own a business? What family businesses can you identify where you live or go to school?

Who knew? When many of us think about family businesses, the first words that come to mind are "Mom & Pop." We think of the small, neighborhood business that may have been around a generation or two. Generally, we think of these as being low-growth or no-growth businesses. Given a few minutes to reflect, we might remember advertisements for S. C. Johnson, "A Family Company"; or recall seeing Bill Marriott in a commercial for the Marriott Hotel chain. Then it starts to register that there are some sizeable family enterprises in the market-place. Now look again at the companies listed by *Family Business* magazine as America's largest family firms—revenues in the billions, employees numbering in the hundreds of thousands. You can find a more extensive list at the magazine's Web site, www.familybusinessmagazine.com. Every one of these firms started and experienced growth as an entrepreneurial venture.

LONG-LIVED FIRMS: POACHED TO PERFECTION?

Longevity of a firm is a desirable objective as prosperous, long-lasting firms con-tribute to **value creation** for the founders, their descendants, employees, commu-nity, and the economy.[1] However, many fail at two critical junctures in the **life cycle** of the firm and its founder. Just as human beings are more vulnerable to illness during the first tender months of their lives and then in mature ages, the survival of business organizations has been most challenging at the start-up stages and then as the firm goes through leadership transitions, especially after long tenures of the founders.[2]

While starting and operating an independent business has long been acknowledged as the cornerstone of economic growth around the world,[3] sur-vival of these ventures at the start-up stage remains worrisome. According to the U.S. Small Business Administration,[4] 637,000 new employer firms were launched, while a staggering 560,000 firms closed their doors in the year 2007. Entrepreneurship scholars and policy makers who are interested in under-standing factors that enable opportunity identification and its exploitation to create something new that adds value to the economy[5] devote considerable efforts to understand the causes of failures of new ventures and provide rel-ated support.

In this book series, an **entrepreneur** is defined as one who creates a new ven-ture, whether in a start-up context or in an established organization (private, pub-lic, or nonprofit). Entrepreneurs are distinguished not because they necessarily came up with the idea, but because they implemented an innovative concept either successfully or unsuccessfully. The innovation could be in the form of

---

[1]Astrachan, J.H., Zahra, S.A., and Sharma, P. (2003). Family-Sponsored Ventures. Presented in New York on 29 April 2003 at the First Annual Global Entrepreneurship Symposium: The Entrepreneurial Advantage of Nations.

[2]McConaughy, D.L. (2000). Family CEO vs. nonfamily CEOs in the family controlled firm: An examination of the level and sensitivity of pay to performance. *Family Business Review, 13*(2): 121–131.

[3]Schumpeter, J.L. (1934). *The Theory of Economic Development: An Inquiry into Profits, Capital Credit, Interest, and the Business Cycle.* Cambridge, MA: Harvard University Press.

[4]http://www.sba.gov/advo/stats/sbfaq.pdf

[5]Shane, S., and Venkataraman, S. (2000). The promise of entrepreneurship as a field of research. *Academy of Management Review, 25*(1): 217–226.

establishing a new venture as done by *founders*, or by adopting new processes or systems within existing organizations, or developing new products or services, for existing or new markets, as done by *corporate entrepreneurs*.[6] From this perspective, founders of the huge firms listed by *Family Business* that we shared at the beginning of this chapter were successful entrepreneurs. Not only did they establish new ventures, they also led these entities through impressive success over generations of products, markets, and process innovations.

Entrepreneurs are not necessarily "born," although evidence indicates that many of those who establish new ventures were found to be raised in families with business owners.[7] Research suggests that while 77 percent of new ventures established in the United States are founded with significant involvement of family in the business, another 3 percent engage family members in business within two years of their founding.[8] This evidence highlights the fact that only about 20 percent of new ventures are established without any significant family involvement. Such ventures may be established by individual or *lone entrepreneurs*, or by *entrepreneurial teams* of nonrelated partners. As depicted in Figure 1.1, the study of entrepreneurship has largely been directed to understand new creations, including new ventures, products or services, markets, and processes— a precarious stage during which family involvement can contribute to making or breaking the business.

Family businesses are organizational entities in which either the individuals who established or acquired the firm *or* their descendants significantly influence the strategic decisions and life course of the firm,[9] leading to success or failure of the business. The family influence might be exerted through management and/or ownership of the firm.[10] As depicted in Figure 1.1, the study of family firms has largely focused on understanding the positive and negative impact of significant family influence in a business, often referred to as the **familiness**[11] of a firm. From

---

[6]Sharma, P., and Chrisman, J.J. (1999). Reconciling the definitional issues in the field of corporate entrepreneurship. *Entrepreneurship Theory and Practice,* 23(3): 11–27.

[7]Fairlie, R.W., and Robb, A. (2007). Families, human capital, and small business: Evidence from the characteristics of business owners survey. *Industrial and Labor Relations Review,* 60(2): 225–245.

[8]Chua, J.H., Chrisman, J.J., and Chang, E.P.C. (2004). Are family firms born or made? An exploratory investigation. *Family Business Review,* 17(1): 37–54.

[9]Chua, J.H., Chrisman, J.J., and Sharma, P. (1999). Defining the family business by behavior. *Entrepreneurship Theory & Practice,* 23(4): 19–39.

[10]Along these lines, in 2008, the European Group of Owner Managed and Family Enterprises (formally known as Groupement Européen des Enterprises Familiales [GEEF]) endorsed the following definition acceptable to a wide variety of family enterprises and across international boundaries. According to GEEF, a firm, of any size, is a family enterprise if (1) the majority of votes is in possession of the natural person(s) who established the firm, or in possession of the natural person(s) who has/have acquired the share capital of the firm, or in the possession of their spouses, parents, child or children's direct heirs; (2) the majority of votes may be indirect or direct; (3) at least one representative of the family or kin is involved in the management or administration of the firm; and (4) listed companies meet the definition of family enterprise if the person who established or acquired the firm (share capital) or their families or descendants possess 25 percent of the right to vote mandated by their share capital.

[11]Habbershon, T.G., and Williams, M.L. (1999). A resource-based framework for assessing the strategic advantage of family firms. *Family Business Review,* 12(1): 1–26.

FIGURE 1.1 Entrepreneurship and Family Business

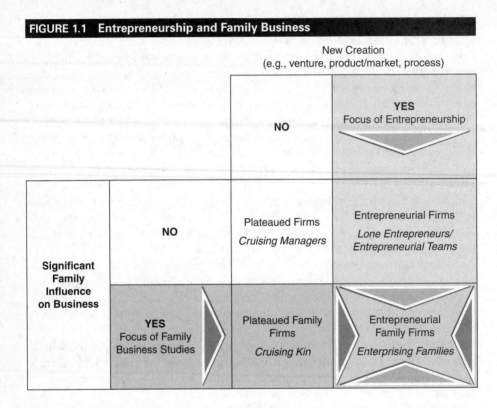

this perspective, all firms on the *Family Business* magazine list are successful family firms as they have sustained the drive and the entrepreneurial spirit that led to their formation. However, not all family firms achieve this level of success. Many fail during birth or in the tender years of infancy. Others survive the birthing process, grow to a certain level, and plateau due to the lack of infusion of new creations, as founders or their kin become comfortable with their employees, markets, and products or services.[12]

With the passage of time, firms can move from one cell to another as shown in Figure 1.1. For example, a firm created by a lone entrepreneur might transition into high family influence as next-generation members join the business.[13] Or, a firm that was launched with significant family involvement at the start-up stage might outgrow that stage to evolve into a lone or team entrepreneurial business, or even to be managed by plateaued kin or nonkin. Also, an entrepreneurial start-up may go into a pause mode in terms of new creations for some years and then regenerate itself to move back into being an entrepreneurial firm.

---

[12]Malone, S.C., and Jenster, P.V. (1992). The problem of the plateaued owner-manager. *Family Business Review,* 5(1): 25–42.
[13]Lansberg, I. (1999). *Succeeding Generations: Realizing the Dream of Families in Business.* Boston, MA: Harvard Business School Press.

This book is focused on **entrepreneurial family firms** that engage in innovative actions across generations of leaders, products, and economic life cycles. Large or small in size, such firms are influenced by enterprising families that create value across generations[14] and achieve longevity while sustaining their firm's competitive advantages over time. With family members significantly influencing strategic decisions of family firms, differentiating between the roles and responsibilities of governance and management is an important and complex issue.[15] While **management** provides leadership of operations and is responsible for the actual work of the company, **governance mechanisms** are aimed at establishing the overall strategy for the firm, including the extent and mode of family involvement in it, setting performance standards and codes of conduct so as to represent the owners of the firm and guide management. At the start-up stage of a firm and in small companies, an owner-manager is generally able to fulfill both roles of management and governance. However, as the firm and family move through life-cycle stages and their relationship becomes more complex, the roles become differentiated, necessitating adoption of varied governance mechanisms.

How can family influence imbue creativity in the very fabric of a firm with an aim toward enduring success? What governance mechanisms must be adopted at different stages of a firm's growth to support the infusion of creativity in a firm? What can be done to ensure that kin and nonkin working in the business do not fall into the trap of cruise control mode? Do entrepreneurial conditions differ in firms with or without significant family influence? What governance mechanisms can be used to ensure that the entrepreneurial spirit of the founders is transmitted across generations of family or nonfamily leaders? We address these issues in this book. Not only do we want you to understand the integral roles played by family in the creation of new ventures, but also our interest extends beyond this time frame as we discuss the positive and negative influences of a family over the life course of a business—both during and beyond the tenure of its founders.

For the firms that survive the first tender years and go through their course of life experiencing growth by beating the odds of failure during economic slowdowns and industry life-cycle changes, the limitations of human life span become a matter of concern as the founders approach retirement years. Alarmed by the challenges to the survival of healthy firms being caused by poor planning of leadership transition, family business scholars have devoted significant efforts to understand the causes of success and failure of such transitions.[16] While these efforts have enhanced understanding of the transition process, its antecedents,

---

[14]Habbershon, T.G., and Pistrui, J. (2002). Enterprising families domain: Family influenced ownership groups in pursuit of trans-generational wealth. *Family Business Review,* 15(3): 223–237.

[15]Gersick, K. (2006). *Generations of Giving: Leadership and Continuity in Family Foundations.* Lanham, MD: Lexington Books. p. 176.

[16]Sharma, P., Hoy, F., Astrachan, J.H., and Koiranen, M. (2007). The practice-driven evolution of family business education. *Journal of Business Research,* 60:1012–1021.

and its consequences,[17] the challenge to fully understand this phenomenon remains.

A recent survey[18] of successful American family companies that generate annual revenues greater than $5 million found that members of the baby boom generation[19] and their elders were anticipating retirement. Nearly 30 percent of the founders who responded were over 65 years of age and another 30 percent were between 55 and 64 years old. Although 80 percent of the senior generation wanted to see the business remain in their family, less than a third developed succession plans, and only about 40 percent identified a successor. A stunning 93 percent had no income diversification, as the family firm was the primary source of income and security of the family.

One could argue that with longer life expectancies, high energy levels, and optimism that are typical of successful founders, perhaps it is too early to worry about leadership transition in many of these firms. However, with shorter business cycles in an economic world where people, information, and goods move freely across national boundaries, the need for continuous regeneration of the business and planning for seamless transitions is critical to ensure the longevity of any business. Against this backdrop, family firms interested in retaining their influence on the strategic direction of a firm across generations must overcome additional challenges. Not only do they need to determine and make the difficult choices of whether to select family or nonfamily members to lead the firm, different generations of family members must also learn how to work together so as to ensure that their influence on the firm enables its smooth functioning. Governance structures must be established to nourish and cherish the entrepreneurial spirit of members throughout different phases of their lives. Given the reigning culture of individualism in many parts of the world today, the changing nature of family structures, and the significantly different life experiences of each generation of family members, learning to effectively work in a multigenerational leadership group creates additional challenges.[20]

In this time of intense competition and challenging economic conditions on a global scale, firms do not enjoy the luxury of pausing to focus on leadership transitions while leaving the enterprise on cruise control, as competitors move quickly to fill in the gap. How can busy entrepreneurs who must engage in continuous efforts to keep at the top of the competitive game find the precious time to prepare the next generation of leaders? How can the vision and burning desire for longevity and continuous regeneration be transmitted to future leaders, when transmittal of such values can be a slow, time-consuming process? How can one train oneself and others to progress from engaging and harnessing personal energy

---

[17]Le Breton Miller, I., Miller, D., and Steier, L. (2004). Toward an integrative model of effective FOB succession. *Entrepreneurship Theory & Practice,* 28:305–328.

[18]http://www.familybusinesssurvey.com/survey/survey.htm

[19]Born 1946 to 1964.

[20]Gersick, K.E., Davis, J.A., Hampton, M.M., and Lansberg, I. (1997). *Generation to Generation: Life Cycles of the Family Business.* Cambridge, MA: Harvard Business School Press.

and efforts to developing an ability of effectively working with others, and then graduating to learning how to work through others?[21] Experience suggests that it takes determination, perseverance, and the most precious of all resources in the life an entrepreneur—time.

DIVERSITY IN START-UP MOTIVES

In 1962, four discount retailers were launched in the United States: Kmart, Target, Wal-Mart, and Woolco. Each of these retailers was an opportunistic adaptation of already existing successful chain stores—Sebastian Kresge's "five-and-dime" stores led to the birth of Kmart; George Dayton of "Dayton Stores" unveiled Target; brothers Frank and Charles of "Woolworth stores" founded Woolco; and "Walton's Family Center" stores of brothers Sam and Bud Walton lead to the creation of Wal-Mart. As the discount retailing industry continues to grow in the United States and globally, all these firms should be getting excited about celebrating their 50th anniversary in a few years. But, life has taken a different course for each of these innovative entrepreneurial creations of the early 1960s.

Woolco is a memory in U.S. history. The chain was acquired by Wal-Mart in 1983. Kmart closed 110 stores in 1994 and later merged with Sears, creating the Sears Holding Corporation in 2005. Today, the merged corporation operates stores under both Sears and Kmart brands. As of January 2007, Target retail chain consisted of more than 1,500 stores generating close to $60 billion in revenues and employing more than 350,000 employees. With aggressive plans to have 2,000 stores by the end of 2010, Target's growth is remarkable. The biggest success story is Wal-Mart, with about 7,200 stores around the world that generated revenues greater than $378 billion in 2007 and employed more than 2.1 million. According to *Family Business* magazine, Wal-Mart tops the list not only of America's, but also of the world's largest family firms.[22] It tops the *Fortune's* Global 500 list[23] of all corporations, leaving huge oil companies such as Exxon Mobil, Royal Dutch Shell, and British Petroleum trailing behind in terms of revenues.

When the Walton brothers built their first Wal-Mart store in Rogers, Arkansas, with Sam and his wife, Helen,[24] putting up 95 percent of the start-up money for this store, no one could have guessed the growth trajectory this new venture was going to experience. Because of this remarkable little engine of economic growth, the Walton family, which controls about 40 percent of the

---

[21]Hoy, F., and Verser, T.G. (1994). Emerging business, emerging field: Entrepreneurship and the family firm. *Entrepreneurship Theory & Practice*, Fall: 9–23.

[22]*Source*: The World's 250 Largest Family Businesses, *Family Business*, www.familybusinessmagazine.com/topglobal.html.

[23]*Source: Fortune Global 500* http://money.cnn.com/magazines/fortune/global500/2007/

[24]Daughter of a prosperous banker and rancher L.S. Robson, Helen Robson (later Walton) was the valedictorian of her high school class and a graduate of the University of Oklahoma at Norman with a degree in business.

company's stock, is the richest family in the world with a net worth in 2007 estimated to exceed $80 billion.

Although gigantic in size and swift in growth, the company is still young in age. Sam's son Rob Walton, now in his 60s, is the company chairman, while Michael T. Duke, who joined the company in 1995, is the president and CEO. Will Wal-Mart endure and join some of the longest-surviving enterprises[25] of the world, such as Japanese innkeepers Hoshi Ryokan, being run by the 46th generation of the founding family; Italian glassmaker Barovier & Toso, managed by the 20th generation of family members; and America's Avedis Zildjian cymbal company, now in the 14th generation of family ownership? Or, will its course follow that of the many promising new ventures that prosper during the lifetime of capable industrious entrepreneurs, linger along for a few generations in the shadow of the founder,[26] only to experience their sad demise? Only time will tell.

If Sam, Helen, and Bud were able to inculcate the entrepreneurial spirit in members of their next generation and successfully pass on the values of integrity, conscientiousness, commitment, and generous sharing in their descendants,[27] perhaps Wal-Mart will prosper for many future generations. On the other hand, if Rob and other members of subsequent generations of Waltons cannot carry on the innovative spirit of the founders or if they begin to cruise on the successes of the past, competitors such as Target and other newer ones will be eager to erode their market share, leading to stagnated growth and eventual demise. What can be done to ensure that family firms such as Wal-Mart continue on a positive spiral in terms of their performance on both family and business dimensions?[28] We address this important question in this book.

Before we get too far into sharing our perspectives on pathways that can enable entrepreneurial growth and longevity of family enterprises, we want to acknowledge that not all ventures are launched with an eye toward perpetuity or growth.[29] Many are launched with an aim to harvest returns through a lucrative sale of the business.[30] For such entrepreneurial ventures, closing an attractive buyout deal may be the ultimate desired objective, indicating a successful closure. Others may have been launched to help support the next generation in preparing for professional careers, with no desire for continuity of the business entity

---

[25]*Source*: The World's Oldest Family Companies, *Family Business,* http://www.familybusinessmagazine.com/oldworld.html

[26]Davis, P.S., and Harveston, P.D. (1999). In the founder's shadow: Conflict in the family firm. *Family Business Review,* 12(4): 311–323.

[27]Chrisman, J.J., Chua, J.H., and Sharma, P. (1998). Important attributes of successors in family businesses: An exploratory study. *Family Business Review,* 11(1): 19–34.

[28]Sharma, P. (2004). An overview of the field of family business studies: Current status and directions for future. *Family Business Review,* 17(1): 1–36.

[29]Hoy, F., and Sharma, P. (2008). Entrepreneurial governance in the family firm. *Family Business Magazine Shareholder's Handbook.*

[30]Tagiuri, R., and Davis, J.A. (1992). On the goals of successful family companies. *Family Business Review,* 5(1): 43–62.

itself.[31] A profitable sale of such a firm, as the next generation graduates with professional qualifications, may indicate an achievement of a lifelong career objective for both generations involved. There are other rational reasons why a profitable enterprise may disappear. Occasionally, there are forces beyond the control of the owners and managers: natural disasters, unexpected economic downturns, premature deaths in the family, no heirs to carry forward the venture, and so on. These are only some examples of reasons why a firm may be not be transitioned across generations of a family.

While not all businesses are created with a desire to perpetuate them after the career and life span of the founders, those desiring to join the successful legacy family firms such as Corning, Fidelity Investments, Hallmark, Laird Norton Tyee, Molsons, and S. C. Johnson, among many others, do not force innovation and family control into an either/or choice. Instead, such entrepreneurial family firms learn to master the "genius of 'and,'" as observed by Collins and Porras in *Built to Last,* and more recently identified by Miller and Le-Breton Miller in their study of century-old firms.[32]

ENTERPRISING FAMILIES AND ENTREPRENEURIAL FIRMS

If a venture is created with a dream to flourish throughout the life span of the founder and last beyond one generation, it is essential to engage in creativity, innovation, and regeneration through different life stages of the firm, family, and individuals involved in it. In this book series, **innovation** refers to the conversion of knowledge and ideas into benefits, which may be for commercial use or the public good, and which may include new or improved products, processes, or services. Leaders of entrepreneurial family businesses possess an orientation toward innovation sparked by an awareness to regenerate for intergenerational value creation. **Family business innovation** is the generation or introduction of novel processes or products as a consequence of interactions between family members of one or more generations.[33]

As depicted in Figure 1.1, entrepreneurship and family business scholars have been drawn to understand two critical stages of a firm's life. Although some notable exceptions exist mainly under the rubric of corporate entrepreneurship studies, a large majority of entrepreneurship scholarship has been focused on seeking and exploiting opportunities to enable the successful creation of new

---

[31]Davis, S.M. (1992). Characteristics of African American family-owned businesses in Los Angeles. *Family Business Review,* 5(4): 373–395; Wong, B., McReynolds, S., and Wong, W. (1992). Chinese family firms in the San Francisco Bay areas. *Family Business Review,* 5(4): 355–372.

[32]Miller, D., and Le-Breton Miller, I. (2005). *Managing for the Long Run: Lessons in Competitive Advantage from Great Family Businesses.* Boston, MA: Harvard Business School Press.

[33]Litz, R.A., and Kleysen, R.F. (2001). Your old men shall dream dreams, your young men shall see visions: Toward a theory of family firm innovation with help from the Brubeck family. *Family Business Review,* 14(4): 341.

ventures.[34] Given the large number of ventures that open and close their doors within the first few years of their life, such attention is clearly warranted.

Family business scholars, on the other hand, have largely been interested in what happens when the founders approach the dusk of their working lives. Succession has remained the most studied topic in this literature throughout its evolution.[35] Given the large number of firms that are to undergo leadership transitions around the world within the next two decades, the low level of preparation to successfully overcome this critical juncture,[36] and succession challenges being ranked as the number one concern of family business owners,[37] attention to succession issues is appropriate.

Although both entrepreneurship and family business studies are adding to our knowledge,[38] not much attention is being paid to what happens after a successful enterprise has been created and before the founder approaches retirement years. One might assume that only good, basic management practices are needed between these two critical stages of firms', founders', and family's life. But such an assumption can only lead to disappointment. Knowledge transfer is sticky and time-consuming.[39] Kindling and nurturing of the entrepreneurial spirit and the transmission and absorption of values take time, diligence, and perseverance. The process of ensuring there is a viable, sustainable enterprise that will last over centuries cannot be undertaken in a hurry. Patient investment of time is required to prepare both the senior and junior generations of leaders for their respective roles in/out of the firm and to brace the firm so that it is well positioned to enjoy sustainable competitive advantages.

SCRAMBLED EGGS: ENTREPRENEURIAL FAMILY FIRMS

Enterprising families[40] seeking transgenerational wealth creation understand the importance of continuous innovation and regeneration through all stages of their existence so as to ensure longevity. Scholars who have given careful thought to

[34]Dyer Jr., W.G., and Handler, W. (1994). Entrepreneurship and family business: Exploring the connections. *Entrepreneurship Theory & Practice*, Fall: 71–83.

[35]Chrisman, J.J., Chua, J.H., and Sharma, P. (2005). Trends and directions in the development of a strategic management theory of the family firm. *Entrepreneurship Theory & Practice*, September issue: 555–575.

[36]http://www.familybusinesssurvey.com/survey/survey.htm

[37]Chua, J.H., Chrisman, J.J., and Sharma, P. (2003). Succession and non-succession concerns of family firms and agency relationships with nonfamily managers. *Family Business Review*, 16(2): 89–107.

[38]Katz, J.A. (2003). The chronology and intellectual trajectory of American entrepreneurship education 1987–1999. *Journal of Business Venturing*, 18(2): 283–300; Sharma, P., Hoy, F., Astrachan, J.H., and Koiranen, M. (2007). The practice-driven evolution of family business education. *Journal of Business Research*, 60: 1012–1021.

[39]Szulanski, G. (1995). Unpacking stickiness: An empirical investigation of the barriers to transfer of best practices inside the firm. *Academy of Management Journal*, 38: 437–441.

[40]Habbershon, T.G., and Pistrui, J. (2002). Enterprising families domain: Family-influenced ownership groups in pursuit of transgenerational wealth. *Family Business Review*, 15(3): 223–237.

whether entrepreneurship and family business studies are distinct or overlapping fields[41] come to the conclusion that for those wanting both prosperity and longevity of their firm, the two have to be woven into a smooth tapestry. Careful understanding and study of different life-cycle stages of individuals, firms, and families is necessary to exploit the development and learning opportunities provided by each stage of life.

As shown in Figure 1.1, most firms start and experience growth as entrepreneurial ventures. Moreover, four out of every five new ventures are created with significant family involvement in the business.[42] Although many founders may not think of the new venture as a family enterprise, family members often participate at the inception as sources of financing, by providing paid or free labor, as customers or suppliers, or as part of the start-up team, as in the cases of Woolco and Wal-Mart. Parents and other relatives make loans or even gifts to the entrepreneur. They may invest and take ownership shares or supply in-kind support by donating furniture, equipment, vehicles, or other tangible items that enable the new business owner to avoid cash outlays. A new entrepreneur may be spinning off her own business from her parents' firm. In a recent study, more than 50 percent of new ventures were found to be created by individuals who had a self-employed family member.[43]

Over time, however, the legend of the founder takes root while the critical roles played by family members merge into the background.[44] For example, while Sam Walton is depicted as a visionary, larger-than-life entrepreneur, he documented the significant role his wife, Helen, his brother Bud, and other family members such as his father, Helen's father and brothers, and their children played in the crucial start-up years of Wal-Mart.[45]

As firms grow, family members may continue to provide capital or may make assets available to collateralize loans. They may have social or professional networks to which they can introduce the entrepreneur. These contacts in turn may facilitate access to funds, to customers, to employees, and to other opportunities. Bill Gates, another celebrated entrepreneur of our time, benefited from the connections of his family. Cringley[46] noted that Mary Gates (Bill's mother) and IBM's chairman John Opel served on the national board of United Way and

---

[41]Hoy, F., and Verser, T.G. (1994). Emerging business, emerging field: Entrepreneurship and the family firm. *Entrepreneurship Theory & Practice,* Fall: 9–23; Zahra, S. (2007). *Looking Outwards: Family Firms & New Business Creation.* Keynote speech at the International Family Enterprise Research Academy's (ifera) annual conference, June, Germany.

[42]Aldrich, H.E., and Cliff, J.E. (2003). The pervasive effects of family on entrepreneurship: Toward a family embeddedness perspective. *Journal of Business Venturing,* 18(5): 573–596.

[43]Fairlie, R.W., and Robb, A. (2007). Families, human capital, and small business: Evidence from the characteristics of business owners survey. *Industrial and Labor Relations Review,* 60(2): 225–245.

[44]Steier, L. (2007). New venture creation and organization: A familial sub-narrative. *Journal of Business Research,* 60: 1099–1107.

[45]Walton, S., and Huey, J. (1992). *Made in America: My Story.* New York: Bantam.

[46]Cringley, R.X. (1992). *Accidental Empires: How the Boys of Silicon Valley Make Their Millions, Battle Foreign Competitors, and Still Can't Get a Date.* Reading, MA: Addison-Wesley.

became good friends. This social connection was instrumental in Microsoft's clinching its first major deal. In maturing companies, members of succeeding generations may help to turnaround stagnant firms or to identify new entrepreneurial options for future growth.[47] As and when the need arises, family members generously provide the physical, financial, social, and emotional resources.[48]

Enterprising families seeking multigenerational survival and success engage in opportunity recognition and exploitation as years roll by. Patient investments of time are made to cultivate a culture that tolerates change and failure so as to embed the entrepreneurial spirit in both the family and its enterprise. Selfless sharing and generous receiving continue through various life-cycle stages of the firm and the individuals in it, although it is recognized that the identity of the giver and recipient, as well as the content of exchanges, changes over time. Entrepreneurial governance in both family and nonfamily firms does not occur exclusively at the creation of a venture or at the time of management and ownership transition. Instead, for longevity of an enterprise, opportunity recognition and exploitation must become the dominant mode. The structure of an organization can make or break the process, and external experts can be of vital help.[49] However, the process must begin with the entrepreneur, and its ripple effects will carry through each life stage of this individual, his/her family, and the enterprise.

VOYAGE OF DISCOVERY

Treat this book as a voyage of discovery. Here, we lift the veil that presents the external face of a business to the commercial world. Behind that veil are the people who make the business what it is and take it where it goes. Entrepreneurs are human—people with strengths and weaknesses, acting on logic and with emotion, applauding each other, and battling each other. In the family business arena, we begin with the recognition that not every enterprise is run as the textbooks would teach us. Those who pretend that family influences do not exist in the business world will experience much frustration and even failure. Our purpose is to find ways to use those influences as pathways to success, not just at the two critical junctures of an enterprise's life—creation and leadership transition—but through all life-cycle changes of the involved individuals, their families, enterprise itself, and the economy.

Understanding how family businesses can be governed in entrepreneurial ways requires more than "war stories." We can provide countless anecdotes about

---

[47]Malone, S.C., and Jenster, P.V. (1992). The problem of the plateaued owner-manager. *Family Business Review,* 5(1): 25–42.

[48]Sirmon, D.G., and Hitt, M.A. (2003). Managing resources: Linking unique resources, management, and wealth creation in family firms. *Entrepreneurship Theory and Practice,* 27(4):339–358; Stewart, A. (2003). Help one another, use one another: Toward an anthropology of family business. *Entrepreneurship Theory and Practice,* 27(4): 383–396.

[49]For a listing of family business consultants in your region, check the Family Firm Institute Web site, www.ffi.org

advantages and disadvantages of working with family members. We can cite phe-
nomenal successes and abysmal failures, comedy and tragedy, hope and despair.
However, useful education offering practical value in life demands that we examine entrepreneurship and family business from a framework that will help you
grasp and manage the complexity of these enterprises and of working with those
you love.[50] Unique cases are fascinating, but overwhelming. It is helpful to find a
lens that will put complexity into perspective.

We use the perspective of life cycles as the foundation for examining the
family and business. We do this because life-cycle models have been found to
have value in understanding problems and opportunities that arise at various
stages and in identifying strategies and tactics that are useful in addressing those
problems and opportunities. Scholars[51] in business administration transferred
life-cycle applications from biologists, first applying them to the introduction and
marketing of new products. Individual, organizational, and family life-cycle
stages have been studied in the literatures of psychology, management, and family
studies. Furthermore, life-cycle models have proven to be of value in studying
organizations, markets, technologies, managers, employees, and other aspects of
business. In this book, we bring together these models to help prepare you to participate in and lead entrepreneurial family firms.

We are especially interested in the governance of the family firm. How are
entrepreneurial attitudes and behaviors infused and executed? Who are the decision makers? How and why do they innovate in new directions? How and when
are nonfamily members brought into leadership roles? Why did four generations
of Fords hold leadership positions in the firm, while Wal-Mart has had only one
Walton in the CEO position? At the time this book is being written, neither company has a family member as CEO, but both have family members serving as
chairman of their respective boards. What does this suggest about family control?

In the chapters ahead, we strive to answer these questions and more in the
context of life cycles. Furthermore, we will look at interactions among life cycles.
What conflicts result from the owner being at one stage and the successor being
at another? How does an entrepreneur reaching maturity respond when taking
over an enterprise with products or markets in decline? What happens when key
executives, organizations, technologies, customers, and owners are all at different
life-cycle stages? What strategies work for governing the firm and for maintaining the family? While our knowledge of life cycles does not guarantee successful
outcomes, it can help in understanding and managing the dilemmas.

The ultimate aim of an enterprise is **value creation**—for the founders
through a sense of accomplishment, growth, and achievement; for the family via a
sense of harmony, security, and growth of the collective; for the business through
sustained profits and growth; and for the community by satisfying customer

---

[50]Jaffe, D.T. (1991). *Working with the Ones You Love: Strategies for a Successful Family Business.*
Berkeley, CA: Conari Press.
[51]Kimberly, J.R., Miles, R.H., and Associates. (1980). *The Organizational Life Cycle: Issues in the
Creation, Transformation, and Decline of Organizations.* San Francisco, CA: Jossey-Bass Publishers.

needs while generating employment and contributing to the societal prosperity. Before we can understand how enterprising families create value for the involved individuals, their families, business, and community, it would be helpful to reflect on the various life-cycle stages.

This introductory chapter is followed by Part A of the book entitled "Entrepreneurial Family Firms: Cycling through the (St)ages." This part consists of five chapters, the first four of which deal with "stages of life" as we examine the life-cycle stages of individuals (Chapter 2), families (Chapter 3), business (Chapter 4), and macro environmental factors such as product, industry, and economy (Chapter 5). This examination better equips us to understand the secrets of enterprising families that enable the individual players, families, and businesses to prosper over many generations. The last chapter of this part (Chapter 6) is devoted to understanding the nature of different forms of resources—human, social, financial, and physical—that are exchanged between family and business as each goes through various life stages.

Part B of the book—"Entrepreneurship through the Stages"—highlights the opportunities, problems, and strategies that can be effectively used at different stages of a venture's life. Chapters 7 to 10 go through the start-up, growth, maturity, and decline/renewal stages. In each of these stages, implications of overlaying the business with other life cycles are discussed as varied resources are exchanged. We discuss how entrepreneurial actions and conditions for entrepreneurship vary across these different stages.

Part C of the book—"Entrepreneurial Family Firms: Success through Life Stages"—consists of two chapters that conclude our voyage. Chapter 11 discusses the governance mechanisms that are likely to sustain and grow the entrepreneurial spirit of an organization, and its leaders are highlighted. In the final chapter, we reflect on lessons learned and directions where the knowledge creation cart might be turned toward next to further enhance our understanding of entrepreneurial governance of family businesses through different stages of life.

Summary

- Innovation and creativity are the lifeblood of entrepreneurial firms.
- Family firms are distinguished from others because of significant family influence in a firm.
- Long-term survival and prosperity for a family business is reliant on intelligent application of entrepreneurial practices by the leaders of family businesses.
- Family-owned and managed businesses dominate most economies in a number of firms.
- Few realize how many large and influential corporations are also family businesses, for example, Wal-Mart and Ford Motor Company.
- Family issues will impact the management and success of a firm and will not be resolved by applying standard business practices.
- Virtually all of us are touched by family businesses in our lives and careers with more frequency than we realize. By understanding the dynamics of the family

and business relationship, we are more likely to achieve personal and professional goals in dealing with those businesses.

- Enterprising families ensure that the entrepreneurial spirit of the founders is nourished through the later generations of family through entrepreneurial family firms that create value across generations.
- Life-cycle models are useful tools for understanding interrelationships in the family enterprise.

Discussion Questions

1. What family businesses have you worked for, purchased from, sold to, or interacted with in any way? Was the family involvement obvious to you?
2. What do you consider to be a family business? A husband and wife working together? Does it require two generations? If a family owns a business, but hires nonfamily managers, is it still a family business?
3. What is an entrepreneurial business?
4. We have argued that even if a business is entrepreneurial at one stage of its life, it does not guarantee that it will be entrepreneurial at the next stage of life. Do you agree? Why or why not? Share examples to highlight your thoughts.
5. Which of the following qualifies as a family business:
   a. A real estate company managed by a mother and son, but the firm is owned by someone else.
   b. A gay or lesbian couple owning and operating a restaurant.
   c. The founder of a lumber company who is passing the ownership to his son-in-law.
   d. A motel franchise owned by an unmarried, cohabiting couple.
   e. A software company started by two unrelated college roommates, financed by their respective parents.
6. Which of your relatives would you like to own and manage a business with? Which one would you never want to be in business with? Why?
7. What did you want to do for a living 10 years ago? If you were to start a business today, what would it be? What kind of business would you like to have 20 years from now?

Learning Exercises

1. Working in a small group of three to four students, analyze the current environmental factors, which can influence a new venture. Given these environmental factors, what kind of businesses would you want to start or which existing business would you want to change? Would you want to involve any family members in your new venture? If so, in what capacity (as part of the management, financial resources, and so on)?
2. Visit the *Family Business* magazine Web site (www.familybusinessmagazine. com). Find other old and successful family firms and describe what they

attribute to their enduring success? Is there any other advice present within the Web site, which would allow them to continue their success?

Other Resources

- Aronoff, C.E., Ward, J.L., and Astrachan, J.H. (Eds). (2002). *Family Business Sourcebook,* 3rd ed. Family Enterprise Publishers: Atlanta, GA.
- *Family Business* magazine, www.familybusinessmagazine.com
- The Family Firm Institute, www.ffi.org
- United States Small Business Administration, www.sba.gov

PART A

ENTREPRENEURIAL FAMILY FIRMS: CYCLING THROUGH THE (ST)AGES OF LIFE

In Chapter 1, we described the dominance and diversity of the family firm phenomenon in the global marketplace and introduced some of the complexities of the relationships between family and business. We also mentioned that life-cycle models are a valuable means to understand the challenges and problems that may arise at different stages in the life of an enterprise, providing cues for the effective governance of these firms. Entrepreneurial family firm leaders have to contend with a multitude of interacting and often conflicting life cycles[1] of individual, family, organization, economy, industry, and products that their venture is involved in over time. Given the scrambled nature of these life cycles in family firms, inappropriate response to changes occurring in one dimension can cause ripple effects in other dimensions as well, creating a negative spiral of performance.

Part A of this book aims to help you understand the lessons that leaders of entrepreneurial family firms can draw from what has been learned in the study of life-cycle models. The first four chapters of this section focus on understanding the individual (Chapter 2), family (Chapter 3), organizational (Chapter 4), and macroenvironmental (Chapter 5) life-cycle models and their influences on entrepreneurial family firms. Chapter 6 discusses various resources that get exchanged between the family and business systems over the course of time in

---

[1]Hoy, F. (1995). The owner and the firm: When life cycles collide. *Small Business Forum*, 13(3): 73–81.

entrepreneurial family firms. This introductory section addresses some fundamental questions related to life cycles and briefly introduces each chapter in Part A of this book.

WHAT IS A LIFE CYCLE?

According to Merriam-Webster's dictionary, **life cycle** is a *series of stages through which something (as an individual, culture, or manufactured product) passes during its lifetime.*[2] It has been described as a navigational chart that gives the latitude and longitude and certain features of the territory, without the geographical detail.[3] It is not a blueprint for the concrete course of a person's life, but we can understand the current pattern of one's life in the context of life-cycle stages. Knowledge of developmental stages is useful to facilitate appropriate action and avoid overreaction when little or no action is needed.[4]

The underlying assumption in models of life-cycle stages is that the lives of human beings, collective social entities such as families and organizations, products, industries, and even economies can be divided into distinct phases or stages. Each developmental stage in life is characterized by unique features offering distinct opportunities and challenges. Gradual incremental development occurring in each stage is punctuated by rapid and discontinuous change as transition is made from one stage to the next. Decisions made in each stage influence the array of possibilities in subsequent stages. It is notable that the choices made at the birth stage have a significant bearing on the trajectory of the life course.[5] A **standard life-cycle** model is displayed in Figure A1 showing the four stages of birth, growth, maturity, and decline, leading to death or renewal.

DO LIFE-CYCLE MODELS *ALWAYS* HAVE FOUR STAGES AS SHOWN IN FIGURE A1?

No, in fact, as you will note in the ensuing chapters, life cycles can be represented in many different ways and can be drawn with more or fewer stages, depending on the users' intent. For example, in the entrepreneurship literature, we might find stages that precede birth, emphasizing the efforts necessary

---

[2]http://www.merriam-webster.com/dictionary/life%20cycle
[3]Levinson, D.J. (1996). *The Season's of a Woman's Life.* New York: Alfred Knopf.
[4]Becvar, D.S., and Becvar, R.J. (1999). *Systems Theory and Family Therapy.* 2nd ed. New York: University Press of America.
[5]Ling, Y., Zhao, H., and Baron, R.A. (2007). Influence of founder—CEOs personal values on firm performance: Moderating effects of firm age and size. *Journal of Management,* 33(5): 673–696.

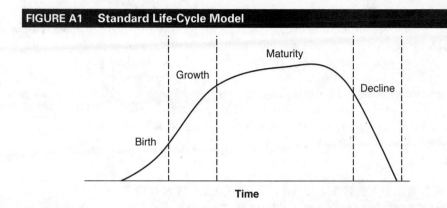

FIGURE A1   Standard Life-Cycle Model

to identify an opportunity and launch a venture. In the study of family enterprises, we focus most frequently on the existing firm and the interactions of family members and nonfamily members during the life of the venture. And we always recognize that not every business follows the same pattern. For example, many never survive beyond the birth stage in order to grow and achieve maturity.

HAVE LIFE-CYCLE MODELS BEEN FOUND USEFUL IN FIELDS OTHER THAN ENTREPRENEURSHIP?

Yes. Although the origins of life-cycle models are in biology, they have been found useful by economists, marketers, social psychologists, and family therapists—to name just a few disciplines that have been captivated by the explanatory power of this approach. Nobel Laureate Simon Kuznets used life-cycle models to develop his S-curves[6] that enable the analysis and quantification of the cyclical nature of production and prices in spans of 15 to 20 years. Social psychologists and family therapists use life cycles to understand the developmental phases of individuals[7] and families.[8] Research findings in these diverse fields indicate that groups of organisms, products, individuals, organizations, and so on behave differently, face different environmental conditions, and engage in different adaptation strategies as they transition from one stage to another.

---

[6]Kuznets, S.S. (1965). *Economic Growth and Structure: Selected Essays.* New York: Norton.
[7]Jung, C.G. (1963). *Memories, Dreams, and Reflections.* New York: Random House.
[8]Carter, B., and McGoldrick, M. (1980). *The Family Life Cycle and Family Therapy.* New York: Gardner Press.

In business literature, life-cycle models were first popularized by Theodore Levitt[9] for understanding life cycles of products, followed by Everett Rogers's[10] technology life cycles used to examine the diffusion of innovation. Subsequently, these models have been used to understand the evolution of products,[11] markets,[12] and organizations.[13] These models help us understand the naturally arising sources of conflicts so that we can be proactive in adopting governance systems to manage these conflicts. Furthermore, in each stage there will be opportunities that entrepreneurial family firm leaders can exploit to create value for their firms.

WHAT ARE THE KEY LIFE CYCLES THAT ENTREPRENEURIAL FAMILY FIRM LEADERS SHOULD KNOW ABOUT?

An understanding of individual, family, organizational, and macroenvironmental life cycles can prepare entrepreneurial family firm leaders for the effective management and governance of their firms.

Individual life-cycle models suggest that human beings go through stages of life influenced by a combination of biological (age) and sociological (era in history through which they are living) imperatives.[14] The personal and professional aspirations of firm leaders depend on their life stage. As different generations of family members get involved in a business, the family firm becomes a ripe arena for conflicts rooted in varied preferences related to the stage of life that each family member is traversing through. Family business experts have observed that when junior-generation members may be struggling to build an identity and career, the senior-generation members may be dealing with issues of maturity and slowing down,[15] leading to disagreements in terms of the extent and nature of entrepreneurial initiatives their firm should undertake.

Business owners and their family members are born, age, and die. So too do the employees and customers of their firms. Savvy leaders know that they cannot afford to see either their employees or their customers as uniform in their wants and needs. The next chapter elaborates on six stages of individual

---

[9]Levitt, T. (1965) Exploit the product life cycle. *Harvard Business Review*, 43, November–December: 81–94.

[10]Everett, R.M. (1971). *Communication of Innovations: A Cross-Cultural Approach.* New York: Free Press.

[11]Day, G. (1981). The product life cycle: Analysis and applications issues. *Journal of Marketing*, 45, Autumn: 60–67.

[12]Kotler, P. (1972). *Marketing Management.* 2nd ed. Englewood Cliffs, NJ: Prentice Hall.

[13]Adizes, I. (1988). *Corporate Life Cycles: How and Why Corporations Grow and Die and What to Do about It.* Englewood Cliffs, NJ: Prentice Hall.

[14]Churchill, N.C., and Hatten, K. J. (1987). Non-market based transfers of wealth and power: A research framework for family businesses. *American Journal of Small Business,* Winter: 51–64.

[15]Jaffe, D.T. (1990). *Working with the Ones You Love.* Berkeley, CA: Conari Press.

life cycles: preadulthood (birth through 15), provisional adulthood (16–20), early adulthood (31–45), middle adulthood (46–60), late adulthood (61–75), and late-late adulthood (over 75). The problems, opportunities, and strategies that entrepreneurial family firm leaders may adopt to deal effectively with each life stage are discussed.

Family life-cycle models attempt to capture the simultaneous changes occurring in a family as the system evolves over time. Unlike individual life-cycle stages that follow a sequential pattern defined by biological markers of human birth and death that are constant for all practical purposes, families are more variable and culturally sensitive. The stages of family development parallel the four stages depicted in Figure A1. These include the formation of new family through marriage or cohabitation (birth), joining of new family members through birth or adoption (growth), parenting of these new family members so as to prepare them for independent lives (maturity), and launching these members to form new families themselves while accepting shifting generational roles (decline).[16]

Family members can only leave by death, even if then, as the shadow cast by previous generations, especially the entrepreneurial founder, prevails in long-lived family firms.[17] While divorce and separation are commonplace in many cultures today, parents forever remain family for their next-generation members. As a family evolves over time influencing the involvement of relatives in business, adaptation in the governance systems becomes necessary. In Chapter 3, we engage you in a discussion of family life-cycle stages and the problems, opportunities, and strengths of each stage.

Organizational life-cycle models maintain that growing organizations go through distinguishable phases of development, each with relatively calm periods of growth interspersed by revolutionary stages of substantial change and turmoil.[18] Although a varied number of organizational life cycle-stages have been proposed in the literature, most of these follow a pattern of birth, growth, maturity, and death or decline as depicted in Figure A1. As evidenced by the list of oldest family firms[19] that we introduced in Chapter 1, unlike for human beings, death is not inevitable for organizations. It may be postponed, perhaps indefinitely, through renewal.[20] However, entropy leading to decline is always a threat, necessitating continuous renewal via innovation.

---

[16]Carter, B., and McGoldrick, M. (2005). Overview: The expanded family life cycle: Individual, family, and social perspectives. In Carter, B., and McGoldrick, M. (Eds.). *The Expanded Family Life Cycle: Individual, Family and Social Perspectives.* 3rd ed. New York: Pearson Publishing.

[17]Davis, P.S., and Harveston, P.D. (1999). In the founder's shadow: Conflict in the family firm. *Family Business Review,* 12(4): 311–323; Nelson, T. (2003). The persistence of founder influence: Management, ownership, and performance effects at initial public offering. *Strategic Management Journal,* 24: 707–724.

[18]Greiner, L.E. (1972). Evolution and revolution as organizations grow. *Harvard Business Review,* 50(4): 37–46.

[19]The world's oldest family companies. *Family Business*, http://www.familybusinessmagazine.com/oldworld.html

[20]Carroll, G.R., and Hannah, J.R. (2000). Density dependence in the evolution of populations of newspaper organizations. *American Sociological Review,* 54: 524–48.

Ideally, as a firm grows in size and complexity, governance changes such as appointing outside directors on the board should be incorporated to continue effective management and value creation by the firm. Family business experts have observed that it is not unusual for strategic imperatives and family life-cycle events to be out of phase.[21] A more detailed discussion of organizational life-cycle stages and related challenges, opportunities, and strategies is provided in Chapter 4.

Macroenvironment cycles are discussed in Chapter 5. These include the economic, industry, and product/service market life cycles that impact the external environment of a firm, determining the opportunities presented and challenges posed. An understanding of these cycles equips an entrepreneur to make significant gains during the high tides so as to survive the low tides.

Economic life cycles refer to the fluctuation—expansion, stagnation, or decline—in a national economy.[22] Considerable efforts are devoted by economists, such as Kuznets mentioned earlier, to capture the cyclical developments in an economy so as to help predict the economic trends in a nation or region. While it is difficult to accurately predict the periodic pattern of an economic life cycle as it is influenced by a large range of variables, generally each economic cycle spans over 15 to 20 years.[23] Entrepreneurial family firm leaders use their understanding of the current trends in an economic life cycle to adjust their priorities and strategies so as to make the best use of the ups and downs in these cycles.

Industry life-cycle models reflect the changes that take place in an industry over time. These models track the collective demand of products in an industry by providing a sense of intensity of competition in a particular market since the breakthrough innovation that made the market possible.[24] Industry life cycles are impacted by economic factors and changes in technology though each industry is not affected equally. Moreover, industries may decline and die in one country or region while simultaneously being born and growing in others. Management thinkers such as Philip Kotler[25] and Michael Porter[26] have enabled our understanding of the factors that influence industry life cycles. Similar to other life cycles discussed earlier, variations in a number of stages in the industry life cycle have been suggested. In general, however, the industry life-cycle models include some variant of the four stages of introduction, growth, maturity, and decline that form the standard life-cycle model.

Product life cycles refer to the succession of stages a product goes through from its inception to when it becomes obsolete in a market.[27] As mentioned

[21]Drozdow, N., and Carroll, V.P. (1997). Tools for strategy development in family firms. *Sloan Management Review*, Fall: 75–88.

[22]http://en.wikipedia.org/wiki/Business_cycle

[23]Kuznets, S.S. (1965). *Economic Growth and Structure: Selected Essays*. New York: Norton.

[24]http://en.wikipedia.org/wiki/Industry_lifecycle

[25]Kotler, P. (1972). *Marketing Management*. 2nd ed. Englewood Cliffs, NJ: Prentice Hall.

[26]Porter, M.E. (1980). *Competitive Strategy*. New York: Free Press.

[27]http://en.wikipedia.org/wiki/Product_life_cycle

previously, one of the earliest applications of life cycle analysis was on products that are believed to pass through a number of phases or stages—introduction, growth, maturity, and decline—going through an S-shaped curve. The introductory stage of a product is generally flat, reflecting the hesitation of buyers to adopt new products. This is followed by rampant growth as the comfort level with and market knowledge of the product increases. Growth then levels off to flat sales in the maturity stage as most or all potential buyers for the product are reached. Growth eventually begins to drop as competitive products and substitutes emerge in the marketplace, beginning new product cycles. As we observed in the case of industry life cycles, the stage at which a product is in one geographic region may vary significantly from its stage in another.[28] Astute business leaders make intelligent assessments of when and how to introduce new products and when to withdraw or replace them. They keep an eye on the life-cycle stage of their products in current markets as well as opportunities in geographically distant markets. Strategies used by entrepreneurial family firm leaders as the offerings of their firms move through different stages of life are discussed in Chapter 5.

RESOURCES ACROSS LIFE-CYCLE STAGES

Family businesses are characterized by the significant influence of family on a firm (and vice versa), leading to the possibility of resource appropriation between family and business over different life-cycle stages. Entrepreneurial family firm leaders complement their knowledge of life-cycle stages with effective management of resources. Chapter 6 discusses various resources involved in the effective management and governance of family firms and how entrepreneurial leaders manage these to create value for their family firms.

---

[28]Porter, M.E. (1985). *Competitive Advantage: Creating and Sustaining Superior Performance.* New York: Free Press.

INDIVIDUAL LIFE-CYCLE (ST)AGES

CONVINCING DAD: INNOVATIONS BY A FOURTH-GENERATION LEADER

When he was 47, Richard A. Lumpkin, hat in hand, marched into his father's office and changed the course of his family's business. Lumpkin, the fourth generation to hold the office of president of Illinois Consolidated Telephone Company, suggested creating a holding company so the heavily regulated, small-town telephone company could branch out into other, unregulated businesses. "Son," said his 85-year-old father, "I wouldn't be for that even if I thought it was a good idea."

Twenty-five years later, that holding company, Consolidated Communications, Inc., was the 14th largest telephone company in the United States. The company reported earnings of over $13 million for 2006 on revenues of nearly $321 million. The firm had 1,100 employees in the states of Illinois and Texas.

"It took some convincing," said Lumpkin, "but my father finally agreed. He had a healthy skepticism. My father was born in 1897, lived to 1989, and ran the company for 60 years. He saw a lot of changes in his lifetime. But he was at the point in his life when he just wasn't very enthusiastic about change."

Neither was his family. Most of the spin-offs started within an 18-month period. The new ventures all lost money for the first five years. Business plans were not working, and the family stockholders were groaning. Lumpkin's mother said to him, "I don't understand why we didn't just stick with the telephone business." Lumpkin replied with a small shrug: "I didn't think we ever left. This is the telephone business. It's just changed."

In the face of his father's resistance, Lumpkin also had some allies. A few years before, his father had approached him with the idea of putting outside directors on the board. "At the time," Lumpkin said, "I think he was really looking for a way to curb some of his son's ambitions. From my point of view, I saw the possibility of allies to make some changes. I agreed quickly." They added three directors—an investment banker, an attorney, and the president of the local university, which was the company's biggest customer. And, ultimately, it was the support of the outside directors that finally convinced the senior Lumpkin that it was time to make some changes.

Two dentists, Dr. Iverson A. Lumpkin and his son, Dr. William C. Lumpkin, incorporated Mattoon Telephone Company in rural Mattoon, Illinois. They overcame a disastrous fire in 1901. From 1906 to 1934, the company engaged in mergers and acquisitions, building what would become Illinois Consolidated Telephone Company. At the age of 27 in 1924, Richard Adamson Lumpkin became general manager upon the death of his father. In turn, Richard Anthony Lumpkin was named president in 1977. When Consolidated Communications, Inc., was created in 1984, company sales were approximately $50 million, coming exclusively from telephone services. The company completed an initial public offering of its stock in 2005. By 2007, Consolidated Communications offered expanded services to residential and business customers in Illinois and Texas, including local, long-distance, and wireless phone services; digital TV, high-speed Internet; pagers; answering service; conferencing; Yellow Pages; and television advertising.

"The family had to be very patient," Lumpkin said. "This was a lot more risk than my family was accustomed to, a lot more unknowns." His father was nervous but kept his faith in his son. To make things more complicated, family dynamics changed completely when the senior Lumpkin passed away in 1989. "While he was alive, he was the sole owner of the company. It was his show," his son said. By the provisions of the father's estate, stock ownership passed to 15 members of the family, scattered across the country. Lumpkin, however, was named the trustee of his father's various trusts, giving him effective control of the company. The board of directors voted to have him succeed his father as chief executive officer.

Lumpkin made sure all members of the family were aware of the new changes in the company, sending out information by mail and bringing managers to week-long family meetings to report on the company's progress. By 1990, the new ventures started turning around. Consolidated's smaller size allowed it to be flexible. Problems were discovered quickly, and new business plans were formed and implemented. "As we were able to show other family members some success, they became more enthusiastic," said Lumpkin. "And, as you know, nothing breeds success like success."

Source: Shu, S.C. (1996). Smart Growth. *Family Business Magazine*, 7(3, Summer): 20–25.

Questions

1. Richard Anthony Lumpkin said that his father "was at the point in his life when he just wasn't very enthusiastic about change." Do you think the life-cycle stages that Richard and his father are going through may influence their attitudes toward change? Why?
2. Why do you think this fourth-generation CEO was so focused on growth and innovation? What do you think would have happened to the company if he had not been?

In the case of Illinois Consolidated Telephone Company, the 47-year-old son and his 85-year-old father were clearly going through different stages of their lives. While the son was eager for the company to undertake major changes so as to regenerate, the father seemed more comfortable in cruising through the golden years of his life. Even Mrs. Lumpkin, the mother, felt unsettled about the changes proposed by her son in an industry in which their family business had enjoyed considerable success. Scholars have noted that there are inherent differences among generations in terms of motivational factors, communication and work styles, thought patterns, and the need for mentoring.[1] Life-cycle application is less about eliminating conflicts that will naturally arise than about understanding the sources of the conflicts. In this case, the timely introduction and capable usage of varied governance mechanisms, based on perceptive understanding and proactive conciliation of these life cycles, led to Consolidated's remarkable growth. But erroneous understanding of any of the cycles at play in this family firm could easily have led to a breakdown on one or more dimensions.

Although the Consolidated case does not elaborate on the firm's employees, these integral stakeholders of the firm also go through life stages. Business owners, whether of family firms or not, cannot afford to see their employees as uniform in their wants and needs. With longer life spans being enjoyed around the world, business organizations are experiencing significant generational diversity among their employees and owners as four generational groups often work side by side,[2] necessitating a clear understanding of life-cycle stages—related constraints and opportunities—so as to adopt and modify how a firm may be governed.

Just as business owners and their family members are born, age, and die, so do their customers. Successful businesses usually segment their markets. Without careful monitoring of the demographic trends[3] in the population it serves, a firm can find itself selling products or services to an ever-shrinking market. In short, an understanding of individual life-cycle stages can better equip an entrepreneur

---

[1]Frankenberg, E. (2004). The next generation really is different. *Family Business,* 5 (4): 16–18.
[2]http://www.familybusinesssurvey.com/survey/survey.htm
[3]Foot, D.K. (1996). *Boom, Bust, & Echo: How to Profit from the Coming Demographic Shift.* Toronto: Macfarlane, Walter & Ross.

to understand the needs, aspirations, and motivations of self, other family members, employees, and customers alike.

This chapter discusses the individual life cycles. A brief tracking of the history of related ideas leads to a model that captures the cycle of human life today. This is followed by a framework to understand the interaction between life-cycle stages and critical strategic issues, such as problems, opportunities, and strategies for success in each life-cycle stage, a model revisited throughout the book.

INDIVIDUAL LIFE CYCLE

An individual's life cycle is generally viewed as the voyage between the two inescapable biological markers of birth and death with different stages during the journey. Each stage, often described as an era or season, has its own distinctive and unifying qualities, although a myriad of variations can prevail. Each stage is influenced by the previous life stage and in turn lays the foundation for the next stage of life.

Interest in understanding the characteristics of the stages of human life dates back to Sigmund Freud (1856–1939), whose internally focused "theory of personality" incorporated the conscious and unconscious influences in the childhood of an individual. Freud believed that childhood influences were enacted throughout the remainder of one's life.[4] Erik Erikson is the next great figure in the study of human development, whose influence surfaced in the 1950s with the publication of his book *Childhood and Society.*[5] Insights from these two intellectual giants have laid a strong foundation for our understanding of the developmental periods in the preadult years of human life—infancy, early and middle childhood, pubescence, and early and late adolescence. The physical, social, cognitive, and psychological changes occurring during each stage are well understood today.[6]

Carl Jung, a Freud disciple, expanded his ideas to incorporate the role of environmental influences on developments throughout the human life cycle.[7] Jung is considered the father of the modern study of adult development, and his works led to the creation of the field of "social psychology." Erik Erikson's enormous influence continues to date and is most visible in the seminal work of Daniel Levinson's classic book *The Seasons of a Man's Life.* The focus of Levinson's book[8] is on "adulthood," divided into two broad eras of early and late adulthood, spanning from about 17 to 45 and 40 to 65 years of age, respectively. This middle stretch of life is preceded by childhood and adolescence (0 to 22) and followed by late adulthood (60 and above).

---

[4]Mannheim, K. (1928, reprinted 1952). *Essays on the Sociology of Knowledge.* Oxford University Press (reprint 1952), provides examples of important early works regarding life-cycle stages.

[5]Erikson, E.H. (1950). *Childhood and Society.* New York: W. Norton & Company, Inc.; Erikson, E.H. (1959). Identity and the life cycles. *Psychological Issues,* 1: 1–171.

[6]http://en.wikipedia.org/wiki/Child_development_stages

[7]Jung, C.G. (1963). *Memories, Dreams, Reflections.* New York: Random House; Jung, C.G. (1964). *Man and His Symbols.* New York: Bantam Doubleday Dell Publishing Group.

[8]Levinson, D.J. (1978). *The Season's of a Man's Life.* New York: Ballantine Books.

While these earlier works were focused on the stages of childhood and a man's adult life, later works by Levinson[9] and Sheehy[10] provide important insights into the life-cycle stages of a woman, enabling a more complete understanding of the individual's life stages. Later in the chapter, we present a model of life-cycle stages that human beings, both women and men, go through today. But, before getting into that discussion, it is important to understand the factors that influence life-cycle stages and the practical consequences of these stages.

WHO DRIVES THE LIFE CYCLE?

Of course, it is the individual whose life it is! Each choice we make ourselves or that others (usually family members) make on our behalf during the dawn or dusk of our lives when we are unable to make choices on our own has the potential to influence not only the overall length of our life's journey but also what we experience and can accomplish in different stages of it. Despite the uniqueness of each individual's life, two factors that have had a significant influence on the length and composition of the journey of humans inhabiting the planet in the 21st century are worthy of mention, as they cast an indelible shadow on all entrepreneurial family firms.

First is the **life expectancy** around the world. Technically, life expectancy is a statistical measure of the average length of survival of a living entity and is often calculated separately for differing genders and geographic locations. In practice, it means the expected age at death for a given human population.[11] Advances in sanitation, nutrition, and medical knowledge have made possible incredible increases in life expectancy around the world in the last century. For example, in the United States, only 50 percent of children born in 1900 could reasonably hope to reach the age of 50. Today, the life expectancy is approximately 77 years of age. There are significant variations around the world as life expectancy varies from 83.52 in Andorra to 32.23 in Swaziland.[12] However, in most advanced nations of the world, the life expectancy has increased significantly.

The second factor influencing the dynamics in today's workplace is the number of women in the workforce. In 2006, of the 118 million women aged 16 years and over in the United States, 70 million (more than 60%) participated in the workforce, as compared to 74 percent men in this age group active in the workforce.[13] Women comprised 46 percent of the U.S. labor force in 2006 and are projected to account for 47 percent of labor force in 2014.

In the United States, there is a significant discrepancy between men and women as life expectancy for men is 73.6 years in comparison to 79.4 years for women.[14] The longer life spans of women have caused a reversal in the total

---

[9]Levinson, D.J. w. Judy Levinson (1996). *The Season's of a Woman's Life.* New York: Alfred A. Knopf.
[10]Sheehy, G. (1976). *Passages.* New York: E.P. Dutton & Co., Inc.; Sheehy, G. (1995). *New Passages: Mapping your life across time.* New York: Ballantine Books.
[11]http://en.wikipedia.org/wiki/Life_expectancy
[12]https://www.cia.gov/library/publications/the-world-factbook/rankorder/2102rank.html
[13]http://www.dol.gov/wb/stats/main.htm
[14]https://www.cia.gov/library/publications/the-world-factbook/index.html

population of men and women in this country. While in 1900, men outnumbered women in the United States (38.8 million vs. 37.2 million), by 1999 women outnumbered men by over 6 million (139.5 million vs. 133.4 million).[15] In 2004 to 2005, women earned 57 to 58 percent of all undergraduate and graduate degrees awarded in the United States, and this number is on an increase.[16]

A reflective examination of the above statistics reveals the consequences of the remarkable advancements in engineering, health sciences, and technology over the past century that have caused substantial changes in the social and economic fabric of our societies. These changes, in turn, have sparked significant modifications in traditional, generational,[17] and gender[18] roles as the combined effects of the biological and sociological imperatives are being experienced in the workplace.

Both men and women live longer today than a century ago. This trend has led to much longer work life spans for both genders. Four popularly labeled (Figure 2.1) generations are simultaneously active in today's workplace.[19] The number of women in the workforce today is larger than a century ago. The combination of longer life expectancies and higher educational achievements of women as compared to men positions them to become a dominant productive force in the economies of most advanced nations.

For business leaders, this means not only learning to plan for and manage their own journey through longer stretches of work lives, but also productively engaging family and nonfamily members of different generations and genders going through different eras of their life. Moreover, they need to understand the varied needs and preferences of a diverse set of customers. We believe that entrepreneurial leaders equipped with an appreciation of the phases of human life cycles can proactively plan the adoption and modifications of structures and policies that become enablers of effective governance of their firms. Given the foundational nature of changes in the composition of the workforce, even the business models of the past two to three decades, based on Levinson's stages of a man's life, are unlikely to lead to success for entrepreneurial family firms. Although life-cycle dynamics have implications for managers of all types of organizations, the added complexity of relatives inside and outside the firm, especially in the case of multigenerational businesses, makes them especially important for the family enterprise.

WHAT DOES THE LIFE CYCLE DRIVE?

As we saw in the case of Illinois Consolidated Telephone Company, the personal and professional plans and dreams of entrepreneurial leaders are influenced by

---

[15]http://www.msu.edu/~bsilver/pls440century.html

[16]http://www.census.gov/Press-Release/www/releases/archives/facts_for_features_special_editions/003897.html

[17]Lancaster, L.C., and Stillman, D. (2002). *When Generations Collide: Who They Are. Why They Clash. How to Solve the Generational Puzzle at Work*. New York: Harper Business Press.

[18]Powell, G.N. (1999). Ed. *Handbook of Gender & Work*. Thousand Oaks, CA: Sage Publications; Powell, G.N., and Graves, L.M. (2003). *Women and Men in Management*. Thousand Oaks, CA: Sage Publications.

[19]http://www.familybusinesssurvey.com/survey/survey.htm

the stage of life each is experiencing at a point in time. Both the age and the era of history that an individual has experienced have a significant bearing on her physical energy and outlook toward work life. Furthermore, one's financial status (earning potential and expense responsibilities), personal and business responsibilities, hours available for professional and personal pursuits, and desired growth or slowdown or exit plans vary significantly depending on the stage of life.

Similarly, the wants, needs, and aspirations of family and nonfamily members of senior and junior generations are likely to vary based on their own life-cycle stages. Business owners cannot afford to see their family or nonfamily employees as uniform in their wants and needs. For example, the motivators for 47-year-old Richard A. Lumpkin were significantly different from those of his 85-year-old father. And the Generation Xers working in Consolidated may be motivated by very different factors than either the father or the son. Moreover, there may be a demographic divide between male and female family and nonfamily managers in a firm. Business leaders today have the challenging task of managing four significantly different generations of employees of both genders. The opportunities and challenges presented to entrepreneurial family firms as the life cycles of the key stakeholders in these firms scramble are discussed later in this chapter. First, we discuss the stages of a human life as being experienced in the 21st century.

INDIVIDUAL LIFE-CYCLE (ST)AGES

In her landmark book *New Passages,* which is based on an extensive study of hundreds of life histories through personal and group interviews, national surveys of professionals and working class people, and findings from over 50 years of U.S. census reports, Sheehy concluded:

> There is a revolution in the life cycle. In the space of one short generation the whole shape of the life cycle has been fundamentally altered. People today are leaving childhood sooner, but they are taking longer to grow up and much longer to grow old. That shifts all the stages of adulthood—by up to ten years. (Sheehy, 1999: 4)

It is important to keep in mind that authors vary in terms of the age brackets and labels they use for the different stages of life. While this may be confusing initially, you will find that the slight variations have little impact on overall conclusions regarding behaviors and conditions.

On the basis of the works of Levinson[20] and Sheehy[21] among others[22] and taking into consideration the changes in generational and gender mix of the

---

[20]Levinson, D.J. (1978). *The Season's of a Man's Life.* New York: Ballantine Books.

[21]Sheehy, G. (1995). *The New Passages: Mapping Your Life Across Time.* New York: Ballantine Books.

[22]Douglas, C. (1991). *Generation X: Tales for an Accelerated Culture.* New York: St. Martin's Press; Foot, D.K. (1996). *Boom, Bust, & Echo: How to Profit from the Coming Demographic Shift.* Toronto: Macfarlane, Walter & Ross; Howe, N., and Strauss, W. (1992). *Generations: The History of America's Future, 1584 to 2069.* New York: Morrow.

FIGURE 2.1 Individual Life-Cycle Stages: The Biological & Sociological Imperative

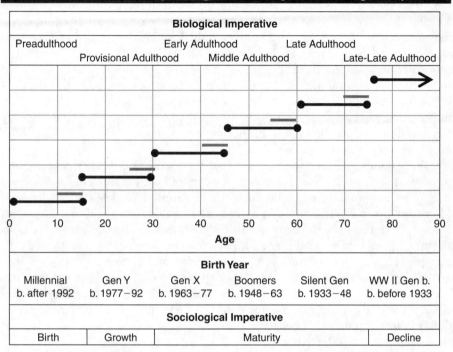

workforce that entrepreneurial family firm leaders have to contend with today, we divide the human life course into six stages (Figure 2.1):

- Preadulthood (birth to 15, currently occupied by the Millennial Generation)
- Provisional adulthood (16 to 30, occupied by Generation Y)
- Early adulthood (31 to 45, occupied by Generation X)
- Middle adulthood (46 to 60, occupied by Baby Boomers)
- Late adulthood (61 to 75, occupied by the Silent Generation)
- Late-late adulthood (76 and over, occupied by the World War II Generation)

Transition periods:
10 to 15 (Preadulthood transition)
25 to 30 (Early adulthood transition)
40 to 45 (Middle adulthood transition)
55 to 60 (Late adulthood transition)
70 to 75 (Late-late adulthood transition)

Although the ages are listed sequentially above, each stage is linked to the next by a five- to six-year transitional phase wherein the bio-psycho-socio features of the previous stage give way to those of the next stage.[23] No doubt, you have noticed our use of the word *(st)ages* in the heading to this section. Our message is that stage and age may have commonalities, but they are not always the same. In Figure 2.1, we have specifically connected age with stage, but you need to analyze your own situation to know when they are identical and when they are different. Individuals vary in the time each takes in a given stage. Some may move to the next stage at the beginning of a typical transitional phase, thereby shortening the duration of stay in the preceding stage, while others may take longer in some stages.

In this book, we take the position that the family and the business are like scrambled eggs; once mixed together, they cannot be unscrambled. As discussed in the last chapter and exemplified by the creation of Wal-Mart, Woolco, and Microsoft, more often than not, ventures are created with family involvement. Before there is a separation, there is already a merger. Family members, both those inside and those outside the company, can be inextricably intertwined, setting precedents, establishing norms of behavior, and setting expectations that artificial practices cannot untangle. Our approach to life-cycle analysis incorporates multiple life cycles that can mesh or conflict with one another. But by identifying potential conflicts in advance, enterprising family business owners may be able to direct the activities of their firms and meet the needs and demands of their families more effectively.

Later, in the next section, we highlight the key features of each of these stages, discussing both the biological and sociological imperatives influencing individuals going through each stage. Problems and opportunities presented in each stage are discussed as we share strategies that can be used to continue developing the various forms of capital needed for success in today's entrepreneurial family firms.

But first, let us respond to the question of how the six stages listed above and depicted in Figure 2.1 relate to the four life-cycle stages in the standard life-cycle model shared in Part A (Figure A1). And why did we choose to use six stages for the individual life cycle, instead of the four stages introduced earlier? Essentially, as we depict in Figure 2.2, the six stages use an expanded, more granular view of the "maturity" stage in the standard life-cycle model. As men and women working in today's businesses belong to these different stages of "maturity," we feel that it is important for you to understand the biological and sociological influencers of these individuals. Dividing the productive work-life stage from ages 30 to 75 into three substages of early, middle, and late adulthood enables a better understanding of ourselves and our coworkers.

---

[23]Levinson, D.J. (1978). *The Season's of a Man's Life.* New York: Ballantine Books.

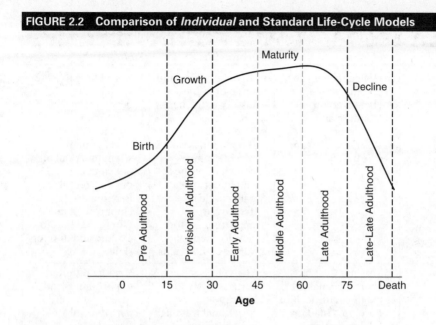

FIGURE 2.2   Comparison of *Individual* and Standard Life-Cycle Models

ENTREPRENEURSHIP THROUGH THE (ST)AGES: A MODEL FOR ANALYSIS

As we noted in Chapter 1, governance of entrepreneurial family firms is designed to establish the overall strategy for the firm, including the extent and mode of family involvement, performance standards, and codes of conduct so as to represent the owners of the firm and guide the management.

Our approach to examining entrepreneurial governance behavior in family businesses, used throughout this book, is through matrices of life-cycle stages and strategic issues (Table 2.1). Across the top of the following chart are the categories *Problems, Opportunities,* and *Strategies*. Along the side are the six stages of human life, each of which is discussed in turn below.

PREADULTHOOD

Preadulthood or childhood spans the formative years from birth to 15 years. In earlier conceptualizations of life-cycle models, this stage stretched to about 22 years; however, the recent changes in science and technology discussed earlier have shortened this phase for most individuals living in industrialized nations. This stage characterizes the most rapid bio-psycho-socio development in life as an individual transforms from a fully dependent newborn baby to become a productive member of the society. Growth occurs simultaneously along physical, social, intellectual, and emotional dimensions.

The family in which a child learns the foundational skills of life has a tremendous impact on shaping the frame of reference of this individual. The values

TABLE 2.1 **Problems, Opportunities, and Strategies by Individual Life-Cycle Stages**

	Problems	Opportunities	Strategies
Preadulthood (Birth to 15 years) Millennials	• High dependence on others • High need for attention and nurturing • Resource and time constraints	• To imbue spirit and pride of family history in the next generation • To embed foundational values of work ethic, conscientiousness, and integrity via patient role modeling • To provide opportunities for development on various dimensions	• Spend time together to enjoy the developments in each other • To understand the passions and strengths about an individual by trying out different things • Part-time employment in different arenas to explore and develop skills
Provisional Adulthood (16–30 years) Generation Y	• Too many career choices available making it difficult to develop a road map • Higher cost of education and living	• High physical energy • Large variety of educational and vocational training opportunities • Fewer responsibilities • Extensive comfort level with digital technologies • Able to manage with part-time or fluid jobs	• Explore different opportunities and career paths through part-time jobs • Launch new businesses in partnership with senior generations to combine digital savvy with life experiences
Early Adulthood (31–45 years) Generation X	• Following behind a large cohort, leaving limited opportunities for full-time employment • Decisions regarding career and family life delayed, leading to late launch in life • Stresses of balancing work and family needs • Realization of reading halfway point in life	• Peak physical performance years • Ability to work with Boomers and Generation Y • Retraining and changing careers widely accepted • Divorce or separation not a stigma in society	• Stable unassuming employees • May be more eager and equipped to launch new ventures based on a good understanding of the needs of two large cohorts, Boomers and Generation Ys

(Continued)

TABLE 2.1 *(continued)*			
	Problems	*Opportunities*	*Strategies*
Middle Adulthood (46–60 years) Baby Boomers	• Lesser digital savvy than younger generation • Fiery and impatient generation with exceptional confidence • Sandwiched between career ambitions and needs of junior and senior generations	• Largest consumer cohort alive today • High confidence, optimism, desire, and ability to succeed • Enjoying good physical health • High confidence and energy to undertake regeneration projects • Approaching phase of life with lesser demands of senior and junior generations	• Begin planning how best to contribute in the remaining 30–40 years of life • Role model enthusiasm for life to junior generations • Launch creative ventures to support the changing needs of this age group
Late Adulthood (61–75 years) Silent Generation	• Have to learn to find ways to contribute productively to family and society • First generation to go through this phase of life feeling so energetic and healthy	• Expanded life stretch with good health and fewer responsibilities of senior and junior generations • Inclusive down-to-earth attitude and manner dispersing calm spirit	• Mentoring junior generations of entrepreneurs • Serving on advisory boards of entrepreneurial family firms • Giving back to society, especially time to help those lacking this resource in current life phase
Late-Late Adulthood (76 and beyond)	• Failing health • Extremely busy next generation with limited opportunities to devote longer time to help this generation	• Find effective ways to make lasting contributions to society that will help beyond limits of human life	• Capture stories of lifetime experiences of this greatest generation alive today

imbued in these formative years influence choices made in the latter course of life. As Christensen and Raynor expressed it:

> We often admire the intuition that successful entrepreneurs seem to have for building growth businesses. When they exercise their intuition about what actions will lead to the desired results, they really are employing theories that give them a sense of the right thing to do in various

circumstances. These theories were not there at birth: They were learned through a set of experiences and mentors earlier in life.[24]

Research suggests that more than 50 percent of the children born in business families are likely to launch new businesses in their life and be successful in running these ventures.[25]

The developmental needs of the young necessitate that adult family members adjust their work and personal lives so as to devote energies and resources to nurture the next generation. As both men and women are active in the workplace today, reducing their available time for family and personal pursuits, many adults are choosing not to indulge in child bearing so as to retain focus on their careers. Some others succumb to the demands of work life after having children and find themselves largely as absentee parents. Unfortunately, the reality of this stage of human life is that a child needs personalized attention and nurturing every single day. However, there are many parents—fathers and mothers—who are successfully able to balance the needs of work and family life.

The distinguishing feature of the Millennials, also referred to as "the Internet generation"[26] (b. after 1992), who are passing through this phase of life, is that this cohort is spending its formative years during the rise of the World Wide Web. They usually have no memory of a pre-Internet world and take for granted services such as e-mail, Wikipedia, Internet forums, MySpace, and YouTube. For them, shopping on the Internet, paying utilities via their computer, checking bank statements, or Internet dating are among the natural order of things. While enjoying great comfort levels with technology and all it offers, many of them are competing for their parents' time and attention, each varying in the success being achieved.

In the context of entrepreneurial family firms, the overlap between the family and business provides excellent opportunities for business leaders to imbue the spirit and pride of the family and its collective history in members of the next generation. Astute leaders of successful family firms have been found to be attentive to the developmental needs of the next generation using every opportunity to instill in them the values of strong work ethic, high integrity, conscientiousness, and a sense of ownership for one's life, which are foundational for success over the course of life.[27] Truett Cathy of Chick-fil-A captured the importance of this stage of human life in *It's Better to Build Boys Than Mend Men.*[28]

For those growing up in family businesses or interested in starting new ventures, this is an opportune time to get a feel for working in business and developing

---

[24]Christensen, C.M., and Raynor, M.E. (2003). *The Innovator's Solution: Creating and Sustaining Successful Growth.* Boston: Harvard Business School Press. p. 17.

[25]Fairlie, R.W., and Robb, A. (2007). Families, human capital, and small business: Evidence from the characteristics of business owners survey. *Industrial and Labor Relations Review,* 60(2): 225–245.

[26]Howe, N., and Strauss, W. (1992). *Generations: The History of America's Future, 1584 to 2069.* New York: Morrow.

[27]Miller, D., and Le-Breton Miller, I. (2005). *Managing for the Long Run: Lessons in Competitive Advantage from Great Family Businesses.* Boston: Harvard Business School Press.

[28]Cathy, S.T. (2004). *It's better to Build Boys Than Mend Men.* Looking Glass Books.

general business skills. It is a time to take on part-time jobs, as they allow opportunities to practice handling multiple responsibilities related to work, school, and personal life, while offering the joys of independent earnings.[29] Moreover, such jobs are an excellent opportunity to develop social skills and better understand one's own strengths and limitations as the foundation for being able to plan developing areas of skill set where more training and practice may be helpful. Working in one's family business or other entrepreneurial ventures provides a great learning experience of watching work life up close with all its positives and challenges.

Toward the end of this stage, the individual is physically a fully developed adult and begins to modify relationships with family members as she begins to explore the world independently. As in all transition phases, an individual wavers from being a child wanting to be nurtured and guided, to asserting independence while locating herself in the productive world of adults.

PROVISIONAL ADULTHOOD

This stage extends from 15 to 30 years of age as a consequence of shortened childhood and longer time taken to make career choices and establish independent homes. Generation Y, treading through this energetic stage of human life today, is faced with bewildering choices, leading to contradictory feelings of abundance and stress. They are finding it harder to develop clear road maps, given the enormity of choices available. Both men and women in this stage are choosing to stay in school for longer durations and returning for further education after brief stints in the workforce. They change majors more times than any of the previous generations.

However, they are facing higher costs of tuition than previous generations. In many instances, their "boomer" parents are becoming "helicopter parents," landing in the offices of their children's advisors or administrators in colleges, causing concern for the developing maturity and social progress of this cohort. Given the downward trend in the economy and rising prices, only a small percentage of them are able to live independently. Thus, they are taking longer to "pull up roots" and leave their parents' homes or return after some time on their own, experiencing the constraints and negative connotations of such choices.

The future seems bright for this cohort as it is smaller than the previous cohort. This opens more opportunities for those in this age group. Moreover, they are highly educated and skilled to manage fluid careers of today. They are on the cutting edge of the digital revolution as cyberspace and multimedia reside in their pockets. Communicating in symbols and ignoring time zones and national boundaries, this cohort, while taking longer to launch into adult life, seems well prepared for the challenges of next few decades.

The entrepreneurial family firms of today have an opportunity to harness the skills of this generation, and many are doing so through co-op and part-time jobs that this generation is seemingly comfortable with as they continue their education.

---

[29]McCann, G. (2007). *When Your Parents Sign the Paychecks: Finding Career Success Inside or Outside the Family Business.* Indianapolis, IN: JIST publishers.

Such jobs provide mutually beneficial opportunities for both the employers and employees. Many opportunities exist for creating new ventures especially as partnerships between the young, physically energetic 20- and 30-year-olds with those in more senior generations who have accumulated rich experience over longer life spans. Adulthood can be delayed, but eventually it has to be experienced. Sometimes between the ages of 25 and 30, an individual makes the transition from provisional to early adulthood.

EARLY ADULTHOOD

This stage spans from 30 to 45 years of one's life. This cohort that is described as Generation X[30] is experiencing life in the shadow of the Baby Boomers (discussed next). They have already experienced the economic downturns of the early 1990s and 2000s. As a consequence, they entered adulthood to be met by short-term employment contracts as long-term job opportunities were not easily available. This is the first living generation where men earned about 20 percent less than their fathers did at the same age. However, the combined family income has increased as more women are entering the workplace and are contributing to the household income. Faced with shortages in employment and more competition due to women entering the workforce, many Generation Xers chose to launch their own ventures.

By the time this cohort gets to their 30s, they have overcome the indecisiveness of earlier years and established their niche in society. For most, crucial decisions about career choices have been made. Enjoying the peak biologically energetic years of the human life cycle, incumbents of this stage either experience rich satisfaction related to love, family life, and occupational advancement or suffer disappointment, as the realization of reaching the halftime point in life strikes.

Those enjoying work and family lives, however, are faced with crushing stresses of balancing the demands from both arenas of life. The disappointed, on the other hand, have opportunities to retrain for another career choice as continuing education is becoming a norm in society. Others unhappy with marital choices have many options, as separation, divorce, and entering into new relationships are well accepted in today's society.

Pragmatic and skeptical, this generation has been observed not to have been inspired or challenged by a collective cause. Health concerns are usually not an issue for this cohort though as adolescents they were plagued by guns, drugs, and AIDS, leading to highest suicide rates of any cohort alive today.

For entrepreneurial family firms, they are an unassuming group and likely to be more stable employees in comparison to either the fiery and impatient Boomers or the following generation of more technology-dependent Generation Y members. As this generation bridges the Boomers and the Generation Y, they are in a good position to understand the perspectives of individuals in these cohorts, thereby having an ability to work well in multigenerational and diverse teams.

---

[30]Coupland, D. (1991). *Generation X: Tales for an Accelerated Culture.* New York: St. Martin's Press.

MIDDLE ADULTHOOD

This stage spans from mid-40s to 60 years of age and is currently occupied by the more than 76 million Baby Boomers in the United States who are enjoying this "age of mastery," according to Gail Sheehy. This generation holds the power of numbers as 4 out of every 10 Americans alive today fall in this category. Thus, they command attention as they are the largest segment of consumers alive.

Parents of this generation, most of whom had experienced the Great Depression and World War II, worked hard and were successful in insulating the Boomers from hardships of life, leading to an extremely confident and optimistic generation. Boomers were the first generation to grow up with television, which solidified a sense of generational identity as they watched similar programs across the country. Both men and women of this generation are highly educated and motivated to succeed. Two paychecks in a household are a norm for this age group, although the philosophy of self-indulgence and instant gratification reigns supreme for many of this cohort.

Enjoying excellent physical health and an optimistic outlook toward life, this generation confidently undertakes major regeneration of their family firms, as exemplified by Richard A. Lumpkin in the opening vignette. Trusted by the senior generation and backed by their own success, they have enabled significant positive developments in the economy. Despite their enthusiastic optimism and success in life, this generation is facing the dual edge of responsibility of junior and senior generations. With increased human life spans, their parents are living longer, but the health of many is beginning to fail. While nursing and "mature living" homes are helping, the responsibilities do add to the stresses of this generation. At the same time, they are ambitious for their junior generation, encouraging them to participate in extracurricular activities and seek better college education. Sandwiched between the needs of the senior and junior generations, this generation is found spending a considerable amount of time in caring for the needs of these generations, while trying to balance their career ambitions.

What was labeled the most serious recession in the post–World War II era began in 2008. Conditions in the global economy, including job losses, business closings, and jeopardized and diminished pension funds, tempered the optimism of this generation. The sandwich threat became real for many who had the care of elderly parents and unemployed children. For some family business owners, this meant the postponement of retirement plans or downsizing of operations or even the closing or sale of the enterprise. Research suggests that entrepreneurial family firms are tenacious. Their preference for low debt, high control through ownership, and long-term orientation often provides the shock absorbers to cruise quietly through low economic times while retaining their employees and contributing to their communities.[31]

---

[31] Astrachan, J.H., Zahra, S.A., and Sharma, P. (2003). Family-Sponsored Ventures. Presented in New York on 29 April 2003 at the First Annual Global Entrepreneurship Symposium: The Entrepreneurial Advantage of Nations.

The large size of the Boomer population segment continued to provide opportunities. Astute entrepreneurial founders such as Donald and Dorris Fisher established ventures like Gap, Inc., in the late 1960s with the intention of catering to the changing needs of the Boomer generation. Subsequent problems encountered by this chain, however, show that entrepreneurial family firms need to change as their target markets progress through life cycles. Nevertheless, given the large size of this generation, ventures aimed to satisfy the needs of this group are likely to do well into the future.

LATE ADULTHOOD

This stage stretches from about 60 to 75 years of age, a stage of life that has been referred to as the "age of integrity."[32] Enjoying good health and having largely completed their duties toward their immediate senior and junior generation, this is the "duck and cover generation" that grew during the threat of thermonuclear war and experienced regular related drills in schools. Having gone through their foundational years before the era of drugs and narcotics, television, credit cards, and washing machines or dryers, women were mostly stay-at-home moms while grandparents lived in the spare room. This was the most fertile of any generation that inhabited the United States and Canada in the 20th century. While women took on the traditional home front jobs earlier in their lives, a remarkable number of them went back to college after their 40s. This cohort produced a number of civil rights leaders such as Fannie Lou Hamer, Martin Luther King Jr., and Malcolm X.

This is a proud, down-to-earth generation that reaches out to people of all cultures, races, ages, and handicaps. They excel at mediating arguments and have a large capacity to listen and ask questions. Retired but not feeling old yet, many of this generation take on part-time jobs, engage in public service, and consult or serve on boards. Enjoying an expanded span of life as grandparents, many individuals of this generation are investing a lot of time and energy in mentoring the junior generations both within their family and beyond. For leaders of entrepreneurial family firms, this generation offers a wealth of knowledge and experience that can be harnessed for the development of other generations alive today.

LATE-LATE ADULTHOOD

This stage extends into the golden years of 75 and older. The current members of this age group have been described as the "Greatest Generation"[33] as they were raised during the Great Depression and fought in World War II. Their love for flying and aviation made them distinct from others as they crowded the armed services. Women of this generation either served in the war or kept the home front intact during it. They married young but delayed family due to war. Those who survived the wars lived in poverty while helping rebuild the industries of

---

[32]Sheehy, G. (1995). *The New Passages: Mapping Your Life Across Time.* New York: Ballantine Books. p. 10.

[33]Brokaw, T. (1998). *The Greatest Generation.* New York: Random House.

America. Gender roles were highly differentiated as women were defined by their motherhood and housewifery skills. In many states, wife and children were treated as the property of a man. Top-down hierarchy was common, and men in this generation were comfortable either receiving or giving orders. While largely out of the active workforce today, the idealistic values of work ethic held by this generation continue to influence our work lives today as evident in the lasting influence of Lumpkin Sr. in our opening case.

For entrepreneurial family firms, capturing the life stories and experiences of this generation can lead to precious advantages of learning from life's experiences. Members of this cohort can use their life savings and learn to find effective ways to ensure that their legacy continues in causes of their choice beyond their lifetime.

ENTREPRENEURSHIP AND FAMILY BUSINESS: BUILDING A NEW MODEL

In this chapter, we introduced you to the concept of life-cycle models and the diverse applications of these models. Leaders of entrepreneurial family firms can prepare themselves to negotiate the problems and opportunities presented by conflicting life cycles that impact their firm. To start this learning process, one must engage in self-reflection of the stages of life and changes experienced along the way.

However, an individual does not operate in vacuum. Family is the first social system that has a foundational life-long influence on an individual. For those born in enterprising families, business is an integral part of the growing-up years. Family business scholars have looked at how the three life cycles—individual, family, and organization—interact. Traditional business education has attempted to eliminate family issues from business management, emphasizing rational decision models. Family business specialists acknowledge that family cannot be removed from the equation in that as Gersick et al. propose,[34] boundaries need to be established. Richard Anthony Lumpkin appears to have been aware for the need of such a distinction. When his father died, he found himself with a diverse set of relations as co-owners. He set forward to carry out his vision but simultaneously did not neglect the family. He communicated to them as aggressively as he did to his staff to have their commitment to the changes he was making. In the next chapter, we discuss the diverse forms of families today and the life-cycle stages they go through. The problems, opportunities, and strategies for dealing with each family life-cycle stage are highlighted.

The body of knowledge in the field of entrepreneurship draws from many disciplines: economics, psychology, sociology, finance, education, engineering, marketing, and others, but perhaps none more so than strategic management. A simple definition of strategy is the process of fitting an organization to its

---

[34]Gersick, K.E., Davis, J.A., Hampton, M.M., and Lansberg, I. (1999). *Generation to Generation: Life Cycles of the Family Business.* Boston: Harvard Business School Press.

environment. In considering the life cycle of an organization from a strategic management perspective, we would ask which actions by the corporation are most appropriate as the competitive, industry, economic, legal and regulatory, technological, and market environments all change.

In the entrepreneurship literature, the focus is primarily on early and late stages of the venture and on the life cycle of the entrepreneur. Scholars investigate conditions in prestart-up, leading to the launch of the firm, the start-up and early growth stages, and the eventual harvesting of the wealth created by the firm. Entrepreneurship can best be thought of as a process. The **entrepreneurial process** is the key to conceptualizing entrepreneurship. As a process, entrepreneurship can be implemented in a wide variety of contexts. The process consists of the following steps: opportunity recognition, concept development, resource needs assessment, resource acquisition, implementation and management, and harvesting or exit.[35]

Life-cycle applications to the entrepreneurs typically seek to determine whether there are uniform or reasonably consistent characteristics that distinguish and enable us to predict entrepreneurs and whether the founding entrepreneurs can make the transition to so-called professional management as the organization grows and matures. Chapter 5 focuses on the life-cycle stages of an organization and how an entrepreneurial spirit can be nurtured and retained to ensure long-term prosperity of these firms.

In subsequent chapters, we examine the macro life cycles that an entrepreneur has to contend with, the forms of capital needed to run a successful venture, and how to develop various forms of capital. The life-cycle models will first be used to determine the strategic issues that arise in family businesses and to identify strategies for addressing those issues. From there, we study the interaction among the stages and how inherent conflicts can be resolved or turned into opportunities.

Summary

- Life-cycle models have been found to be of value for theory and practice in a wide variety of disciplines.
- Entrepreneurs have to simultaneously contend with individual, family, organizational, product, industry, and economic life cycles.
- Four stages of a life cycle include birth, growth, maturity, and decline or renewal.
- Progress made in the 20th century has led to increases in life expectancy and in the number of women in the workforce, leading to longer life and work spans.
- Six stages of human life can be traced each with its unique features and lasting about 15 years in length.
- An understanding of individual life-cycle stages helps an entrepreneur govern the firm under his charge and manage the diverse workforce more ably.

---

[35]DeTienne, D. R. (2008). Entrepreneurial exit as a critical component of the entrepreneurial process: Theoretical development. *Journal of Business Venturing,* In Press.

Discussion Questions

1. What are the advantages and disadvantages of using a biological analogy for describing a product? For an organization?
2. This chapter referred to several types of life cycles (the owner, employees, customers, etc.). What are some others, and how could you apply a life cycle to them?
3. On the basis of their mutual life stages in 1982, how do you think Richard Adamson Lumpkin and Richard Anthony Lumpkin were able to have a meeting of minds?
4. What do you think will happen to Consolidated Communication when Richard Anthony Lumpkin steps down as CEO?

Learning Exercises

1. Using the individual life-cycle model presented in this chapter, map the life-cycle stages that each member of your family is currently going through. Ask them what they consider to be the most significant events in each decade of their life.
2. While analyzing the data collected for Learning Exercise 1, do you find any significant differences among male and female respondents? Why do you think this is?
3. Many life-cycle models have been developed besides the four-stage graph presented in Figure 2.1. Find an article or book with another model and explain how it compares to the one in this chapter.

Other Resources

- Aizes, I. (1988). *Corporate Life Cycles: How and Why Corporations Grow and Die and What to Do about It.* Englewood Cliffs, NJ: Prentice Hall.
- Foot, D.K. (1996). *Boom, Bust, & Echo: How to Profit from the Coming Demographic Shift.* Toronto: Macfarlane, Walter & Ross.
- Gersick, K.E., Davis, J.A., McCollom-Hampton, M., and Lansberg, I. (1997). *Generation to Generation: Life Cycles of the Family Business.* Boston: Harvard Business School Press.
- Lancaster, L.C., and Stillman, D. (2002). *When Generations Collide: Who They Are. Why They Clash. How to Solve the Generational Puzzle at Work.* New York: Harper Business Press.
- McCann, G. (2007). *When Your Parents Sign the Paychecks: Finding Career Success Inside or Outside the Family Business.* St. Paul, MN: JIST Publishers.
- Sheehy, G. (1995). *New Passages: Mapping Your Life across Time.* New York: Ballantine Books.

CHAPTER 3

FAMILY LIFE-CYCLE STAGES

AT WHAT POINT DOES A FAMILY ENTERPRISE TRULY DEFINE ITS FUTURE?

I think the term "family business" is about as useful as MS-DOS. We need new "Windows" on the world of families and the enterprises they control. Here is my attempt to open the "Gates" of understanding about the very different enterprises that are blithely described as "family businesses."

I take a developmental approach to this subject, meaning there are stages to traverse before we get to "Family Business 2.0."

Stage 1: First things first: We start with a family—no family business yet, just a family.

Stage 2: Some families have a member who begins a venture, a start-up. Usually this term applies to a for-profit business, from a paper route to a venture-funded high-tech firm. But it also applies to other realms of activity: not-for-profits (think Linux) and politics (think Kennedy, Clinton, Bush, Dole). Now we have a start-up, which may or may not become a "family business." Consultant Ed Cox has described "family business" as a venture in which "more than one family member has a significant investment (financial or emotional) or participates significantly in the operation or management decisions. . . . 'Family' can mean people related by blood or marriage or lifetime commitment."

Stage 3: Once a family venture begins to grow, the owners add employees but generally keep all or a controlling share of ownership. As the business grows, managers are added, but the founder/owner remains active in management. Now we have an owner-managed business. At this stage, the values of the family begin to determine the overall culture of the enterprise.

Too often, at this stage, scholars and other commentators think only of the enterprise the family has created and ignore the family who created it. Some scholars differentiate between "enterprising" families and other families who control capital. Some families are stewards of their capital, while others are consumers, whose businesses exist primarily to sustain their consumer needs. Only a few are truly enterprising families—those that are committed to recognizing opportunities that will enhance both the business's and the family's human, intellectual, and financial capital and will carry these legacies from one generation to the next.

Stage 4:   At some point, the family's financial capital may reach a substantial amount, as may the size of the company's workforce. This is a critical developmental stage for any family enterprise. This is also the time to establish governance structures for both the family and the business in which these values can be communicated to the family, the business, and the community.

At this stage—"Family Business 2.0"—the family business truly defines its future. Supported by its guiding principles, with the culture and values of the founding family embedded in all of its relationships, a family business may endure for decades. In order to assess the possibility of success of any family-controlled enterprise, we need to know more about the "operating system."

Source: Narva, R.L. (2004). Family Business 2.0. *Family Business Magazine,* 15(3):79.

Questions

1. Which do you think comes first, the family or the business? Why?
2. Would Narva's model apply the same to a couple who start a business when they have small children and to a couple who start their business after they have retired from other careers?

Family or business—which comes first? It depends on at what stage of an individual's and family's life cycle the business is created. As Richard Narva mentions in the comments presented above, each individual is born in a family—so family comes before the business. As an example, the birth families of Bill Gates and Richard Stallman existed before the launch of Microsoft in 1975 or Linux in 1991. But Gates started his own family much later in 1987 when he married Melinda Ann French,[1] and Stallman has not yet started his family life, instead referring to his "Free Software Movement" as his "23-year-old child."[2]

On the other hand, for William Clay Ford Jr., the executive chairman of the board of Ford Motor Company, established by his great-grandfather Henry Ford, or for Mukesh Ambani,[3] the second-generation leader of Reliance Industries

---

[1]http://en.wikipedia.org/wiki/Melinda_Gates
[2]http://www.stallman.org/extra/personal.html
[3]http://en.wikipedia.org/wiki/Mukesh_Ambani

who is being touted as one of the richest men in the world today, the families in which they were born were involved in a business, and the two systems were scrambled together. For others such as Melinda Gates, who married Bill Gates after Microsoft was well established, or Lisa Ford (wife of William Ford Jr.) or Nita Ambani (wife of Mukesh Ambani), who married the later-generation family business leaders, given the intertwinement of the two systems, the family and business essentially came as a package deal. Each context is thus unique.

As we mentioned in Chapter 1, members of the founding family significantly influence the strategic decisions and life course of a firm, leading to its success or failure. In turn, the performance of a firm influences the family life and dynamics. To fully comprehend the governance mechanisms that can lead to effective harnessing and managing the inherent richness of entrepreneurial opportunities throughout the life cycle of a business, it is important to understand the life-cycle stages of an individual, family, and business. Chapter 2 elaborated on the life-cycle stages of an individual, and the next chapter focuses on the stages that a business goes through and the interactions among the systems of individual, family, and business.

Family is the focus of this chapter. We reflect on the rapidly altering landscape of families in our changing world, then discuss the powerful influence of the family throughout the personal and professional life of an entrepreneur and his/her business. Armed with this foundational understanding of families that further reveals the scrambled nature of family and business, we address the stages of a family life cycle and the inherent problems, challenges, and opportunities of each stage as they relate to enabling (or disabling) the entrepreneurial urges of family members. The appendix to this chapter introduces you to "family genograms," a powerful tool used by family experts[4] to elucidate and understand family dynamics and developmental processes across generations.

FAMILIES OF THE 21ST CENTURY

What is a family? As Narva suggested, many of us think of "family" as people related by blood or marriage or lifetime commitment. On the basis of our experiences, each of us develops a perspective on what defines a family. We also develop beliefs about what a *typical* or the most prevalent form of family is, and which of the various forms in existence is *optimal* or most effective for the well-being and development of family members. Unlike any other organizational system, families incorporate new members only by birth, adoption, commitment, or marriage, and members can leave only by death, even if then. Although familial roles and functions may be fulfilled by other individuals in cases of death, separation, or divorce, relationships in a family are personal, emotional, and idiosyncratic, making it essentially impossible to replace family members.

In the opening line of his classic novel *Anna Karenina*,[5] Leo Tolstoy observed, "Happy families are all alike; every unhappy family is unhappy in its own way." As

---

[4]McGoldrick, M., Carter, B., and Garcia-Preto, N. (Eds.) (in press). *The Expanded Family Life Cycle: Individual, Family, and Community Perspectives.* 4th ed. New York: Pearson.

[5]Tolstoy, L. (1946). *Anna Karenina.* New York: World.

if following a cue from this observation, single-model advocates of family studies believed that families must conform to one model to effectively perform its functions. Efforts were devoted to search for the most effective family form that would result in happiness. Nearly 100 years after Tolstoy's observation, another Russian writer, Vladimir Nabokov, observed in his novel *Ada*[6] : "All happy families are more or less dissimilar; all unhappy ones are more or less alike," thereby suggesting that optimal families come in different shapes and forms. Froma Walsh,[7] a leading family scholar, observed, "It appears Nabokov got it right (as) research attests to the potential for healthy functioning in a variety of family arrangements." Other family studies experts[8] support this view, observing that there are many ways to go through life in a caring and productive manner, and no specific family structure is ideal. Essentially, the composition of a family can vary along the following dimensions:

- Blood relationships
- Gender of focal couple
- Generations
- Legal status
- Cohabitation

As we discuss later in this chapter, the forms of family structures in a society influence the entrepreneurial opportunities that might be pursued with success.

As our interest is in the interface between family business and entrepreneurship and how families enable or disable the pursuit of entrepreneurial dreams of individual members, we define *family as a group of people affiliated through bonds of shared history and a commitment to share a future together while supporting the development and well-being of individual members*. Family provides the context to allow each individual member to develop and master appropriate skills at each stage of life so as to enable effective interaction with other social systems.[9]

FAMILIES OVER TIME

Parallel to the dominant forms of economic activity—preindustrial, industrial, postindustrial—family structures in the last century have gone through three distinct eras.[10] Extended multigenerational families were more prevalent in the preindustrial agrarian era, then they were replaced by the nuclear families in the industrial era, followed by a wide variety of family structures in the postindustrial

---

[6]Nabokov, V. (1969). *Ada or Ardor: A Family Chronicle.* New York: McGraw-Hill.

[7]Walsh, F. (2003). Changing families in a changing world: Reconstructing family normality. In Walsh, F. (Ed.). *Normal Family Processes: Growing Diversity and Complexity.* New York: The Guilford Press.

[8]McGoldrick, M., Carter, B., and Garcia-Preto, N. (Eds.) (in press). *The Expanded Family Life Cycle: Individual, Family, and Community Perspectives.* 4th ed. New York: Pearson.

[9]cf. Becvar, D.S., and Becvar, R.J. (1999). *Systems Theory and Family Therapy.* Lanham, MD: United Press of America.

[10]Walsh, F. (2003). Changing families in a changing world: Reconstructing family normality. In Walsh, F. (Ed.). *Normal Family Processes: Growing Diversity and Complexity.* New York: The Guilford Press.

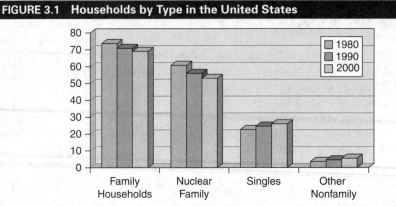

FIGURE 3.1 Households by Type in the United States

Source: U.S. Census Bureau, *Current Population Reports.* From *Statistical Abstract of the United States, 2002 and 2006.*

era experienced today. Of course, the evolutionary patterns of economies and families vary among countries and regions of the world.

The extended multigenerational family form became typical in the preindustrial times, which were marked by a dependence on agriculture as the main form of productive activity. Limited developments in sanitation, health, and family planning led to unexpected deaths, shorter life spans, and unplanned pregnancies. These factors necessitated that multiple generations of a family coreside so as to cope with the uncertainties of their times and to ensure the well-being of members with limited incomes.

The industrial times marked by economic prosperity fostered the emergence of nuclear families with a breadwinner father and a homemaker mother. Average household size became smaller as adult children established separate households. As mentioned in the last chapter, the last few decades have witnessed an increase in the average life span of individuals and in the number of women entering the workforce. As a consequence of longer life spans, families began to experience three and frequently four or five generations of family members simultaneously going through different stages of life. The level of prosperity in the economy and the availability of additional options such as seniors' homes increasingly enable adults in the family to maintain separate households. While some resilient families [11] continue to function effectively using the extended and nuclear family forms, others creatively forge a variety of family arrangements as each strives to build caring and committed relationships for its members.

With data available today (Figure 3.1), it is evident that amid this changing socioeconomic landscape, various family forms coexist. More variety in the family and household forms provides both distinct opportunities and challenges for aspiring entrepreneurs.

---

[11]Walsh, F. (2003). Family resilience: Strengths forged through adversity. In Walsh, F. (Ed.). *Normal Family Processes: Growing Diversity and Complexity.* New York: The Guilford Press.

POWER OF FAMILY INFLUENCES

Entrenched and tenacious, family influences are powerful. Family is the social institution that provides the first natural context within which individual identity, beliefs, and values are framed and attitudes are formed. Moreover, one's family provides the first opportunities to develop physical, social, emotional, and intellectual skills. Families, therefore, have the potential to indirectly influence all the major personal and professional decisions made by individuals throughout their life course, including whether or not the entrepreneurial spirit is nurtured, whether related aspirations come to fruition or not, what form these aspirations take (such as the establishment of a new venture or using entrepreneurial skills in an existing organization), and the extent of success achieved. The traditions of a family can be tools or constraints. The first generation of a family enterprise makes history. The second generation has the responsibility to assess that history and determine how best to make its own mark. [12]

Most of us experience at least two sets of family life. The first set is the **family of origin** into which we are born or adopted and spend the preadulthood and part of the provisional adulthood years of our lives. The second set is the **family/ies of attachment**, which refers to the new family or families we launch during the course of our life by partnering with another individual and, in most cases, by extending to include members of junior and/or senior generations. It is in this family that the majority of a person's life is spent. As we discuss below, both the families of origin and attachment significantly and sometimes directly influence an individual's career and life decisions, including those concerned with pursuing entrepreneurial opportunities.

FAMILY OF ORIGIN

Does family business really, as Narva contended, begin with the family? Research supports his contention as the literature on entrepreneurship shows us that for many people an entrepreneurial attitude is infused in the family womb at early ages. The family of origin has ample opportunities to provide an environment necessary to develop the personality traits and skills required for entrepreneurs to succeed and to imbue values and beliefs influencing attitudes related to the relative roles of family and business. Let us discuss each of these in turn.

ENTREPRENEURIAL PERSONALITY

According to Johns and Saks,[13] personality is the relatively stable set of psychological characteristics that influences the way individuals interact with

---

[12]Corbetta, G., and Claudio, D. (1993). Steering the development of family businesses: A survey of 45 Italian firms. In Henry Welt (Ed.). *Family Business: A Generation Comes of Age*, Proceedings of the 1993 Family Firm Institute Conference, New York.

[13]Johns, G., and Saks, A.M. (2005). *Organizational Behavior: Understanding and Managing Life at Work*. Toronto: Pearson Prentice Hall.

their environment. It summarizes an individual's distinctive style of dealing with the world and reacting to people, situations, and events.

There is mounting evidence of an enduring relationship between personality and career success across life spans. Scholars at the University of California at Berkeley[14] conducted a set of three multiple longitudinal intergenerational studies spanning more than 60 years. They collected data on personality, general mental ability (intelligence), work, and family life of participants at five different points in their life spans.[15] Findings point toward the influence of both intelligence and personality traits on career success achieved at all stages of life. The effect of personality was lasting and explained success even when controlling for intelligence. Results of this study and others suggest that career success is significantly related to high levels of conscientiousness, emotional stability, and extraversion. Although the results for agreeableness and openness to experience are not as consistent, there are indications that high levels of openness to experience and low levels of agreeableness point toward career success.

Parallel to this history of personality research, entrepreneurship scholars devoted significant efforts to understand how personality traits relate to entrepreneurial individuals and their success.[16] The driving questions for these scholars were the following: Why do some individuals launch new ventures while others, seemingly with similar mental abilities and background, do not? And, of those who launch new ventures, why do some succeed while others fail? Trait scholars in entrepreneurship believed the answer lay in understanding the personality traits of individuals and began an arduous search for "the entrepreneurial personality."

A meta-analytical review by Zhao and Siebert[17] of available research on personality factors of entrepreneurs and nonentrepreneurs revealed that entrepreneurs[18] scored high on the dimensions of conscientiousness, emotional stability, and openness to experience, but low on agreeableness. No difference between entrepreneurs and nonentrepreneurs was found in terms of extraversion scores. We elaborate more on these topics in Chapter 6, where we take up the discussion of different forms of capital, including human and emotional capital. But, for now, do you wonder where personality comes from?

Research provides evidence that personality is influenced by genetics.[19] However, psychologists continue to debate the relative importance of disposition

---

[14]Judge, T.A., Higgins, C.A., Thorensen, C. J., and Barrick, M.R. (1999). The big five personality traits, general mental ability, and career success across the life span. *Personnel Psychology,* 52:621–652.

[15]Ages of participants in different data collection waves ranged from ranging from age 12–14; 15–18; 30–39; 41–50; and 53–62.

[16]Ireland, R.D., and Webb, J.W. (2007). A cross-disciplinary exploration of entrepreneurship research. *Journal of Management,* 33(6): 891–927; Gartner, W.B. (1988). Who is an entrepreneur is the wrong question. *Entrepreneurship Theory & Practice,* 12(4).

[17]Zhao, H., and Seibert, S.E. (2006). The big five personality dimensions and entrepreneurial status: A meta-analytical review. *Journal of Applied Psychology,* 91:259–271.

[18]In this study, entrepreneur is defined as someone who is the founder, owner, and manager of a small business and whose principal purpose is growth.

[19]Bouchard Jr., T.J. (1994). Genes, environment, and personality. *Science,* 264:1700–1701; Bouchard Jr., T.J., and Loehlin, J.C. (2001). Genes, evolution, and personality. *Behavior Genetics,* 31(3):243–273.

(genetic traits) versus situation (family or organizational setting) on an individual's personality. For our discussion, however, the family of origin is well positioned to influence personality both through disposition and through situational factors.

Entrepreneurial skills are the abilities required to create value in the context of a new venture or an established organization. They include creativity, innovation, opportunity identification and assessment, risk management, resource leveraging, bootstrapping, and guerrilla capabilities. These skills are often expressed in various forms of intelligence, such as

- Creative intelligence to come up with and recognize new ideas
- Practical intelligence to identify ways to develop them
- Analytical intelligence to determine whether or not to develop them
- Social intelligence to understand and communicate these ideas with others.[20]

Skills may be developed through educational programs and guidance of mentors. Perseverance and practice are needed to hone these skills. The entrepreneurship literature indicates that opportunities to develop venture creation skills and intelligence frequently emerge from founders' experiences in incubator organizations. In the present context, a **family incubator** is the unit in which an individual acquires foundational skills that can be transferred to other contexts and enable the successful pursuit of entrepreneurship.

There is evidence that the occupations of parents influence career choices of their children.[21] Entrepreneurs often have parents or close relatives who own or have owned businesses. Experience with and knowledge of those businesses may help trigger ideas or the desire for a new venture. Such "passing along of opportunities" while keeping them within a family helps fulfill the entrepreneurial desires of two generations, providing the satisfaction of mentoring to the senior generation while enabling a somewhat protected launch of the junior-generation member's entrepreneurial career.

Along similar lines, a study of 190,000 firms in the United States[22] concluded that the children of business owners are substantially more likely than others to become self-employed. More than half of the business owners who responded to the survey had a self-employed parent before starting their businesses, although fewer than half of them had worked in their parents' business. However, those who had work experience in their family businesses before launching their own venture were more likely to succeed.

This suggests that growing up in a family with self-employed parents or close relatives infuses confidence within next-generation members for launching new

---

[20]Sternberg, R.J. (2004). Successful intelligence as a basis for entrepreneurship. *Journal of Business Venturing,* 19(2): 173–188.

[21]Bandura, A. (1977). *Social Learning Theory.* Englewood Cliffs, NJ: Prentice Hall; Barling, J. (1990). *Employment, Stress, and Family Functioning.* New York: Wiley.

[22]Fairlie, R.W., and Robb, A. (2007). Families, human capital, and small business: Evidence from the characteristics of business owners survey. *Industrial and Labor Relations Review,* 60(2): 225–245

businesses. It might also increase the likelihood of identifying opportunities around which to launch new ventures. It must be kept in mind, however, that while being a member of a family that owns an established business offers a potential to acquire general and specific business skills, this potential is realized only by actually working in the business and by honing these skills rather than by watching them from a distance, regardless of the proximity of this distance. Experiential learning can only come from experience!

However, as you may know from experience, working with members of our family of origin is not always a smooth ride. Research on father-son and father-daughter dyads provides some evidence of one of the reasons underlying such turbulence. Using a life-cycle perspective, Davis and Tagiuri conducted a study of 89 father-son dyads working together in business.[23] Results indicated that there are swings in the quality of work relationship between fathers and sons, as a function of their respective life-cycle stages. When both father and son are going through life stages when social interactions are easy and they are comfortable with their self-identity, the relationship with each other is harmonious and effective. Conversely, when both father and son are going through life stages wherein identity confusion reigns, relationships tend to be relatively problematic.

Dumas's research on father-daughter dyads in 18 family firms indicated that in comparison to the relationship in father-son dyads, father-daughter relationships are more harmonious.[24] However, the role carryover from family to work is higher in this case as both fathers and daughters find it more difficult to transition from parent-child relationship to that of business associates.

It must be noted however that both of these studies were conducted in the 1980s. As more women are receiving professional education, joining the workforce, and establishing larger numbers of new ventures as compared with men, the nature of relationships between fathers and daughters might have changed. Evidence of this change comes from studies attempting to understand the relative importance of successor attributes that founders report as important in the next-generation leader. Of the 30 attributes that founders were asked to rate in terms of importance, gender and birth order were rated as the two least important attributes.[25] Integrity and commitment to business topped the list of desirable next-generation attributes. From a life-cycle perspective, relationships between all family members are likely to undergo swings over the course of life.

Can individuals whose family of origin does not include a self-employed member become successful entrepreneurs? Of course! Some extremely successful venture founders like Dhirubhai Ambani of Reliance Industries and Fred DeLuca of Subway restaurants did not grow up in business families. However, they did acquire

---

[23]Davis, J.A., and Tagiuri, R. (1989). The influence of life stage on father–son work relationships in family companies. *Family Business Review*, 2(1): 47–74.

[24]Dumas, C. (1989). Understanding of father–daughter and father–son dyads in family-owned businesses. *Family Business Review*, 2(1): 31–46.

[25]Chrisman, J.J., Chua, J.H., and Sharma, P. (1998). Important attributes of successors in family businesses. *Family Business Review*, 11(1): 19–34.

and hone their entrepreneurial skills outside of the family environment by engaging in smaller entrepreneurial exercises. It is not unusual to find that business founders engaged in entrepreneurial behavior before starting their businesses. This can take the form of opening a lemonade stand, taking on a newspaper delivery route, and selling belongings on eBay.com. For example, Fred DeLuca's mother shared that as a young boy Fred would buy a comic book for 50 cents, read it, resell it for dollar, buy two more comic books, read them, resell each for a dollar again, and so on, pocketing some change for a soft drink to enjoy while reading the comic books.[26] Similar entrepreneurial sparks often form the background stories of business founders. Family of origin plays a significant role in whether such sparks are nourished or not.

VALUES, BELIEFS, AND ATTITUDES REGARDING ENTREPRENEURSHIP

"Attitude is a little thing that makes a big difference," remarked Winston Churchill, and he was right! Research shows that attitudes influence individual behavior. In turn, attitude is a product of our beliefs and values. Johns and Saks[27] represented this relationship as follows:

$$\text{BELIEF} + \text{VALUE} \;\rightarrow\; \text{ATTITUDE} \;\rightarrow\; \text{BEHAVIOR}$$

Attitude is described as a fairly stable evaluative tendency to respond consistently to some specific object, situation, person, or category of people.[28] **Values** are broad tendencies to prefer certain states of affairs over others and determine what an individual considers to be good or bad. **Beliefs** govern the pathways that we think will lead to the desired outcomes. Research indicates that people settle in occupations that are a good fit with their beliefs and values.[29] For the purpose of our discussion, it is important to note that both values and beliefs are acquired early in life.[30] Thus, the family of origin significantly influences our beliefs, values, and attitudes, including those toward entrepreneurship, independent business ventures, and the relative role of family and business.

John Ward, one of the first scholars to write about family businesses, noted in his classic 1987 book *Keeping the Family Business Healthy* that all families have to make a basic choice in their philosophical orientation or beliefs regarding the relative role of family and business so as to resolve dilemmas of the competing needs of these two social institutions. While Ward focused on existing family firms, his fundamental idea can be used to understand the basis of decision making regarding the role of family in new ventures as well. He observed that depending on whether family or

---

[26]Video: *Introduction to Franchising: The Subway Story.*

[27]Johns, G., and Saks, A.M. (2005). *Organizational Behavior: Understanding and Managing Life at Work.* Toronto: Pearson Prentice Hall, P. 109.

[28]Johns, G., and Saks, A.M. (2005). Ibid.

[29]Judge, T.A., and Bretz, R.D. Jr. (1992). Effects of work values on job choice decisions. *Journal of Applied Psychology,* 77: 261–271.

[30]Schwass, J. (1993). Conflict in the family business: A European perspective. In Henry W. (Ed.). *Family Business: A Generation Comes of Age.* Proceedings of the Family Firm Institute Conference, New York.

TABLE 3.1 Beliefs Regarding the Relative Role of Family and Business			
		Predominance of business	
		Yes	No
Predominance of family	Yes	**FB** Family Business First	**Fb** Family First
	No	**fB** Business First	**fb** Neither family nor business first

Source: Inspired by Ward, J.L. (1987). *Keeping the Family Business Healthy.* Family Enterprise Publishers Inc.; Whetten, D. (2007). Keynote speech at the Family Enterprise Research Conference, Monterrey, Mexico.

business needs are given precedence in decision making, firms can be described as Business first, Family first, and Family Enterprise first. These are depicted in Table 3.1 as Bf (Business family), Fb (Family business), and FB (Family Business). In addition, we add the fourth possible choice as fb (small f, small b) to encompass those enterprises in which neither family nor business is the fundamental basis of decision making. Examples might include life-style ventures launched by single individuals where decisions are guided by individual preferences rather than either by family or by business needs. Or, such an orientation might be found in later generational family firms as businesses are changed under the leadership of nonfamily members while family separates itself from the operations of the business, devoting time to other individual or collective pursuits such as philanthropy, travel, and so on.

Those with a "Family first" orientation would employ all family members seeking to join the enterprise regardless of their qualifications or contributions to the business. In such cases, the needs of the family supersede those of the business. On the other hand, a "Business first" orientation would prompt employing family members in the business only if the benefits to the business of such employment are higher than the involved costs. Others, who give equal importance to both Family and Business (big F, big B), might attempt to develop opportunities within or related to the business so as to best utilize the inherent strengths and interests of family members interested in contributing to the business. Similar guiding beliefs are used when determining the distribution of dividends or absorbing losses that might occur in the business or the extent of the investment of time, money, and emotional capital that family members might be willing to make in a new venture created by a family member.

In a study[31] of 732 Spanish small- and medium-sized family firms with 50 to 500 employees, Basco and Rodríguez found that about 46 percent firms followed a "Family Enterprise first" orientation emphasizing both family and business concerns; 26 percent used a "Business first" orientation; while another 28 percent placed limited importance to both family and business issues in their management and

---

[31]Basco, R., and Rodriguez, M.J.P. (2009). Studying family enterprise holistically: Evidence for integrated family and business systems. *Family Business Review,* 22(1): 82–95.

governance. In comparison to the Business first firms, Family Enterprise first firms that emphasized both family and business, with relatively more importance to family issues, performed better on family dimensions and as well as Business first firms on the business dimensions. This is the first evidence suggesting the importance of the tangible performance implications of different orientations in family firms.

Another significant way in which family beliefs and values influence attitudes toward business is in terms of time perspectives, that is, whether an individual tends to focus decisions on the past, present, or future.[32] Research suggests that those with a present time perspective operate on shorter planning horizons as they tend to be focused on current pleasures and consumption. For others guided by the past time perspective, recall of past events and related costs and benefits experienced influences decision making. Individuals guided by the future time orientation operate on longer time horizons as their decisions are based on a consideration of the future consequences of decisions.

Individuals and families with a future time perspective are more likely to invest in new venture start-ups as these entities usually take high investments of resources in the first few years before fruits can be harvested. Narva mentioned that once a business is established and substantial financial capital is invested in it, families either act as consumers of capital and stewards of the business, or commit to recognizing new opportunities aimed to enhance the value of the business from one generation to the next. We contend that it is family values on time perspective that determine whether family members treat the business as an entity to be **Consumed**, **Cruised** through, or re-**Created**.

Guided by the present time perspective, *consumers of family business* are focused on using the business to support their current consumption needs. Those anchored in the past time perspective operate in the founder's shadow, treating the business as sacred ground that should not be disturbed or changed. Such individuals attempt to *cruise* through life without undertaking any major changes to the business. Given changes in the life cycles of industries, products, and economy that we discuss in Chapter 5, such individuals often find themselves at the helm of permanently failing organizations.[33] **Enterprising families**[34] who are committed to transgenerational wealth creation have been found to be future oriented. While they preserve the core entrepreneurial values of the founders, they embrace change and *create (and re-create)* the business, as their decisions are driven by the future possibilities of business and its growth potential.[35]

---

[32]Orlikowski, W.J., and Yates, J. (2002). It's about time: Temporal structuring in organizations. *Organization Science*, 13(6): 684–700; Strike, V., and Sapp, S. (2007). Owner Type, Temporal Orientation, and Risk-Taking. Presented at the Academy of Management Annual Conference, Philadelphia, PA.

[33]Meyer, M.W., and Zucker, L.G. (1989). *Permanently Failing Organizations*. Newbury Park, CA: Sage Publications.

[34]Habbershon, T.G., and Pistrui, J. (2002). Enterprising families domain: Family-influenced ownership groups in pursuit of trans-generational wealth. *Family Business Review*, 15(3): 223–238.

[35]Collins, J.C., and Porras, J.I. (1994). *Built to Last: Successful Habits of Visionary Companies*. New York: Harper Business.

Resilient family firms that survive through generations of leaders and multiple life cycles of changes in the economic and social landscape embrace the future time perspective. In some instances, family champions are needed to redirect the focus of an enterprise from the past into future orientation. The Falck Group of Italy is one such example. This firm was founded in 1906 as a steel company and grew to become the largest privately owned steel producer in Italy in the 1950s and 1960s. After suffering losses in the 1970s and 1980s, it successfully exited from the steel industry in the 1990s, re-creating itself. Today, it has emerged as one of the major players in the renewable energy business in Europe. Salvato et al., who traced the 174-year history of the Falck Group, going back into the developments in the family and entrepreneurial spirit imbued over generations, concluded:

> The critical role of far-sighted *"family champion of continuity"* is found central in redirecting the family from its anchoring in past activities to focus on future entrepreneurial endeavors. While commitment to the founder's business continues, the family champion aided by business savvy and astute non-family executives ably modifies its meaning of "continuity of the founder's business" from "steel production" to "continuity of the entrepreneurial spirit of the family," hence preserving institutional identity.[36]

In short, family beliefs, values, and time orientation regarding the relative role of business and family influence the success and potential for longevity of entrepreneurial ventures undertaken by family members. In turn, the performance of the business has a significant influence on the life of family members, careers they adopt, and the endowments of various forms of capital that they are able to enjoy in life. Thus, both family and business are open systems that are scrambled together—each affects the other.

WITHIN-FAMILY DIFFERENCES

If families of origin have the profound effects on their members we discussed above, why do we find individuals from the same family so dissimilar in their personalities, skill sets, and orientation toward entrepreneurship?

Research on birth order sheds light on some of the reasons for such observed differences. **Birth order** refers to a person's rank by the sequence of birth among his or her siblings.[37] An influential series of studies on birth order and its relationship to innovation was conducted by Sulloway.[38] Examining the birth order, the extent of innovation in their discoveries (incremental or quantum leaps), and ease (or difficulty) with which they supported scientific breakthroughs in a sample of more than 3,000 scientists, he concluded that biological

---

[36]Salvato, C., Chirico, F., and Sharma, P. (2009). A farewell to the business: Championing exit and continuity in entrepreneurial family firms. *Entrepreneurship and Regional Development*.

[37]http://en.wikipedia.org/wiki/Birth_order

[38]Sulloway, F.J. (1996). *Born to Rebel: Birth Order, Family Dynamics, and Creative Lives*. New York: Pantheon; Kluger, J. (2007). The power of birth order. *Time*, October 29: 43–48.

(or functional[39]) firstborns prefer the status quo, while later-born siblings go against the convention and are "born to rebel." Sulloway's research revealed that in comparison to firstborn scientists such as Sir Charles Lyell and Louis Agassiz, later-born scientists such as Charles Darwin and Alfred Wallace were 4.4 times more likely to go against the conventions and support liberal scientific break-throughs. Moreover, their own innovations were more pathbreaking in nature.

Sulloway explained these findings in terms of the niche of shared environment that each child carves in his/her family of origin. He argued that siblings born of the same parents, although living in the same household, experience life differently. In the universal quest for parental attention, each child is placed in a competitive arena with others for this limited yet coveted resource. On the basis of their sequence in the birth order, each child adopts a different niche strategy to increase his/her proportion of parental attention and other shared familial resources.

The firstborn child enters the family with little competition from other siblings and finds the best way to gain parental attention is to meet their expectations and desires. Soon this child finds out that this strategy gets duly rewarded and begins to favor the status quo, making the firstborns more conservative in their approach while being less likely to support innovations or be entrepreneurial. This feeling is further reinforced for firstborn males in families that follow the principle of **primogeniture**.[40] This guiding value accords the common law right to the firstborn son to inherit the entire estate, to the exclusion of other siblings. In his special position as the future heir, he receives particular attention from parents as they attempt to prepare him for leadership of the family and its business. This attention further strengthens his desire to refrain from change and maintain the status quo.

For the next sibling who enters the family, the niche strategy of obedience and meeting parental expectations has already been taken by the firstborn. This child quickly finds out that adopting the same niche strategy as that of the elder sibling does not bring the desired goal of parental attention as parents are not wowed by the same performance the second or third time around. Instead, breaking the norms and challenging the status quo work better to gain their attention. Thus, later-born children adopt the strategy of rebelling against the status quo, which turns out to be a good preparation for engaging in innovative and entrepreneurial careers. From this stream of research and reasoning, it follows that in comparison to other children, a larger proportion of the youngest siblings are likely to be entrepreneurial. However, evidence from studies on female entrepreneurs[41] suggests that about half of these entrepreneurs are firstborns. These conflicting results suggest a need for more research to fully understand the relationship between birth order and entrepreneurial tendencies of an individual.

---

[39]Functional firstborns are those who may be biologically later born in sibling ordering, but are raised as firstborns due to circumstances within a family. Examples include siblings significantly far apart in age such that the biological firstborn has already left home by the time the later born enters the family. In such instances, the later born effectively grows up as if she or he was the firstborn.

[40]http://en.wikipedia.org/wiki/Primogeniture

[41]Henning, M., and Jardim, A. (1977). *The Managerial Woman.* New York: Anchor Press/ Doubleday; Hisrich, R.D., and Brush, C.G. (1984). The woman entrepreneur: Management skills and business problems, *Small Business Management,* 22: 30–37.

The childhood and preadulthood years of an individual's life provide ample opportunities to the families of origin to influence the development of skills, values, and attitudes so as to prepare the child to achieve his or her full potential. In general, business founders are most often those who have received much parental attention during childhood and preadulthood years of an individual's life cycle. However, this attention is directed toward setting higher expectations while providing opportunities to develop independence and a sense of responsibility, thereby sowing the seeds for **entrepreneurial orientation**[42] in the next generation of family members.

Family/ies of attachment exert a significant influence on the major decisions of an individual's life. The foundation of this family starts with **mate selection** as individuals decide to partner with another to set up a new family together. Research on mate selection[43] suggests that a committed partner exerts a great deal of influence on the personal and professional life of an individual. Kaye, a developmental psychologist, observed that "the effect of marriage choices on subsequent generations' opportunities is greater than any of those factors a parent can influence more directly. It may be as great as all the other factors combined." This potential of deep-rooted and long-lasting influence of a selected marriage partner (or committed significant other) has been well understood and astutely used in political and business dynasties.[44] In some instances, a family or an individual may acquire financial capital through marriage and use the money as seed capital for establishing entrepreneurial ventures. However, the money is rarely significant to last beyond one generation or provide a lasting legacy. Instead, acquiring intellectual, human, social, and emotional forms of capital is what determines the potential success of an entrepreneurial career.[45]

Marriages frequently occur at the stage of provisional adulthood. Individuals are working to establish an independent identity, separate from the family of origin. A spouse's attitude toward the risk of starting or owning a venture may profoundly impact the founder or successor and may directly affect the success of either the business or the marriage.

Narva's Stage 1 is accurate in many ways. While some founders launch a business without any familial help, more often than not, an individual enjoys the support of his partner and other relatives through loans and investments, cosigning for debt, working in a struggling business at no pay, handling personal chores for the entrepreneur while that person builds the company, and in many other ways. The term **co-preneurs** has come into vogue to describe husbands and wives who form companies together. As compared with lone founders, co-preneurs combine the talents of a couple. As each has experienced a different family of origin, they can draw upon double the family incubator experiences and networks, thereby adding foundational strength to such business partnerships and ventures formed through them.

While a mate has many opportunities and pathways to influence the choices of a venture launched by an entrepreneur and the potential of its success, in an era

---

[42]Lumpkin, G.T., and Dess, G.G. (1996). Clarifying the entrepreneurial orientation construct and linking it to performance. *Academy of Management Review,* 21: 135–72.

[43]Kaye, K. (1999). Mate selection and family business success. *Family Business Review,* 12(2): 107–115.

[44]Landes, D.S. (2006). *Dynasties.* New York: Penguin Books.

[45]Hughes, J. (1997). *Family Wealth: Keeping It in the Family.* Princeton, NJ: Bloomberg Press.

marked by a divorce rate currently near 50 percent and the rate of redivorce at over 60 percent, the termination of a marriage causes emotional distress,[46] difficult negotiation, and resettlement issues. In the case of co-preneurs, further issues of whether or not to continue as business partners arise. Although there is scant information available on ex-spouses working together as co-preneurs,[47] research indicates a glimmer of hope as many such couples continue to work effectively as business partners after their marriages or committed relationships fail.

As an entrepreneur moves through different stages of a life cycle, the importance of the role played by the next generation in the context of the entrepreneurial venture begins to increase. Despite the longer life spans enjoyed today, the hard fact remains that humans die while organizations can potentially live into perpetuity. The limited life spans of individuals make the longevity and success of the founder's creation (the venture) depend on the career aspirations and entrepreneurial abilities of the next generation of family members.

Meyer and Allen[48] conducted extensive research on commitment and suggested that there are three motivating reasons for an individual to feel committed toward a course of action, such as pursuing a career in one's family business:

- Affective commitment (based on desire)
- Normative commitment (based on a sense of obligation)
- Continuance commitment (based on perceived need)

Junior-generation members, drawn to pursue careers in their family firms due to affective commitment based on their belief and acceptance of organizational goals and a desire to contribute toward them, have been found to be successful leaders of these firms.[49] Such individuals are more likely to engage in the *re-creation* of their business and undertake entrepreneurial initiatives. Others drawn by normative commitment based on feelings of obligation toward their family of origin to continue the family enterprise mostly adopt the *cruise* mode that we described previously. The third category of juniors drawn to pursue careers in their family businesses is compelled neither by feelings of desire nor by those of obligation. Instead, these juniors are motivated by continuance commitment, that is, a perception of significant loss of opportunity costs if they do not pursue such a career. These individuals have been found to be the least effective of the three categories of junior-generation leaders for family enterprises.[50] It is these individuals who are most likely to adopt the *consume* mode toward their family business.

[46]McGoldrick, M., and Carter, B. (2003). The family cycle. In Walsh, F. (Ed.). *Normal Family Processes: Growing Diversity and Complexity*. New York: The Guilford Press.

[47]Cole, P.M., and Johnson, K. (2007). An exploration of successful copreneurial relationships post divorce. *Family Business Review,* 20(3): 185–198; Olsen, P. (2008). The ex factor. *Family Business Magazine,* Winter: 49–51.

[48]Meyer, J.P., and Allen, N.J. (1991). A three-component conceptualization of organizational commitment. *Human Resource Management Review,* 1: 61–89.

[49]Sharma, P., and Irving, G. (2005). Four bases of family business successor commitment: Antecedents and consequences. *Entrepreneurship Theory and Practice,* 29(1): 13–33.

[50]Irving, P.G., Marcus, J., and Sharma, P. (2007). Predictors and Behavioural Consequences of Family Business Successors' Commitment. Presented at the *Academy of Management* meetings in Philadelphia.

Family business scholars[51] use the term **familiness** to describe the stocks of social, human, financial, and physical capital resources in a firm that result from the interactions between family and business. Over time, levels of these stocks can either increase or decrease, in one or both systems. While the reduction of stocks indicates a negative or **constrictive** influence of one system on the other, enhanced stocks reflect positive or **distinctive** influences. Short-term imbalances in the flows of capital between a family and its business are to be expected. For example, at the venture creation stage or during economic downturns or redevelopment of a business, family members may be willing to lend the human, social, or financial capital in their possession for the survival of the business.[52] However, this is usually done with an expectation of returns over the longer term that may extend across generations, leading to intergenerational reciprocity.[53]

In today's era marked by varied forms of family structures, different members of the same family of origin are likely to experience different forms of family structures through the course of their life. As each set of experiences provides unique learning opportunities and challenges, ideas for entrepreneurship can come from any member of a family at any time in their life cycle. Therefore, an understanding of the family life-cycle stages and their likely influences on the entrepreneurial process is important for aspiring entrepreneurs. We now turn to this discussion.

ENTREPRENEURSHIP THROUGH FAMILY STAGES

The family life-cycle model is designed to capture the simultaneous changes in individual life cycles of family members as the system evolves over time.[54] Understanding normal developmental processes and transitions in a family can help an entrepreneur recognize opportunities, plan resource mobilization, and evaluate the impact of venture creation or re-creation decisions on both family and business.[55] Although each family is unique, researchers have found remarkably similar patterns of behavior by applying life cycle or stage of development models to the study of families.[56] Think of the family life cycle as circular and repetitive—one can start at any point to tell the story of a family.[57]

[51]Habbershon, T.G., and Williams, M. (1999). A resource-based framework for assessing the strategic advantages of family firms. *Family Business Review*, 12(1): 1–25; Sharma, P. (2008). Familiness: Capital stocks and flows between family and business. *Entrepreneurship Theory & Practice*, 32(6): 971–977.

[52]Sirmon, D., and Hitt, M.A. (2003). Creating wealth in family business through managing resources. *Entrepreneurship Theory & Practice*, 27: 339–358.

[53]Wade-Benzoni, K.A. (2002). A golden rule over time: Reciprocity in intergenerational allocation decisions. *Academy of Management Journal*, 45(5): 1011–1028.

[54]McGoldrick, M., and Carter, B. (2003). The family cycle. In Walsh, F. (Ed.). *Normal Family Processes: Growing Diversity and Complexity*. New York: The Guilford Press.

[55]Aldrich, H.E., and Cliff, J.E. (2003). The pervasive effects of family on entrepreneurship: Toward a family embeddedness perspective. *Journal of Business Venturing*, 18: 573–596.

[56]Becvar, D.S., and Becvar, R.J. (1999). *Systems Theory and Family Therapy*. New York: University Press of America.

[57]McGoldrick, M., Carter, B., and Garcia-Preto, N. (Eds.) (in press). *The Expanded Family Life Cycle: Individual, Family, and Community Perspectives*. 4th ed. New York: Pearson.

TABLE 3.2 Comparison of Stages in Three Family Life-Cycle Models		
Four-Stage Model Used in This Chapter	*Becvar and Becvar's Nine Stages*	*McGoldrick, Carter, and Garcia-Preto's Six Stages Model*
	1. Unattached adult	i. Between families: Young adulthood
Birth of a family of attachment	2. Newly married couple	ii. Joining of families in marriage: Young couple
Growth through birth or adoption	3. Childbearing 4. Preschool age 5. School-aged children 6. Teenage children	iii. Family with young children iv. Families with adolescents
Maturity as juniors prepare for independent lives	7. Launching career 8. Middle-aged parents	v. Families at midlife: Launching children and moving on
Decline in family size as juniors leave home	9. Retirement	vi. The family in later life

There are many life-cycle models, with varying numbers of stages (Table 3.2). Becvar and Becvar[58] use a nine-stage model aimed to understand an individual in the context of family development. Alternatively, McGoldrick et al.[59] find a six-stage model to be helpful as their interest is in understanding the processes to be negotiated as a family expands or contracts. To grasp the relationships between family and business, we find a four-stage family development model that roughly parallels the four stages of a standard life-cycle model introduced in Part A to be helpful (Figure 3.2). These stages are as follows:

- Birth of a family of attachment
- Growth through birth or adoption
- Maturity as juniors prepare for independent lives
- Decline in household size as juniors leave home

We start from the family of attachment when two individuals make a commitment to launch a new family through marriage or cohabitation, and one or both of these members harbor entrepreneurial career aspirations either within their family business or by launching a new venture. This is followed by growth in the number of family members through birth or adoption. The third stage involves preparing the next generation for independent lives, which in turn leads to a decline in family size as juniors leave home.

---

[58]Becvar, D.S., and Becvar, R.J. (op. cit.) use nine stages—Unattached adult; newly married couple; childbearing; preschool-age; school-age child; teenage child; launching center; middle-age parents; retirement.

[59]McGoldrick, M., Carter, B., and Garcia-Preto (op. cit.) use six stages—Young adulthood, young couple, families with young children, families with adolescents, families at mid-life, and family in later life.

FIGURE 3.2 **Comparison of *Family* and Standard Life-Cycle Models**

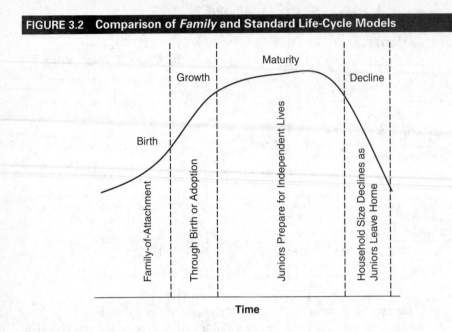

BIRTH OF A FAMILY OF ATTACHMENT

Given that **entrepreneurship** is the process of creating value by bringing together a unique combination of resources to exploit an opportunity and the pursuit of this opportunity without regard to resources controlled, the launch of a new family of attachment by partnering with another individual is an entrepreneurial event in itself as the two individuals combine their resources to set up a new life together while being unsure of the risks involved or resource implications of their partnership.

This is a stage of confluence of resources and skills of a couple as each brings individual strengths and limitations into the partnership. For those eager to engage in entrepreneurial pursuits, this stage affords the support of resources from the partner while the new venture is being established. Also, there is a potential of gaining new insights, perspectives, and support from the partner and the extended family as the collective resources and social networks can now become available to an entrepreneur.

While this stage of family life brings opportunities for larger pools of resources, skills, and social networks, there are also more family members involved in a couple's life. Depending on their attitudes toward entrepreneurship, either there may be more support available for entrepreneurial pursuits or there may be more people to dissuade one or both partners from treading on risky entrepreneurial paths. Table 3.3 summarizes the problems faced, potential opportunities, and strategies available to entrepreneurially oriented individuals at each stage of family life.

TABLE 3.3 Family Life-Cycle Stages

	Problems	*Opportunities*	*Strategies*
Birth of a family of attachment	• Reaching compromises about the rules for the new family unit regarding career and family issues might be emotionally stressful • Attitudes of partners toward entrepreneurial pursuits might vary, needing time-consuming discussions to reach meaningful compromises	• Combined resources of the couple and two families of origin can provide support to undertake entrepreneurial initiatives • Larger combined family size, without direct responsibilities of caring for seniors or juniors, provides added capital for venture creation • Family may provide human capital for a venture	• Opening up to new experiences and ideas • Encouraging each other to experience and absorb new ways of viewing life • Understanding that this is perhaps the ripest time for entrepreneurial pursuits with high physical energy, combined resources, and few responsibilities
Growth through birth or adoption	• Financial and physical demands on family resources are high • Establishing new roles and rules to attend to increased needs for child care and balance work commitments	• Expand social networks • Extend intellectual capital and learn new skills • Increased awareness of needs of families going through this phase of life reveals new product and service needs in the marketplace • Grow socially, emotionally, and intellectually as a family	• Reconnect with extended family members and develop new social networks with parents of other young children • Learn new skills and increase intellectual capital • Share new experiences as a family to imbue openness to experiences in all family members • Begin assigning responsibilities to children
Maturity as juniors prepare for independent lives	• Shifting parent-child relationships necessitate readjustments and may cause stress • Junior generation's exposure to new ideas, values, and workplaces leads to questioning of family ways of thinking and doing	• Lowered resource constraints and more time available to the couple to pursue entrepreneurial initiatives • Opportunities to expose the next generation to business and work life within and outside the family firms	• Using new experiences of the next generation to rethink (renew or modify) family's natural ways of thinking and doing • Encourage building and practicing of skills such as multitasking, conscientiousness, and openness to experience in the next generation

(continued)

TABLE 3.3   Family Life-Cycle Stages *(continued)*

	Problems	*Opportunities*	*Strategies*
Decline in household size as juniors leave home	• Needing to redevelop family roles after children have left home • Questioning whether a couple has grown well together or separately • Caring for one or more parents	• Lesser stain on financial resources and time allows the family to take on new activities • Giving back to family and community while gaining through new experiences	• Spread entrepreneurial spirit in members of the next generation of the family and community • Expand own experiences through travels and starting or recreating new ventures with junior family or nonfamily members

GROWTH THROUGH BIRTH OR ADOPTION

Family scholars observe that if a couple chooses to launch into this stage of parenthood, the family is established as a more permanent system.[60] If a couple separates before having children, they dissolve their family unit. Once children are born into the system, even if the couple chooses to end their relationship, they will forever be the family of origin for their children, who are also likely to remain connected to the extended families of both individuals.

For an entrepreneur, the addition of a child (or children) in a family means that the business has the potential of continuing as a family business beyond the founder's life span. There are now more responsibilities to cater to, and the growth and stability of a venture become more critical as resource needs of a family increase. Moreover, the caretaking of young children is demanding in terms of time and energy, and the availability of both partners for entrepreneurial pursuits lessens. If members of an extended family live in the vicinity, they often assist with child care responsibilities. However, with increasing geographic mobility, such opportunities are becoming less common. Where they are available, they may add more voices and perspectives on child care and the role of family and business—at times creating more emotional stress for entrepreneurial pursuits. With increased needs from the family system, this is not necessarily the most logical time to engage in entrepreneurial pursuits, as such initiatives are likely to add to the collective stress in both the family and the business systems.

Each stage of family life offers opportunities for entrepreneurs. As in the previous stage, as the child grows up, the family needs continue to change, alerting an entrepreneurially oriented parent toward new and unmet product or service needs of the families at this stage of life. The founding of ventures such as child care centers, facilities for sporting events such as hockey arenas and synchronized swimming pools, and cleaning and shopping services often goes back to the needs the founders felt at this stage of their family life. This stage of family

---

[60]McGoldrick, M., Carter, B., and Garcia-Preto (in press). Ibid.

life provides an opportunity to significantly influence the attitudes of the next generation of family members through role modeling and sharing new experiences together as a family.

MATURITY AS JUNIORS PREPARE FOR INDEPENDENT LIVES

This is the stage when the next-generation family members reach the provisional adulthood stage and begin to explore their individual identities in work and family life. At this stage, many junior-generation members take on part-time jobs and begin to experience work life, including balancing school and job issues. They now become capable of traveling independently of their parents. The shifting of parent-child relationships begins, requiring a new set of roles and rules.[61] The family now has more collective time available, and resource constraints begin to ease as the junior members need less time from their parents. Instead, they begin to contribute (albeit in small ways) to the family resource pool. Despite the myth of adolescent rebellion, research suggests that most adolescents remain close to their parents and begin to admire and understand them better as they enter the workplace.[62]

Through work experiences or friendships, junior family members interact with other social systems outside of their family of origin and bring new ideas into the family. These ideas provide opportunities to review and rethink the established modes of behavior and thinking in a family. Such questioning of the status quo, while challenging at times, leads to either strengthening family beliefs or modifying them. Furthermore, as juniors experience life outside their family through work, social, and educational experiences, they may recognize ideas for new ventures or for regenerating their family firms.

For entrepreneurs with established businesses and for junior members in such families of origin, this is a good time to experience work life within or outside their business. As suggested by research findings on father-son and father-daughter dyads, at this stage of life, the decision to work within or outside the family business should be guided by the nature of the relationship between the parent and the child. Regardless of whether the junior works within or outside the family business, the experience helps both generations to determine whether or not a career within the family business would be of interest to the junior and beneficial to the business and family. The general and specific business skills, work ethic, and experience gained are likely to come in handy to the junior in any career he or she ends up pursuing.

For many entrepreneurs who may have missed spending time with children because of the needs of business, this stage of family life provides a good opportunity to get to know the children and imbue in them skills and attitudes necessary for entrepreneurial success. Overall, this stage offers renewed opportunities to create or re-create existing firms, as more family members are now available to contribute to such pursuits.

---

[61]Becvar, D.S., and Becvar, R.J. (1999). Op. cit.

[62]McGoldrick, M., Carter, B., and Garcia-Preto, N. (in press). Op. cit.

DECLINE IN HOUSEHOLD SIZE AS JUNIORS LEAVE HOME

This phase is marked by the largest number of exits from and entries into a family, as children leave home to launch independent lives. In many cases, their partners enter family life, bringing new values and ideas with them. As the next-generation members establish their independent households, the couple in the "empty nest" face each other again.[63] For some, the needs of aging parents might begin to assert themselves.

As summarized in Table 3.3, each stage of life offers challenges and provides opportunities. Enterprising individuals and families find ways to enjoy each stage of life by focusing on new and exciting learning experiences, enabling continuous growth of self and other family members. This attitude helps in the development of an entrepreneurial orientation in a family that is nurtured in each generation and transmitted into succeeding generations. Referred to as **family entrepreneurial orientation**,[64] its source, presence, or absence across generations of a family can be effectively captured through *genograms*.[65]

A **family genogram** is a visual representation that simultaneously captures the family tree,[66] key relationships, and events in a family's development over time. Popularized by McGoldrick and Gerson, a genogram goes beyond a traditional family tree to incorporate hereditary tendencies and psychological factors that punctuate relationships.[67] It provides a view into a family that captures the historical multigenerational perspective of a family life, including patterns of relating and functioning transmitted down the generations. The negative events such as untimely deaths, chronic illnesses, job losses, divorces, and separations and positive ones such as marriages, birth of children, and launch of new ventures can be highlighted.

Genograms are popular tools used by professionals to deal with social interactions in families. Family scholars and clinicians search for patterns that recycle in the form of new developments in a family. Medical[68] genograms are used to evaluate health risks of individuals. For those interested in the business system, a family genogram provides an understanding of a family's entrepreneurial orientation, its history in an industry and business, and key family stakeholders involved in the firm. It highlights the disruptions in the past that may underlie the surface tensions being experienced in a business, the significant influencers of a family member, and potential heirs and claimants to the business.[69] A genogram is

---

[63]Becvar, D.S., and Becvar, R.J. (1999). Ibid

[64]Cruz, C., Nordqvist, M., Habbershon, T.G., Salvato, C., and Zellweger, T. (2006). A conceptual model of trans-generational entrepreneurship in family influenced firms. International Family Enterprise Research Academy, Jvväskylä; Koiranen, M. (2007).

[65]McGoldrick, M., Gerson, R., and Petry, S. (2008). *Genograms: Assessment and Intervention.* 3rd ed., New York: W. W. Norton.

[66]Family tree is a chart representing family relationships starting from the oldest generations at the top to the newer generations at the bottom.

[67]http://en.wikipedia.org/wiki/Genogram

[68]http://en.wikipedia.org/wiki/Genogram#Medicine

[69]Poza, E. (2007). *Family Business.* Mason, OH: Thomson, South-Western.

often accompanied by a table, highlighting the key dates and events in the life cycle of a family and its business. In Appendix A (at the end of this chapter), we share more information on genograms, including steps to prepare these and an example.

Summary

- A family is a group of people affiliated through bonds of shared history and a commitment to share a future together while supporting the development and well-being of individual members.
- The most prevalent form of family structure has changed over the last century. While the extended multigenerational form was most common in the preindustrial era, the nuclear family became the most dominant form of family in the industrialized era. Today, various forms of families can be found.
- There is no one optimal form of family structure, as different types of family forms can provide a nurturing environment in which family members are able to grow and develop.
- Most individuals experience two sets of family life during the course of a life— family of origin and family of attachment. Both sets of families have significant influence on the attitudes, behaviors, skill development, and entrepreneurial orientation of individuals.
- Family of origin is the family in which we are born or adopted and spend the preadulthood and a part of provisional adulthood years of our life.
- Families of attachment refer to the new family or families we launch during the course of our life by partnering with another individual and in most cases by extending to include members of junior and/or senior generations. It is in this family that the majority of an individual's life is spent.
- Personality is the relatively stable set of psychological characteristics that influence the way individuals interact with their environment.
- Entrepreneurs score high on conscientiousness, emotional stability, and openness to experience, but score low on agreeableness.
- Family influence on an individual's entrepreneurial aspirations can be positive or negative.
- Families go through distinct life-cycle stages. Each stage poses problems and provides opportunities for aspiring entrepreneurs.
- Enterprising families and individuals use each stage of the family life cycle to develop entrepreneurial abilities and skills.
- Genograms are an effective tool to capture a family's entrepreneurial orientation.

Discussion Questions

1. Entrepreneurial attitude is infused in family members at early ages. True or false? Why? How? Elaborate with examples from your own experiences as well as from scholarly research.
2. What are the most important personality traits for entrepreneurial success? How might each of these traits be developed in an individual at various life stages?

3. What might an individual and family do to develop the following?
   a. Creative intelligence
   b. Practical intelligence
   c. Analytical intelligence
   d. Social intelligence.

Learning Exercises

1. Using a chronology of key events from the perspective of three different family members, draw a genogram for your family of origin. What can you detect in terms of the extent and pathways to entrepreneurship that exist in your family?
   [HINT: You may find it useful to go through Appendix A before doing this exercise.]
2. For each stage of the family life cycle discussed in this chapter, think of two more problems, opportunities, and strategies that might be used by a family to develop the family entrepreneurial orientation.

Other Resources

- Bellow, A. (2003). *In Praise of Nepotism: A Natural History*. New York: Doubleday.
- McGoldrick, M., Gerson, R., and Petry, S. (2008). *Genograms: Assessment and Intervention*. 3rd ed. New York: W. W. Norton.
- McGoldrick, M., Carter, B., and Garcia-Preto, N. (Eds.) (2010 in press). *The Expanded Family Life Cycle: Individual, Family, and Community Perspectives*. 4th ed. New York: Pearson.
- Geneology charts: http://www.misbach.org/
- Hughes, J.E. (2007). *Family: The Compact among Generations*. New York: Bloomberg Press.
- Poza, E. (2007). *Family Business*. Mason, OH: Thomsen South-Western
- Walsh, F. (2003). *Normal Family Processes: Growing Diversity and Complexity*. New York: The Guilford Press.

Family Genograms

As discussed in this chapter, a family genogram is a visual representation that simultaneously captures the family tree,[70] key relationships, and events in a family's development over time. Various software programs[71] are now available to create genograms. The Multicultural Family Institute,[72] a nonprofit educational institution devoted to research, training, and consultation for family systems, has a comprehensive Web site with standard genogram symbols used to depict familial relationships. Different types of genograms can be developed depending on the nature of interest, such as genealogy, medicine, psychology, family studies, or management.

STEPS TO PREPARE A GENOGRAM

As we are interested in using genograms to understand the entrepreneurial orientation of a family and the extent of familiness (distinctive or constrictive) that a family member is likely to encounter in pursuit of entrepreneurial aspirations, the following steps can be used to develop such a genogram:

i. The first step is to become familiar with the standard genogram symbols used to depict family members and key events in a family. Below are examples of the commonly used symbols and legends in genograms (Figure A1). You may also find it useful to consult the Web site of the Multicultural Family Institute[73] to explore symbols used for denoting interaction patterns among family members and the software programs available to develop genograms.

ii. A few general rules to keep in mind are the following:

   a. Males are denoted by a square and females by a circle.

   b. Members of the same generation are listed in a horizontal line.

   c. Siblings are listed according to their birth order with the oldest at the left.

   d. Mates of the siblings are placed to their right, using a horizontal line attached to each sibling. In case of multiple relationships, all mates of an individual are shown along the same horizontal line starting from the first committed relationship.

   e. Members of the next generation (children) are linked to their parents via a vertical line. Thus, each generation is represented along a horizontal line of its own with the senior generation in a line above and juniors in a line below.

---

[70]Family tree is a chart representing family relationships starting from the oldest generations at the top to the newer generations at the bottom.

[71]http://en.wikipedia.org/wiki/Comparison_of_genealogy_software

[72]http://www.multiculturalfamily.org/genograms/genogram_symbols.html

[73]http://www.multiculturalfamily.org/genograms/genogram_symbols.html

FIGURE A1 Genogram Symbols

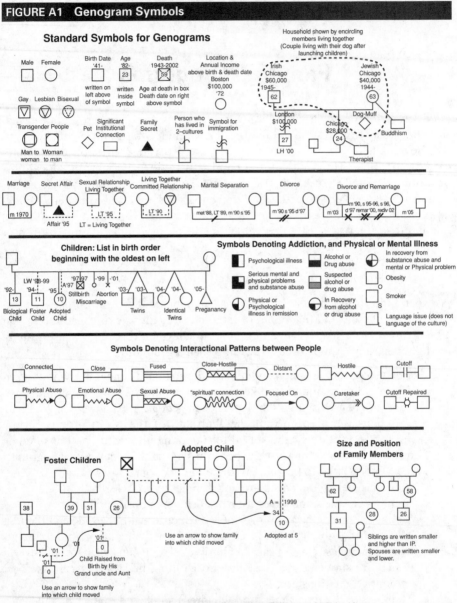

Source: http://www.multiculturalfamily.org/genograms/genogram_symbols.html

iii. With this background preparation, identify the first individual in the family to launch an entrepreneurial venture and list the members of his/her generation both from the family of attachment (mates) and family of origin (siblings).

iv. Note the key dates of entry and exit of the family members in a family by developing an accompanying table to record these events and dates.

Researchers often find that perspectives of key events in a family and business often vary among family members, and related discussions can bring up sensitive family issues. While these differences provide an understanding of the extent of the importance with which events in family life have registered in an individual's mind and help explain the basis of decision making, *they necessitate a need to gain clear approval of all family members before engaging in this exercise and maintaining strict confidentiality of collected data.*

v. Once the family members and key dates of their entry or exit from a family are recorded, legends are used to depict the business start-ups and major positions in the firm, emotional relationships among key members, and physical ailments (if any).

AN EXAMPLE OF A GENOGRAM

Below is an example of a genogram (Figure A2) and accompanying table of key events (Table A1) for the Italian Falck family and the group.

With this information, you should be able to develop a genogram for your own family to understand the extent and pathways of the prevailing familial entrepreneurial orientation.

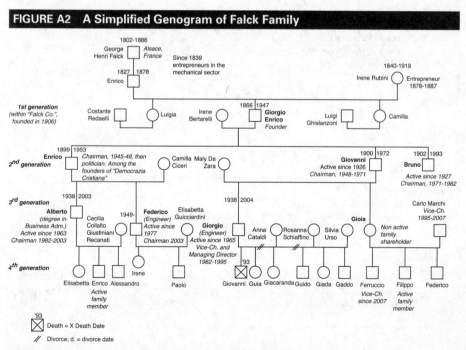

FIGURE A2   A Simplified Genogram of Falck Family

Source: Salvato, C., Chirico, F., and Sharma, P. (2007). A Farewell to the Business: De-escalation Strategies and Business Exits in Family Firms. Presented at the 3rd EIASM Workshop on Family Firm Management Research, Jönköping International Business School, Sweden.

TABLE A1 A Selection of Some Key Events in the Early Life Cycle of the Falck Family and Group

	Business-Related Key Events	Family-Related Key Events
1833	Georges Henri Falck (1882–1886; originally from Alsace) is invited to Lombardy as a technical adviser to the iron manufacturer Gaetano Rubini. The company is renamed Rubini, Falck, Scalini e Comp, as Falck invested some of his money into the venture to assure his commitment to the venture.	He moves with his wife, Alsace, and son Enrico.
1863		Enrico Falck (1827–1893) marries Irene Rubini, daughter of a patriarchal ironmaster. They have two daughters and one son.
1878	Enrico dies. Irene Rubini Falck runs the business until her son, Giorgio Enrico (1866–1947), takes over in 1893.	
1906	Giorgio Enrico establishes the Società Anonima Acciaierie e Ferriere Lombarde (AFL), the first steel company started by a Falck family member.	Enrico marries Irene Bertarelli and they have three sons, Enrico (b. 1899), Giovanni (b. 1900), and Bruno (b. 1902).
1908	Start-up difficulties, the general Italian industrial crisis (1907), and a subsequent drop in demand instigate the first serious company crisis.	
1912	Falck decides to concentrate on scrap or broken iron rather than imported steel and to reduce bank involvement in capital in favor of building private ownership; both strategies shaped firm's leadership in steel industry for decades	
1916	Falck constructs its first hydroelectric plant financed through wartime profits. In-house electric production enables the company to avoid large-scale foreign imports of iron ore	
1930	The next generation of Falck family members, Giorgio's sons Enrico, Giovanni, and Bruno, joins the Board of Directors.	Enrico and wife, Camilla, have two sons, Alberto and Federico; Giovanni and wife, Maly, have a son, Giorgio, and a daughter, Gioia; Bruno has no children.
1934	New division Servizi Idroelettrici created to handle expansion into power	

(continued)

TABLE A1 *(continued)*	
Business-Related Key Events	*Family-Related Key Events*
1941	Falck launches new energy production program leading to 15 power plants by mid-1950s.	
1945	Enrico becomes the chairman of Falck. Falck produces almost 3% of Italian national output of electricity.	
1948	Enrico resigns from Falck to pursue politics. Giovanni takes over as the chairman, a position he holds until 1971.	
1950s	High level of investments in new furnaces, production lines, and rolling mills.	
1960s	Major expansion in steel production and radical technological innovations	
1963	Alberto Falck enters the family business, later becoming the leader of both family and business	

CHAPTER 4

BUSINESS LIFE-CYCLE STAGES

CHANGE: INEVITABLE PART OF SURVIVAL

Many of us who run or are part of a family business know that if our company is not capable of change, it will not survive. For a lot of us, though, change is often difficult to accept, especially when it comes about as a result of succession.

My family's company, Arbill Safety, a national supplier and manufacturer of safety products and services based in Philadelphia, has been through those changes. My grandfather, Robert Bickman, started the business in 1945. It served primarily as an industrial laundry until my grandfather's customers convinced him to start selling them gloves.

In 1964, the business was passed down to my father, Barry Bickman, who again initiated change. With the establishment of the Occupational Safety and Health Administration in the 1970s, my father saw a chance to transform Arbill from a glove company into a comprehensive supplier of personal protective equipment that firms would need to comply with OSHA regulations. Arbill grew from a company that sold just gloves to one that sold gloves, kneepads, hard hats, respirators, and more. It also began offering its own product line.

Arbill changed once again in 2004, when my father appointed me president and CEO.... How did we manage our transition? Part of it has to do with the fact that even though my grandfather, my father, and I have had different approaches to bringing Arbill into the future, we all have shared one common goal—to keep Arbill one step ahead of our customers' needs.

My father had a rule: Work outside of the family business before working for Arbill. He believed strongly that his children needed to be independent and have experiences outside the family realm.

I began working for a start-up electronic publishing company after graduating from Syracuse University in 1993. The job enabled me to take part in launching and sustaining a new business. . . . [T]he experience allowed me to better understand the challenges my grandfather must have gone through when he began Arbill 60 years ago.

[After joining Arbill, it] took some time to adjust to working for my father. I had to remind myself that at work, my father was my boss and not my dad. I found myself constantly questioning him and getting a lot of "nos" when I would propose new ideas. Eventually, I realized I had to approach him differently. I began proposing that we "test" my ideas; I learned how to approach him with several ideas rather than trying to sell him on just one.

I also began planning what I would need to do to demonstrate to my father, my fellow employees, and my customers that I was qualified to become the company's future leader. There were several things I did to prepare that I would recommend to any potential successor:

- Get an MBA.
- Set goals.
- Join a support/networking group.
- Realize early on that you have the capacity to change.

The change in leadership was announced to the company in September 2004. My father made the announcement and explained why the change was necessary and how it would benefit the company. In October, I presented my five-point strategic plan to the management team and then to the entire staff. A clearly communicated strategic plan can be a great way to demonstrate your leadership style and your vision for the company.

We are in the process of evolving from a safety products supplier to a supplier of safety solutions and strategies that will help customers better protect their workers. Our staff shares a sense of teamwork, a spirit of cooperation, and the drive to perform at a high level.

Source: Copeland, J. (2006). Keeping the company on the right track. *Family Business,* Autumn, 17(4): 40–42.

Questions

1. Do you agree that a family business must change with each generation to survive? Why or why not?
2. What do you think about Julie Copeland's strategies for preparing herself to take over leadership of the company?

===

Now we treat the company as a living entity. Similar to a family, an organization, whether for profit or not,[1] is nothing if not the people who breathe life into it. But it is also more than an accumulation of its individual members and, in some ways,

---

[1] Please note while our focus in this book remains on for-profit entities, you may choose to adapt the information to alternate organizational entities that are or wish to become enterprising organizations.

takes on a life of its own. The venture founder may be a lone entrepreneur such as Robert Bickman of Arbill Safety or Richard Stallman of Linux's Free Software Movement. In other instances, a firm may be founded by an entrepreneurial team of nonkin such as Bill Gates and Paul Allen of Microsoft. However, most new ventures are created by enterprising family members such as brothers Sam and Bud Walton of Wal-Mart, or by father and son teams such as Drs. Iverson and William Lumpkin, who started the Mattoon Telephone Company, which later became the Illinois Consolidated Telephone Company you read about in Chapter 2. In these founding teams, family members combined their talents and resources to launch a new venture.

The new venture that survives the hazardous birthing period often experiences some early and rapid growth. Later, it matures and, as happens with each individual who is a part of the organization, it may decline and die. People are the lifeblood of an organization. Although each individual is bounded by the limitations of human life span and must go through the cycle of birth, growth, maturity, and death, each has the capacity to renew the company so as to extend its life beyond that of an individual leader. In that sense, an organization is similar to a family, as both can live in perpetuity, as individual players come and go.

While a family firm might continue across generations of leaders, it may or may not occupy the same market, product, or industry space over time. Firms like the Zildjian Cymbal Company (established 1623) and Tuttle Farms (established 1635–38) continue in the same industry[2] in which they were established centuries ago. Others, such as Arbill Safety, occupy different niche positions within the industry of their founding. In such cases, the major shifts in market and product positioning were synchronized with the changing of the generational leadership guard. Still others regenerate and move into a completely different industry after a few generations of leadership, as in the case of the Italian Falck Group,[3] whose genogram was shared in the last chapter. This suggests that for the family firm, entrepreneurial change may occur at times of succession, but may also be needed at other times in the development of the firm. There seem to be different pathways to regenerate family firms and succeed against the backdrop of changing economic and sociological landscapes.

In this chapter, our focus is to uncover the secrets of enterprising families who retain their entrepreneurial spirit across generations. In such firms, each generation is driven by the desire to pass a renewed organization to the following

---

[2]Cymbal manufacturing for Zildjian (http://www.zildjian.com/EN-US/home.ad2) and strawberry and vegetable farming for Tuttle Farms (http://www.tuttlesredbarn.net/history.html)

[3]Italian Falck Group was established as a steel company in 1906, ascended to become the largest privately owned steel producer in Italy in the 1950s and 1960s, and suffered significant losses in the 1970s and 1980s, leading to business exit from the steel industry in the 1990s. This was followed by successful entry into the renewable energy business. Today, it is a leading player in this industry.

generation. What is common among these firms? How are leaders of such firms different from others who plateau or cruise through a generation without adding much value to the enterprise? Or, how are they different from those with an entitlement mind-set who focus on consuming or harvesting their inherited bounty, leading to phrases like "shirtsleeves to shirtsleeves in three generations"?[4] What pathways of regeneration do enterprising families use? How are these pathways chosen? How do they succeed amid the diversity of individual talent and family membership? These questions, and more, are addressed in this chapter.

SUSTAINING ENTREPRENEURSHIP ACROSS GENERATIONS

Generational transition is often described as a relay in which a baton is passed from one generation to the next.[5] In the context of entrepreneurial firms, to effectively pass the baton of entrepreneurial spirit across generations of family, members of both generations must be well prepared for their respective job of handing and taking over the family firm.[6] Similar to the relay races, the timing and communication[7] between the two generations must be well managed, too. Churchill and Hatten[8] described the four sequential stages of this transition as follows:

1. Owner-managed business
2. Training and development of the new generation
3. Partnership between generations
4. Transfer of power.

Arbill Safety follows this stereotypical pattern of family firms as Robert Bickman, the founder, recognized an initial opportunity and launched a new venture providing industrial laundry services (see Table 4.1). Later, his customers encouraged him to start selling them industrial gloves. While new to this business, he exploited this opportunity, leading the growth of his owner-managed business from laundry services into product (gloves) sales.

---

[4]Other similar phrases include the following: "The first generation creates, the second inherits, the third destroys" (Germany); "From the stable to the stars and back again" (Italy); and "From peasant shoes to peasant shoes in three generations" (China).

[5]For example, Dyck, B., Mauws, M., Starke, F.A., and Mischke, G.A. (2002). Passing the baton: The importance of timing, sequence, technique, and communication in executive succession. *Journal of Business Venturing,* 17: 143–162. The analogy of baton passing has also been found useful in elaborating the processes involved in CEO succession in nonfamily firms. For example, Vancil, R.F. (1987). *Passing the Baton: Managing the Process of CEO Succession.* Boston, MA: Harvard Business School Press.

[6]Sharma, P., Chrisman, J.J., and Chua, J.H. (2003). Predictors of satisfaction with the succession process in family firms. *Journal of Business Venturing,* 18(5): 667–687.

[7]In running relay races, the baton must be passed between runners *within a certain zone* usually marked by triangles on the track—passing of baton too early or late can lead to disqualification. Also, teams often use *auditory signals* such as "Stick!" to indicate their readiness to hand over or accept the baton.

[8]Churchill, N.C., and Hatten, K.J. (1987). Non-market-based transfers of wealth and power: A research framework for family businesses *American Journal of Small Business,* Winter: 51–64.

TABLE 4.1 Generational Entrepreneurship at Arbill Safety

Source of Opportunity		*Customer Need*	*Regulation Change*	*Expanding Industry*
Service/Product lines[9]	Industrial laundry services (founding business)	Product sales (industrial gloves)	Sale of comprehensive personal protective equipment + Manufacturing of own product line (TruLine)	Safety product sales + Safety training + Safety services + Geographic expansion
Year in which each family member joined the business	Robert Bickman (1945) 1st generation	Barry Bickman (1964) 2nd generation	Julie Copeland (1995) 3rd generation	
Year of major (re-) creations and family member at the helm	Robert Bickman New *service* venture created (1945)	Robert Bickman From service to Product Sales (1957)	Barry Bickman Expansion of product lines + Manufacturing (1970)	Julie Copeland New *service products* + Market expansion (2004)
Time between joining and new creation		Robert Bickman 12 years	Barry Bickman 6 years	Julie Copeland 9 years

Almost 20 years after the business was founded, Robert's son Barry joined the business. The father-son team worked together for a few years with the tacit knowledge and experiences of the senior passed along to the junior, ensuring both generations were ready to pass along the baton of the family firm. In enterprising family firms, it is quite common to find that major shifts occur each time there is a leadership change. Following this pattern, six years after joining the business and going through stages 2 and 3 mentioned above, Barry shifted the company's core into a new product line. Then his daughter followed a similar path as she joined the business and later redefined its nature after gaining experience.

Arbill Safety is a firm oriented toward future growth and value creation as indicated by Julie Copeland's remark: "We all have one shared common goal—to keep Arbill one step ahead of our customers' needs." While each generation is sensitive to the opportunities that the changing environment is presenting and eager to exploit them, the firm leaders nurture and protect the spirit of excellence and cooperation among their employees. Arbill Safety's

---

[9]http://www.arbill.com/info/default.aspx

entrepreneurial leaders thereby follow the dictum of "preserve the core/stimulate progress" that Collins and Porras found were used by the visionary leaders of long-lasting companies.[10] In the context of family firms, Miller and Le-Breton Miller[11] found that firms that manage to maintain leading positions in their respective industries over extended periods of time maintain a good balance between building *community* within the enterprise, while ensuring *connections* with external environment are nurtured as well.

In Arbill Safety, major regeneration occurred a few years after each junior generation joined the business, enabling each generation to add a unique dimension to the business beyond the shadow of the founder or previous-generation leader. But this was not done in haste. Each successor took time to get to know the business and learn from the senior while exploring opportunities for new directions. This reminds us of the family motto of another enterprising family, the Metzlers, who recently celebrated the 333rd Anniversary of their family's private bank, B. Metzler seel. Sohn & Co. KGaA. According to Fredrich von Metzler, one of their current leaders, their family follows "Festina lente"—Latin for "Hurry slowly." He explained that while decisions are made after calm consideration of all factors, they are resolutely implemented.[12]

It is worth noting that at Arbill the senior generation fostered an environment for encouraging the succeeding generation to be entrepreneurial. As you may recall from the last chapter, entrepreneurs are distinguished from other successful individuals because of their "openness to new experiences." By requiring his daughter to gain educational credentials and external work experience, Barry Bickman exposed her to new ideas and experiences, thereby enabling the development of confidence that was needed to gain legitimacy and succeed in their entrepreneurial firm. Drawing upon his experiences with family businesses around the world, educator and consultant John Ward strongly endorsed outside family experience for the junior-generation family members in his classic book *Keeping the Family Business Healthy.* He suggested that

> outside tenure will prepare the successor to guide the family business into a future that is more complex and challenging than the present. The overall benefits of such outside experience to successors include: learning their market value as measured by salary, establishing a professional identity apart from the family business, making "youthful" mistakes away from the watchful eyes of the family and future colleagues, developing expertise and self-assurance, knowing they have been evaluated and/or promoted exclusively on their own merits, and finding out that the grass is not always greener in other businesses. (1987: pp. 60)

[10]Collins, J.C., and Porras, J.I. (2002). *Built to Last: Successful Habits of Visionary Companies.* New York: HarperBusiness Essentials.

[11]Miller, D., and LeBreton-Miller, I. (2005). *Managing for the Long-Run: Lessons in Competitive Advantage from Great Family Businesses.* Boston, MA: Harvard Business School Press.

[12]Voyles, B. (2008). A once and future bank: The Metzler family celebrates their bank's 333rd anniversary. *Family Business,* Spring: 96.

In Arbill Safety, we see a company that grows, matures, but avoids decline and death through entrepreneurial actions that have been sustained from one generation to the next. As we discuss in more detail in Chapter 10, such transitions are not automatic. There are many reasons why businesses do not continue from one generation to another:

- There are no heirs.
- Members of the successor generation decide on alternative careers.
- The owners receive a compelling offer from someone who wants to purchase the business.
- Environmental conditions—legislative, technological, economic, etc.—prevent the business from being viable.

For surviving family companies, maintaining an entrepreneurial spirit across generations of family leaders requires technique and communication.[13] Just as for relay race runners, the baton must be passed "within a certain zone" when both junior and senior generations are ready for their respective roles of handing and takingover the firm's leadership. Passing the baton either too early or too late can lead to disappointments. The technique refers to learning to work with the other and, as Julie Copeland recommended, realizing that you have a capacity to change. Communication refers to the senior generation's vocal support for the leadership and change actions being initiated by the new leader.

Although some firms survive by stability through generational transitions, the dynamics of the global economy often call for the renewal of firms for long-term prosperity. To prepare you to help create and nurture an entrepreneurial spirit in your family firm, we believe an understanding of life-cycle stages of a firm will be useful—a discussion we engage in next.

THE ORGANIZATIONAL LIFE CYCLE

Organizations change over time. But they grow at different rates. While some follow the biological patterns of life-cycle stages of birth, growth, maturity, decline, and possibly death, others do not. It is important to keep in mind that the metaphor of life cycle is not perfect for describing organizational life over time, as each organization is unique in many ways.[14] Nevertheless, it is a useful conceptual tool to help entrepreneurs make sense of the developments in their ventures over time. The issues that need attention at the creation stage

---

[13]Dyck, B., Mauws, M., Starke, F.A., and Mischke, G.A. (2002). Passing the baton: The importance of timing, sequence, technique, and communication in executive succession. *Journal of Business Venturing,* 17: 143–162.

[14]Kimberly, J.R., and Miles, R.H. (1980). *The Organizational Life Cycle: Issues in the Creation, Transformation, and Decline of Organizations.* San Francisco: Jossey-Bass Publishers.

are significantly different from those faced in each of the later stages of a company's life. Problems encountered and opportunities presented vary at each stage of life.

Years of research have gone into how variables emerge and change as organizations form, grow, and disappear. Several stage models have been presented in the marketing, strategy, and entrepreneurship literatures. Typically, entrepreneurship scholars focus on smaller businesses, even including stages that precede the actual launch of a firm[15] (more on this in Chapter 7), while strategy scholars focus on large corporations and the postcreation stages of organizational life.[16] For the purposes of studying family business, however, we are interested not only in the creation of new firms but also in keeping the existing organization's entrepreneurial character across generations of leadership. That is, our interest extends not only to the business and its stages but also to those family members who have significant influence on the business over time. Family business scholars[17] tend to overlay the developmental stages of an individual, family, and their firm.

Models vary, but there are almost always at least four stages: introduction (birth), growth, maturity, and decline (death). Similar to individual and family life-cycle stages, organizations also go through transitional phases between stages. Each stage is marked by its specific characteristics and incremental changes in organizational practices, sometimes referred to as **evolutions**.[18] In contrast to the gently flowing evolutions, the transitional stages involve substantial turmoil and quantum changes in organizational life referred to as **revolutions**.[19] We introduce each of the four stages with a discussion of key features of each stage, problems encountered, opportunities presented, and strategies that may be useful for entrepreneurial firms (Table 4.2).

---

[15]Churchill, N.C., and Lewis, V.L. (1983). The five stages of small business growth. *Harvard Business Review,* May–June: 30–50. The five stages for small business identified in this article are existence, survival, success, take-off, and resource maturity.

[16]Adizes, I. (1988). *Corporate Lifecycles: How and Why Corporations Grow and Die and What to Do about It?* Englewood Cliffs, NJ: Prentice-Hall. This book provides corporate executives with a manual for engaging in strategic actions by understanding the stage at which their companies were functioning or transitioning.

Chandler, Jr., A.D. (1962). *Strategy and Structure: Chapters in the History of the American Industrial Enterprise.* Cambridge, MA: MIT Press. This study depicts four broad stages in the lives of four large US companies.

[17]Gersick, K.E., Davis, J.,A., Hampton, M.M., and Lansberg, I. (1997). *Generation to Generation: Life Cycles of the Family Business.* Boston, MA: Harvard Business School Press.

[18]Greiner, L.E. (1972). Evolution and revolution as organizations grow: A company's past has clues for management that are critical to future success. *Harvard Business Review,* July–August; Miller, D., and Freisen, P.H. (1982). Structural change and performance: Quantum versus piecemeal incremental approaches. *Academy of Management Journal,* 25(4): 867–892.

[19]Greiner, L.E. (1972). Evolution and revolution as organizations grow: A company's past has clues for management that are critical to future success. *Harvard Business Review,* July–August; Miller, D., and Freisen, P.H. (1982). Structural change and performance: Quantum versus piecemeal incremental approaches. *Academy of Management Journal,* 25(4): 867–892.

TABLE 4.2 Organizational Life-Cycle Stages		
	Problems	*Opportunities*	*Strategies*
Birth	• Liabilities of newness • Resource constraints • Finding and retaining customers • Delivering goods/ services on time • Energy and time of founding team	• Easier to be flexible and creative • Centralized decision making—no losses in the transmission of messages • Ability to know the customers, suppliers, and employees well	• Take incremental steps of newness instead of quantum leaps • Use creative ways to handle resource constraints such as supplier or customer credits • Utilize all available resources such as co-op students and underemployed family members
Growth	• Mismatch between revenues and expenses; demand and supply; personnel available and skill sets needed • Competitors react more aggressively	• Stable customer base • Various pathways to grow • Leadership talents and growth potential of founding team and employees begin to emerge	• Align guiding values, internal structures, and systems to ensure internal and external fit • Explore growth pathways to follow • Leadership development opportunities
Maturity	• Firm and its leaders may become complacent • Inertia • Fit with external and internal environment weakens	• Identify different pathways to grow products and/or markets • Process improvements • Addition of new team members is likely to help infuse energy in others as well	• Understand the causal factors leading to slow or no growth • Renewal measures must be guided by the underlying causes
Decline	• Obtaining capital • Attracting and retaining talent • Policies and procedures may inhibit creativity • Competitors encroachment on markets and employees • High financial and emotional stress	• Use accumulated assets of maturity • Shed unproductive resources • Move into new products and/or markets	• Engage the junior generation and use their fresh insights to plan and help renewal • Explore new beginnings using social networks

LIFE-CYCLE STAGES

BIRTH

This stage is focused on the creation of a new enterprise. Over 40 years ago, Stinchcombe[20] coined the term **liabilities of newness** to describe the difficulties that are encountered because of new learning that must take place when a venture is created. This phrase describes the problems that newly formed organizations face, which render them prone to failure.[21] By definition, such creation involves newness on three key dimensions:

1. Products or services
2. Markets
3. Personnel or core team involved.

Is all "newness" equally new?[22] As indicated in Figure 4.1, the degree of newness on each three key dimension might vary from one venture to another, leading to eight levels of degrees of newness shown in the eight regions of this figure.

Some ventures may be launched to deliver new products or services in an existing market with which the founders are well familiar. Such ventures are focused on *product expansion*—regions 2 or 6. Depending on whether the founding team is experienced in working together or not, the degrees of newness in adopting this strategy can vary. Robert Bickman's move to start selling gloves to his industrial laundry customers is one such example. Another venture may be launched by an entrepreneur or by an entrepreneurial team to open new markets for existing products or services, that is, *market expansion*. Depending on whether the venture team has previously worked together or not, the degrees of newness in market expansion can vary significantly. Canadian-based company Research in Motion's[23] move to begin selling Blackberry smartphones in Asian-Pacific or European markets is an example of market expansion.

The highest levels of liabilities of newness are likely to be faced by *absolutely new* ventures (region 8 in Figure 4.1) launched by an inexperienced entrepreneurial team that is working together for the first time, to bring new products or services to an unfamiliar market. The learning curve in such cases is likely to be very steep, and chances of failure are high. Perhaps this is one reason why new ventures are often launched by enterprising family members working together as it reduces one significant degree of newness (of team members) in an already challenging situation where founders must deal with newness along markets and/or products/services dimensions.

---

[20]Stinchcombe, A.L. (1965). Social Structure of Organizations. pp. 142–193. In March, J.G. (Ed.). *Handbook of Organizations*. Chicago: Rand McNally and Company.

[21]Schoonhoven, C.B. (2005). Liability of newness. In Hitt, M.A., and Ireland, R.D. (Eds.). *The Blacwell Encyclopedia of Management: Entrepreneurship*. Volume III. London: Blackwell Publishing.

[22]Sharma, P., and Chrisman, J.J. (1999). Towards a reconciliation of the definitional issues in the field of corporate entrepreneurship. *Entrepreneurship Theory & Practice, 23*(3): 11–27.

[23]http://www.rim.com/ Research in Motion is based in Waterloo, Ontario, Canada.

> **FIGURE 4.1** Degree of Newness in a Venture: Products/Services, Markets, Team

	Existing Products /Services	New Products /Services
Existing Markets	**1. *Existing business*** *(OLD or experienced team)*	**2. *Product / Service Expansion*** *(OLD entrepreneurial team)*
	5. *Existing business*	6. *Product Expansion*
	NEW Entrepreneurial Team	
	7. *Market Expansion*	8. **ABSOLUTELY NEW**
New Markets	**3. *Market Expansion*** *(OLD entrepreneurial team)*	**4. *New Products /Markets*** *(OLD entrepreneurial team)*

At the birth stage, survival is the primary problem for the firm. Owners-managers work to ensure that they can obtain customers for the firm's products and services, and deliver these in a timely and efficient manner so as to expand the customer base. The business is highly dependent on the energy and talents of the founders and the resources that can be marshaled. It is encouraging to note that there is some recent evidence that family businesses have a higher rate of survival in the birth stage than nonfamily businesses. Researchers Littunen and Hyrsky attributed this success to the focus owners placed on survival and family well-being over profitability and market position.[24]

What some see as problems represent opportunities to entrepreneurial individuals. Successful entrepreneurs possess the "can-do" optimistic attitude that proves extremely valuable at this tender stage of venture creation. As we noted in Chapter 1, opportunity recognition is at the core of entrepreneurship. For a company with growth potential, the founders will identify and seek to satisfy unmet customer needs. Creativity and flexibility are key words at this stage as it is much easier to be nimble at this stage than at any other stage in an organization's life. The different forms of intelligence that we alluded to in the last chapter—creative, practical, analytical, and social[25]—prove helpful to successfully negotiate this stage of organizational life cycle.

Prior research has shown that certain strategies occur more frequently in some stages than others. Entrepreneurs often benefit from traversing incremental steps of newness rather than quantum leaps, as would be the case in "absolutely

---

[24]Littunen, H., and Hyrsky, K. (2000). The early entrepreneurial stage in Finnish family and nonfamily firms. *Family Business Review*, 13(1): 41–54.

[25]Sternberg, R.J. (2004). Successful intelligence as a basis for entrepreneurship. *Journal of Business Venturing,* 19(2): 173–188.

new" ventures (Figure 4.1). Such steps might involve working in a market, and/or with a team, and/or with products or services that one is already well familiar with, instead of simultaneously trying to negotiate the liabilities of newness related to all three of these key dimensions.

As flexibility and creativity lie at the heart of the start-up's competitive advantages, new ventures may be able to adapt and customize to meet customer needs and penetrate the market. Entrepreneurs can be expected to invest in research and development, finding new ways to satisfy customers. Management guru Tom Peters famously stated, "Anything worth doing is worth doing poorly." By that he meant: get your product or service into the hands of the customer. They are the best way to learn what is wrong with what you are selling. When you identify problems, work hard and fast to find solutions. This is the stage for product improvement and flexibility to better meet customer needs. We found this in the case of Robert Bickman of Arbill Safety as he listened to his customers and adapted according to their needs. When his customers asked for industrial gloves, the industrial laundry services provider stepped up to help and was well rewarded for his flexibility.

Creative ways to manage under tight resource constraints must be discovered. Founders such as Fred DeLuca (of Subway) discovered the power of "supplier credit" on payments as he would get the supplies a day or two ahead of when the payments were due.[26] This small slack in time proved helpful to him during cash-crunched formative stages of Subway. Others are able to negotiate favorable customer credit terms or convince an angel investor (usually a family member or an associate who knows the individual well) to contribute to the new venture resources. Familiness often comes in extremely valuable in this early stage of an organization's life as a family's resources are called upon to help sustain the young venture.[27]

Founders typically govern in a centralized fashion, making quick decisions to respond to changes in their environment. The liability of newness limits access to alliance partners, so many entrepreneurs use the talents and complementary skills available within their family networks to start ventures in partnership across generations. In short, the start-up of new ventures tests the creative mettle and perseverance of entrepreneurs and their family members. In Chapter 7, we focus more on this stage of family firms.

GROWTH

The venture that has established a niche for itself moves into the growth stage. A sufficient number of customers have accepted its products and services, and it has satisfied their needs enough to retain its business. It is now a workable business entity.

As the firm becomes more established and begins to grow, perhaps rapidly, other problems arise. The balance between revenues and expenses may be mismatched in quantity, timing, or both. Cash may be flowing in, but not necessarily

---

[26]Video: Introduction to Franchising—The Subway story. Young Entrepreneurs Organization.

[27]Aldrich, H.E., and Cliff, J.E. (2003). The pervasive effects of family on entrepreneurship : Toward a family embeddedness perspective. *Journal of Business Venturing*, 18(5): 573–596.

enough to sustain the growth, or not in a timely manner when it is needed for payments. Financing may follow expansion, but may have been needed to expand.

The demand and supply may be mismatched too—at times stocks might pile up, while at other times customers may be lining up with not enough stocks to satisfy their needs. Similar mismatches may be experienced in personnel—current employees may be stretched to their limits, but there is not enough work or revenue to hire another employee. The firm takes on more obligations, but may not have the number or skill set of employees to satisfy these obligations. Given the expanding nature of the business, additional pressure might come from competitors as those who earlier ignored a small start-up may react more aggressively to a growing challenger.

Roles and responsibilities of employees remain unclear as the enterprise and its leaders are fully consumed in production, marketing, or customer relations. Founders may realize that they or some of their loyal employees—family or nonfamily members—are not well equipped to deal with the increased complexity that comes about as a consequence of growth. They may not be ready or able to take the additional emotional strain of terminating the employment of loyal family or nonfamily employees, even though their capabilities may not be best suited for a growing business. Cracks of strain among founders and employees might begin to appear. In family firms, these strains easily carry over into the family.

The company can be stretched so thin that it loses the flexibility that had been an advantage at the time of founding. Some firms outgrow their resource base and may find liquidation to be the necessary course of action, while others persevere thriving on the opportunities that growth presents. The firm should be gaining recognition for its brand name and building customer loyalty. Processes get established and roles of key members of the entrepreneurial team begin to gel as strengths and limitations of each member begin to surface.

Enterprising individuals and families do not rest on their accomplishments. Instead, they continue to explore different alternatives for growth by moving vertically, horizontally, or diagonally along dimensions as shown in Figure 4.1. Base products may be improved, and new ones are introduced to increase market share. Growth may come not only from product and service sales to repeat customers, but also through acquisitions in current or new markets, sometimes on the international scene. As the company goes through growth against the backdrop of resource constraints, the creativity of employees, family and nonfamily members alike, is put to test. This reveals those capable of moving to higher sets of responsibilities and others with whom the firm must part ways.

If the company survives and begins to grow, it should keep an eye both on being effective and efficient; that is, it must develop a good fit with both its external and internal environments. Research reveals that organizations with well-fitting components of values, structures, and strategies perform better in the longer term than those with ill-fitting parts.[28]

---

[28]Miller, D., and Friesen, P. (1984). *Organizations: A Quantum View.* Englewood Cliffs, NJ: Prentice-Hall; Greenwood, R., and Hinings, C.R. (1988). Organizational design types, tracks and the dynamics of strategic change. *Organization Studies,* 9: 293–316.

Effectiveness refers to gaining and retaining good relationships with key external stakeholders. An example would be staying close to customers and understanding their changing needs. While the focus of a firm may be on manufacturing or honing the offered services in the earlier stage, it may place greater emphasis on marketing in the growth stage. Given the significant importance of social capital to entrepreneurial ventures, it is often helpful to begin active participation in one's professional networks. Many entrepreneurs find it valuable to join their local chambers of commerce, industry associations, or family business centers at this stage. Others retain close contacts with universities through strategies such as hiring co-op students or encouraging student projects to be conducted on their growing enterprise. Such linkages not only help bring new energy and ideas into an organization, but also help astute entrepreneurs know their value in locating one of the most precious resources for their organization—talented, capable employees who fit well with the culture of the firm.

To improve profit margins, owners should find more efficient means of operating the business internally as well. Organizationally, managers must be able to take over the routine functions of an enterprise so as to leave the leaders the time to explore growth and strategic issues. Many entrepreneurs have trouble moving from the "doing it oneself" stage to "working through others" stage, as the skills required are significantly different in the two work styles.[29] Family firms eager to retain an entrepreneurial spirit across generations and entrepreneurial individuals eager to continue on the growth trajectory take the time and effort that are required to learn the new skills so as to work effectively through others and become true leaders of their organization.

Amid all the chaos and excitement that come with growth, reflective entrepreneurs let the basic philosophical orientation of their families guide growth decisions of their enterprise. As discussed in the last chapter, four basic orientations are Family first (Fb), Business first (fB), Family Business first (FB), or neither family nor business (fb) first (Table 3.1, Chapter 3). This stage of the organizational life cycle is an opportunity to align guiding orientation with the extent of family involvement in the management and ownership of a firm, adopted structures, and strategies.[30] More details on these are discussed in Chapter 8.

MATURITY

Just as with individuals, maturity can strike different organizations differently. In this stage, an organization has established its niche with loyal customers, kinks in production processes or service offerings have been straightened, employees have well-established roles, and cash flow is not a problem anymore. The company provides stable income and a lifestyle that the founding team feels

---

[29]Hoy, F., and Verser, T.G. (1994). Emerging business, emerging field: Entrepreneurship and the family firm. *Entrepreneurship Theory & Practice,* Fall: 9–23.

[30]Hienerth, C., and Kessler, A. (2006). Measuring success in family businesses: The concept of configurational fit. *Family Business Review,* 19(2): 115–134; Sharma, P., and Nordqvist, M. (2007). A typology for capturing the heterogeneity of family firms. *Best Paper Proceedings of the Academy of Management* meetings in Philadelphia.

comfortable with. The business is successful but not growing much. The excitement and uncertainty of the launch and growth periods are history now. At this stage, owners frequently feel they have earned the right to reap the benefits of hard work.

Some organizations stay in this stage for extended periods of time as long as they are managed reasonably well and the environment continues to support their market niche.[31] Many mid-sized lifestyle family firms settle in this stage of organizational life cycle with low or slow growth rates in later years. Oftentimes, the owners express frustration with being bored and plateaued[32] but do not feel they want to go through the birth or growth phases all over again. Firms with entrepreneurial leaders, however, continue to explore opportunities for individual and organizational growth. As seen in our opening vignette for this chapter, while the founder settled into maturity in the industrial gloves business, the firm gained entrepreneurial momentum again once his son joined the business, leading to its renewal into expanded product lines and manufacturing.

For many companies in the maturity stage, **problems** will be encountered in the midst of success.[33] The company is likely to have significant investments in fixed assets. Some of those assets become physically worn out or technologically obsolete. Costs increase. The fit between the organization and its environment may become loose, as macroenvironmental forces impose change. Inattention to the changing environment may be caused by reduced intelligence gathering or ineffective processing of new information. Products and services tend to become commoditized for mature companies, resulting in price competition and lower margins. Industries may also be aging, opening the door for new competitors and substitutes.

Internally, processes that were put in place to manage growth may become misfits in the low-or no-growth stage of maturity. These may exhibit themselves as extreme process orientation or bureaucratic red tape in an organization. Uncertainty about the level of interest of future generations in the business may cast serious doubts in the family founder's mind as to whether investments in the firm are the best avenues for familial wealth creation and conservation.

Opportunities abound in the maturity phase for an entrepreneurial venture. Successor products to those on which the firm was founded can be rolled out. Information technology can help managers learn more about their customers to determine what else they need, so that the company can generate repeat business. Mature companies are attractive to foreign manufacturers as distributors.

The pathways to innovation must be chosen **strategically**, however. As seen in the examples of both Arbill Safety and Illinois Consolidated Telephone Company, sometimes the stepping aside of the incumbent from the leadership

---

[31]Churchill, N.C., and Lewis, V. L. (1983). The five stages of small business growth. *Harvard Business Review,* May–June: 30–50. The five stages for small business identified in this article are existence, survival, success, take-off, and resource maturity.

[32]Malone, S.C., and Jenster, P.V. (1992). The problem of the plateaued owner-manager. *Family Business Review,* 5(1): 25–41.

[33]Miller, D. (1994). What happens after success: The perils of excellence. *Journal of Management Studies,* 31(3): 325–358.

of the firm might be necessary. Entrepreneurial individuals recognize and have the courage and foresight to change leaders as necessitated by the changing environment.

However, if the cause of stunted growth is in factors such as market saturation, product obsolescence, and demographic or social changes that are beyond the control of an enterprise, altogether different measures for renewal may be necessary. As the margins begin to narrow, some firms engage more heavily in advertising and promotion, efforts to differentiate products, and price cutting. While such measures may provide a temporary boost to morale within an organization, longer-term regeneration is more likely to come from changing in more fundamental ways. The more entrepreneurial firms seek ways to innovate and grow in the dimensions of Figure 4.1 that are still open to them. Evidence of this occurs in geographic expansion, quality improvement, and market segmentation.

However, all good things must come to an end. All products and services have a shelf life, making regeneration of a firm imperative. The successful entrepreneur often engages in actions counter to prevailing patterns. And, of course, entrepreneurial behavior is all about unpredictable disruptions. Joseph Schumpeter,[34] one of the seminal contributors to entrepreneurship theory, coined the term **creative destruction** to explain how entrepreneurs introduced radical new products, services, or business concepts that would destroy the status quo. Over time, that innovation would achieve equilibrium, leaving it vulnerable to destruction by the next entrepreneurial action.

DECLINE

Decline is the stage when a firm moves from no or slow growth to negative growth as it begins losing its customers. Financial strain begins to be felt and may manifest itself first as inadequate return on capital. If left unattended, it may worsen into a firm's inability to pay its bills when they are due, a condition referred to as **insolvency**.[35] If this negative trajectory continues, **bankruptcy** may have to be declared. This is a legally declared condition of a firm's inability to pay its creditors, leading to a restructuring or even termination of the firm.

In Chapter 10 of this book, we elaborate on various forms of decline, causal factors, and strategies that are likely to prove helpful in this stage of a firm's life cycle. Below, we highlight some of the key problems of this stage, the opportunities it presents, and strategies that enterprising families use to renew their firms.

If the company slips into decline, obtaining capital again can be a problem. Companies toward the end of their mature stages have, over time, created and imposed policies and procedures that represent bureaucracy in its worst form. The rules are prohibiting entrepreneurial action, regardless of whether the leaders of the firm are still family members or nonfamily managers. Failure to innovate is

---

[34]Schumpeter, J.L. (1934). *The Theory of Economic Development: An Inquiry into Profits, Capital Credit, Interest, and the Business Cycle.* Cambridge, MA: Harvard University Press.

[35]Altman, E.I. (1971). *Corporate Bankruptcy in America.* Lexington, MA: Lexington Books.

associated with excess capacity because new opportunities are not identified and exploited. The company desperately needs an influx of fresh ideas and capable individuals to implement them, but such talented employees, whether family or nonfamily members, are not eager to join a sinking vessel. Competitors find a window of opportunity to attract customers and perhaps even capable employees away from the failing company.

Family firms have been found to be remarkably undiversified as over 90 percent of the family's worth and financial security may be tied to the firm.[36] Given the overlaps between family and business systems, as the firm slides down the negative spiral, it may create a domino effect on relationships within the family too. Stress may build up among family members, leading to emotional turmoil and sometimes the breakup of families.

Late-maturity-phase companies face decline or renewal. Although we would like to think that enlightened and entrepreneurial business owners and their successors would initiate renewal strategies when the firm enters a decline stage, there are many barriers to renewal in family firms. Jaffe identified the following barriers:

- Employees retained for loyalty, not results.
- People will not confront the founder.
- Focus on politics and power, not environment.
- Oriented toward past, not future.
- No new blood.
- No innovation of products or systems.
- Focus on existing markets and customers.
- Employees lack abilities to handle new demands.[37]

However, entrepreneurial firms find **opportunities** to regenerate in this stage. Many such firms use this stage to shed unproductive resources and prune the firm's asset base. Others may overcome decline in demand for one product or in a particular market segment by moving into alternate areas offering high growth rates so as to ensure that the firm continues on a positive trajectory. A mature business that has established a strong reputation and image with its customers can build on that foundation to support renewal in new and innovative growth areas.

In sharp contrast to the **liabilities of newness** faced by the fledging firm at birth stages, entrepreneurial leaders know how to harvest the **assets of maturity**. The leadership team has experience, with higher levels of self-efficacy and deeper pockets of networks to draw from. This may be an opportune time to bring in junior family members and/or outsiders for a fresh set of renewal ideas.

After an astute assessment of the internal strengths and weaknesses of the firm, life-cycle stages and goals of key family members, and external environmental

---

[36]http://www.familybusinesssurvey.com/survey/survey.htm

[37]Jaffe, D. T. (1990). *Working with the Ones You Love*. Berkeley, CA: Conari Press.

conditions, they may decide it is time to harvest the wealth created by the business for the family by divestiture, asset reduction, or selling to new owners. But, as indicated above, the reputation of the firm and residual customer loyalty might suggest initiatives, such as new product introductions. Given the high failure rate of newly created ventures, renewal of firms is perhaps a more favorable option than many others. In Arbill Safety's case, we saw major shifts in the mission and purpose of the business to penetrate new markets with unmet needs and growth potential.

Richard H. Brien cogently observed a generation ago that "at some time in the life of every organization, its ability to succeed in spite of itself runs out." Although many factors can lead to the decline of an organization, a management team often has a significant role to play.[38] Family enterprises are uniquely endowed to reap the benefits of reputation across generations of leadership and balance out the liabilities of newness being faced by one generation, with the assets of maturity of the other generation, to continue their firm on a positive entrepreneurial path.

LIFE-CYCLE SCRAMBLES—INDIVIDUAL, FAMILY, ORGANIZATIONAL

Given the intertwinement of family and business systems, family business scholars and practitioners have long understood the need to simultaneously capture the developments in the life-cycle stages of key individuals, their families, and business. Such an exercise must start by identifying the family and non-family stakeholders who have the potential to significantly influence the strategic directions of a firm.[39] The resource- and time-strapped entrepreneur faces the question of who the salient stakeholders are to whom she must pay attention so as to ensure the smooth functioning of the entrepreneurial firm.[40] A recent survey of 200 family firms in the north-western states of the United States revealed that in comparison to others, family business owners who pay significant attention to the goals and wishes of their family members are likely to enjoy higher profitability in comparison to their competitors.[41] Similar results have been found in a recent Spanish study of 732 firms, which found firms that attend to both family and business stakeholders do better on both family and business dimensions, in comparison with firms attending only to the business dimension.[42]

[38]Argenti, J. (1976). *Corporate Collapse: The Causes and Symptoms.* New York: John Wiley & Sons; Hedberg, B.L.T., Nystrom, P.C., and Starbuck, W. H. (1976). Camping on seesaws: Prescriptions for a self-designing organization. *Administrative Science Quarterly,* 21: 41–65.

[39]Freeman, E. (1984). *Strategic Management: A Stakeholder Approach.* Boston, MA: Pitman.

[40]Mitchell, R.K., Agle, B.R., and Wood, D.J. (1997). Toward a theory of stakeholder identification and salience: Defining the principle of who and what really counts. *Academy of Management Review,* 22(4): 853–886.

[41](2008). Laird Norton Tyee Northwest Family Business Survey. http://familybusinesssurvey.com/

[42]Basco, R., and Peréz Rodríguez, M. (2009). Studying the family enterprise holistically: Evidence for integrated family and business systems. *Family Business Review,* 22(1): 82–95.

FIGURE 4.2 The Three-Circle Model of Family Firms

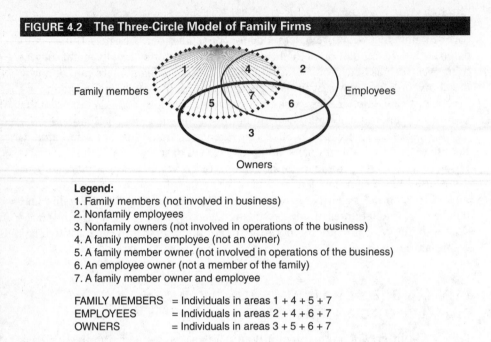

Legend:
1. Family members (not involved in business)
2. Nonfamily employees
3. Nonfamily owners (not involved in operations of the business)
4. A family member employee (not an owner)
5. A family member owner (not involved in operations of the business)
6. An employee owner (not a member of the family)
7. A family member owner and employee

FAMILY MEMBERS	= Individuals in areas 1 + 4 + 5 + 7
EMPLOYEES	= Individuals in areas 2 + 4 + 6 + 7
OWNERS	= Individuals in areas 3 + 5 + 6 + 7

IDENTIFYING THE SALIENT STAKEHOLDERS

Various efforts have been made to visualize and identify influential stakeholders of family firms and capture the relationship between a family and a business.[43] The earliest conceptualizations took the form of triangles with three apexes, representing individual, family, and business.[44] The next set of attempts to capture this relationship used overlapping S-curves for the life cycles of the current and next generation of family leaders.[45] But, it was the overlapping three circles model developed by Davis[46] in his doctoral dissertation in 1982 that gained widespread acceptance (Figure 4.2).

The model helps capture the various forms of family involvement in a business.[47] The overlaps add the complications and opportunities, showing seven distinct

[43]Sharma, P., and Nordqvist, M. (2008). A classification scheme for family firms: From family values to effective governance to firm performance. In Tapies, J., and Ward, J.L. (Eds.). *Family Values and Value Creation: How Do Family-Owned Businesses Foster Enduring Values.* New York: Palgrave Macmillan Publishers. http://www.palgrave.com/products/title.aspx?PID=300866

[44]Davis, P.S., and Stern, D. (1981). Adaptation, survival and growth of family business: An integrated systems perspective. *Human Relations,* 34(3): 207–224.

[45]Churchill, N.C., and Hatten, K.J. (1987). Non-market-based transfers of wealth and power: A research framework for family businesses. *American Journal of Small Business,* Winter: 51–64; Hoy, F. (1995). The owner and the firm: When life cycles collide. *Small Business Forum,* 13(3): 74.

[46]Davis, J.A. (1982). *The Influence of Life Stage on Father-Son Work Relation in Family Companies.* Ann Arbor, MI: University Microfilms, Inc.

[47]Chua, J.H., Chrisman, J.J., and Sharma, P. (1999). Defining the family business by behavior. *Entrepreneurship Theory and Practice,* 23(4): 19–39.

categories of family involvement in business. It has proven to be a helpful heuristic to understand the unique challenges and advantages of these firms. Both practitioners and researchers have found this model to be of significant help.

As simple as the three intertwining circles shown above appear to be, they actually portray distinct groups engaging in complex interactions. They help distinguish between the internal stakeholder and the external stakeholder of the firm. Those involved with a firm as either employees[48] (receive wages), owners (shareholders), or family members are referred to as *internal* stakeholders. Others not linked to a firm through employment, ownership, or family membership, but who can influence the long-term survival and prosperity of a firm, are referred to as *external* stakeholders.[49]

Each internal stakeholder of the firm can occupy one and only one of the seven possible sectors. The diversity of internal stakeholders becomes evident by developing a **stakeholder map**.[50] This is done by plotting the internal stakeholders in their respective position and by identifying the ones who are currently most salient for the firm. Stakeholders like the junior-generation family members who are likely to become salient over the passage of time can also be identified. In a firm owned and managed by a lone entrepreneur such as Robert Bickman, the center of the figure—segment 7—is occupied by this *controlling owner*,[51] who may also be the patriarch or matriarch of the family. In other cases, ventures may be run by an entrepreneurial team of kin or nonkin. For kin-run ventures, the membership of this core segment may be shared by members of the same generation such as siblings or cousins,[52] or by members of different generations such as parents and their children, grandchildren, nieces, or nephews. The diversity of occupants within each segment can be further captured by using legends.

As an example, the stakeholder map is shown in Figure 4.3 for Nadia's Interior Designs (NID). NID is a partnership between Nadia Kovenski; her husband, Rick Kovenski, and their daughter Erica; and Nadia's friend Peter. While Nadia, Peter, and Erica work in the business, Rick is a nonactive owner who provides informal support to the venture. The Kovenskis have three other children. The older two, a boy and a girl, are employed in the business, but the younger daughter is not. There are five other employees in the firm, two of whom are managers. The business is enjoying rapid growth.

---

[48]The term "employees" is used broadly and includes all levels of employed workforce in a firm.

[49]Sharma, P. (2001). Stakeholder Management Concepts in Family Firms. Proceedings of 12th annual conference of International Association of Business and Society, Sedona: AZ, pp. 254–259.

[50]Sharma, P., and Nordqvist, M. (2008). A classification scheme for family firms: From family values to effective governance to firm performance. In Tapies, J., and Ward, J.L (Eds.). *Family Values and Value Creation: How Do Family-Owned Businesses Foster Enduring Values.* New York: Palgrave Macmillan Publishers. http://www.palgrave.com/products/title.aspx?PID=300866

[51]Gersick, K.E., Davis, J.,A., Hampton, M.M., and Lansberg, I. (1997). *Generation to Generation: Life Cycles of the Family Business.* Boston, MA: Harvard Business School Press.

[52]Gersick, K.E., Davis, J.,A., Hampton, M.M., and Lansberg, I. (1997). Ibid.

FIGURE 4.3 A Stakeholder Map for Nadia's Interior Designs (NID)

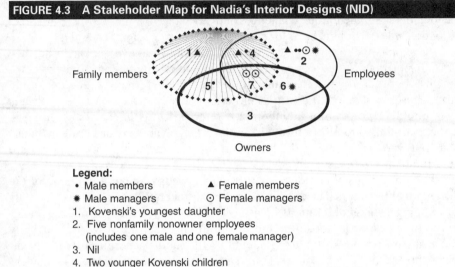

Legend:
- • Male members   ▲ Female members
- ✳ Male managers   ⊙ Female managers
- 1. Kovenski's youngest daughter
- 2. Five nonfamily nonowner employees
       (includes one male and one female manager)
- 3. Nil
- 4. Two younger Kovenski children
- 5. Rick
- 6. Peter
- 7. Nadia and Erica

The perspectives of incumbents in each of the seven sectors of the three-circle model are likely to vary. The three-circle model helps one to understand why conflicts arise over capital and also how capital can be used to resolve conflict and make organizations more effective. By developing a stakeholder map, an entrepreneur is able to identify the source of power of each individual and the underlying source of varied perspectives. In addition, the key stakeholders whose family and individual life-cycle stages must be paid particular attention to can be identified. Such an understanding helps determine the pathways and appropriate timing for undertaking entrepreneurial regeneration of the firm.

Once the key stakeholders are identified, an entrepreneur who has a foundational understanding of individual, family, and organizational life-cycle stages is equipped to consolidate this information by identifying the life-cycle stage of the venture, key individuals involved in it, and their respective family stages (Table 4.3). For example, in the case of NID, the business is in the growth stage. The life-cycle stages and perspectives of all four owners (occupants of segments 5, 6, 7), potential owners in segment 4, and key nonfamily managers from segment 2 must be understood. To gain a consolidated understanding of the extent of resources that are likely to be available to the family firm through these key individuals, the individual and family life-cycle stage of each must be plotted. This can be done by adding the names of each key individual into the appropriate cell in the table shown below to let the overall picture emerge. Of course, it is important to keep in mind that the ages shown in Table 4.3 are approximates and may vary among individuals and families.

TABLE 4.3 Life-Cycle Scrambles		
Organizational Life-Cycle Stages	*Family Life-Cycle Stages*	*Individual Life-Cycle Stages*
Birth	Establishing a family of attachment	Preadulthood (0–15)
Growth	Growth through birth or adoption	Provisional adulthood (16–30)
Maturity	Family matures as juniors prepare for independent lives	Early adulthood (31–45) Middle adulthood (46–60) Late adulthood (61–75)
Decline	Decline in household size as juniors leave home	Late-late adulthood (76 +)

By reviewing the problems and opportunities of each of the occupied stages, an entrepreneur can develop strategies that are likely to help with continuous renewal of a firm. Furthermore, the appropriate timing of taking on new initiatives is likely to become more evident too. If the key individuals are going through demanding personal life stages, it may not be the best time to launch into major renewals of the business. On the other hand, if the business is going through a resource-intensive phase of a life cycle, a savvy entrepreneur tries to avoid intensive resource demands on the family side.

With a good sense of the key players, their individual and family life-cycle stages, and the stage at which her venture currently lies, the entrepreneur has a good understanding of the internal positioning of the family firm. But, as you may recall, the entrepreneurial family firms are not only well aware of their internal strengths and weaknesses, they also maintain a keen interest in the environmental forces outside their family firm. In the next chapter, we provide a foundational understanding of the key macroenvironmental factors and their respective life-cycle stages.

Summary

- New ventures may be created by lone entrepreneurs and by entrepreneurial teams of kin or nonkin. Most of them are launched with the significant influence and involvement of family in business.
- Four stages of organizational life cycle are birth, growth, maturity, and decline. While some organizations follow this typical pattern, entrepreneurial family firms renew themselves to avoid stagnant maturity or decline.
- Various pathways to renew are available to family firms including moving into new products, services, or markets.
- The liabilities of newness cause steep learning curves, but successful entrepreneurs learn how to complement them with assets of maturity. This is done

either by negotiating newness in incremental steps or by teaming up with others who complement the entrepreneur with their assets of maturity.

- While renewal may be undertaken by existing leaders, in entrepreneurial family firms it is often synchronized with the transition of leadership to the next-generation family or nonfamily leaders.
- Generational leadership transition is described as a relay in which a baton is passed from one generation to another.
- Enterprising families ensure that their next generation is well prepared to lead their family firms through changing economic and sociological life-cycle changes. Preparation through education training and external and internal work experience is mandatory in such firms.
- Firms with a good fit between guiding family values, adopted governance structures, and pathways to growth enjoy performance advantages.
- The three circles model is an effective tool to understand the roles and perspectives of key stakeholders of a family firm.
- Stakeholder maps are an efficient way to understand who the salient stakeholders are now and those likely to become important in the future.

Discussion Questions

1. Julie Copeland of Arbill Safety suggests a four-point preparation plan for family business successors:
   - Get an MBA.
   - Set goals.
   - Join a support/networking group.
   - Realize early on that you have the capacity to change.

   How effective do you think this plan is likely to be in gaining the trust and confidence of key stakeholders of an entrepreneurial family firm? Is this plan likely to work in all family firms? Are there any missing components of the plan that need to be considered?
2. What similarities and differences do you find in the two cases of Arbill Safety and Illinois Consolidated Telephone Company (Chapter 2) in terms of strategies used to prepare the family and business for the pursuit of entrepreneurial opportunities?
3. Research suggests that most entrepreneurial ventures are created with the significant involvement of family members. Why do you think this is? What are the likely challenges and advantages that ventures created by family members, in comparison with those created by nonkin entrepreneurial teams, encounter?
4. We have argued that liabilities of newness may be effectively negotiated in incremental steps or by teaming up with others (kin or nonkin) who complement the entrepreneur with their assets of maturity. Do you agree with this strategy? Why?
5. Would working with kin be any different from working with nonkin? How? Would you prefer to work with members of your family or not? Why?

6. What are the four basic guiding philosophical orientations of a family firm? What strategies might a growing firm adopt to synchronize its familial values with firm structure and policies?
7. How would you recognize that a family business has reached the maturity stage of the life cycle? What renewal strategies are available at this stage?

Learning Exercises

1. Locate an entrepreneurial family firm in your community. Interview the CEO of this firm, develop a stakeholder map for this firm today, and learn how the positioning of key stakeholders is likely to change over the next decade. What talents and skills are likely to be needed to successfully operate the above firm 10 years from now? Remember to ask about the major strengths, weaknesses, opportunities, and threats that the firm faces.
2. Locate a long-established family firm in your community and find out what pathways of growth in terms of market and products/services offered the firm has followed. (Hint: To locate family firms, you may find it useful to contact the local chamber of commerce for some ideas, leaders of established businesses, or those of family business centers in your region. Commercial bankers are another good source to locate such long-lived firms in a community).

Other Resources

- Gersick, K.E., Davis, J.A., Hampton, M.M., and Lansberg, I. (1997). *Generation to Generation: Life Cycles of the Family Business.* Boston, MA: Harvard Business School Press.
- Greiner, L.E. (1972). Evolution and revolution as organizations grow: A company's past has clues for management that are critical to future success. *Harvard Business Review,* July–August.
- Ward, J.L. (1987). *Keeping the Family Business Healthy: How to Plan for Continuing Growth, Profitability, and Family Leadership.* Marietta, GA: Family Enterprise Publishers.
- http://www.arbill.com/info/default.aspx

CHAPTER 5

PRODUCT, INDUSTRY, ECONOMIC LIFE-CYCLE STAGES

PLANNING VERSUS INTUITION: ANTICIPATING BUSINESS AND PRODUCT CYCLES

Research the market. Assess your core strengths. Write a business plan. Go out and follow your plan—and with a little luck and a lot of hard work, you have a business.

That's how entrepreneurship is taught in business schools. But Michael and Steven Roberts have gone about building their businesses in a very different, much more intuitive way. These two St. Louis brothers built a business empire of nearly 70 LLCs currently worth around $820 million, in a dizzying series of zigs and zags, with one project leading to another or another two. Where most business people would have stuck to a single niche, the Roberts brothers have pursued all kinds of businesses—encompassing an array of ventures that includes real estate development, political consulting, TV stations and cell phone towers.

Michael, 57, chairman and CEO, describes himself as "the visionaire" of the team. Steven, 55, the president, is the "functionaire," Michael says.

Even when they were kids, growing up in a middle-class St. Louis family, the sons of a post office executive and a first-grade teacher, Michael knew how to put a bit of a spin on their entrepreneurial ventures. They didn't just cut grass, he says, "we had a lawn service." They didn't wash cars, "we had a car spa." Then brother Steven would work out the details with him.

The Roberts brothers started their business ventures in 1974, the year Michael graduated from law school. Through the '80s and '90s, they kept . . . connecting . . . dots, often developing the expertise to run a particular business venture only after the opportunity developed.

They got into the shopping center business, for example, when an old Sears store came on the market in an African American neighborhood of St. Louis. They converted the old store into a shopping center and office building. They applied for a local television license that the Federal Communications Commission had earmarked for minority ownership, and then signed a deal with the then-new Home Shopping Network, which forced local cable providers to carry the channel under common carriage regulations—a tactic they repeated in a number of other cities, sometimes with HSN providing the financing. Later, when digital cell phone spectrum became available, they used cash from HSN to buy some of the spectrum that had been reserved for minority businesses.

Younger brother Mark Roberts is general manager of Roberts Marriott Hotel in Dallas, while sister Lori Roberts is an administrative assistant at Roberts' St. Louis headquarters. Michael Jr. is already working in the family business as a vice president for business development and head of the hotel group, and he says he expects all his siblings and cousins . . . will eventually join the firm. The business is so flexible, Michael Jr. says, that they are all likely to find a niche that matches their interests and abilities.

And what's next for the Robertses? Michael Jr., who seems to have inherited the "visionaire" gene from his father, says he sees the Roberts Companies as a *Fortune* 500 firm some day. "I want to be a world leader," Michael Jr. says. " I want to have the company operating in such a way where we have a wonderful team [and] I cannot worry about having to be in the office physically all the time, and travel the world and influence people, and teach them the way I've been taught about wealth and authority and building legacies. I believe I can pull it off."

Source: Voyles, B. (2007). Building an empire through intuition. *Family Business*, 18(3): 50–53.

Questions

1. How do the Robertses complement each other in their entrepreneurial styles? Do you think they may be in conflict on some goals or strategies for their business? What might those be?
2. Is Michael Jr. a born entrepreneur? How could a family business owner pass on a "visionaire gene"?

Enterprising brothers Michael and Steven Roberts are what we label habitual entrepreneurs, also known as serial entrepreneurs. They have made a habit of creating new ventures. Instead of engaging in careful planning, these entrepreneurs appear to be propelled by intuition. Reading their story, it feels that they are traversing through life stages in a corridor[1] of entrepreneurial opportunities. Their enthusiastic pursuit of continuous growth has infected other family members too, leading to the ascension of this family from modest beginnings to a multimillion dollar net worth, within one generation.

Habitual entrepreneurs have held an equity stake in two or more businesses that they have established, purchased, or inherited.[2] In their book *The Innovator's Solution,*[3] Christenson and Raynor observe that

> we often admire the intuition that successful entrepreneurs seem to have for building growth businesses. When they exercise their intuition about what actions will lead to the desired results, they really are employing theories that give them a sense of the right thing to do in various circumstances. These theories were not there at birth: They were learned through a set of experiences and mentors earlier in life.

Research suggests that not only do such individuals nurture their entrepreneurial skills through all stages of life, but also they are alert to the opportunities in their environment and able to find market information that helps exploit opportunities.[4]

Many economists and corporate strategists contend that business leaders such as Michael and Steven Roberts are less likely than others in society to be taken by surprise by new developments because they monitor environmental trends. They continue to identify and exploit opportunities as they violate patterns. With multiple family members engaged in the enterprise, they are able to use the talents, eyes, and ears of many trusted individuals to scan the environment. In life-cycle terms, enterprising families regenerate their ventures continuously by coming up with new innovative projects to retain the attention of current customers while adding to their repertoire of offerings to meet emerging needs in the market. In addition to keeping a close eye on the environmental trends, they are also aware of the developments in the markets regarding products and industry life-cycle changes. Such knowledge helps them decide the pathways to growth—product, service, or market expansion for the current undertakings (Figure 4.1, Chapter 4). In this chapter, we introduce you to the key environmental trends and also the product and industry life-cycle stages. Strategies to navigate the uncertainties posed by changes in trends and life-cycles stages of products or industry are discussed.

---

[1]Ronstadt's Corridor principle (introduced in Chapter 3) suggests that the mere act of starting a venture enables entrepreneurs to see other venture opportunities they could neither recognize nor take advantage of until they had started their initial venture.

[2]Ucbasaran, D., Westhead, P., and Wright, M. (2005). Habitual entrepreneurs. In Hitt, M.A., and Ireland, R.D. (Eds.). *The Blackwell Encyclopedia of Management: Entrepreneurship*. Malden, MA: Blackwell Publishing. pp. 138–141.

[3]Christensen, C.M., and Raynor, M.E. (2003). *The Innovator's Solution: Creating and Sustaining Successful Growth*. Cambridge, MA: Harvard Business School Press. p. 17.

[4]Kirzner, I.M. (1973). *Competition and Entrepreneurship*. Chicago: University of Chicago Press.

MACROENVIRONMENTAL TRENDS

From the Roberts' case, we learn that changing environmental trends are a major source of new business ideas and that it is critical for entrepreneurs with high-sustained growth aspirations to be sensitive to such changes.[5] This sensitivity to changing trends is evident from the following description of Roberts Tower, the most recent undertaking of this entrepreneurial family:

> Roberts Tower[6] will be more than luxury living; it will also be selectively smart living. Located in the heart of revitalized downtown St. Louis, Roberts Tower will offer premiere, environmentally intelligent residences. It will not only feature the finest appointments and amenities— including personal concierge service from the adjoining Roberts Mayfair Hotel—it will also reduce energy use by up to 75%. Designed to achieve LEED Gold Certification and constructed from responsible, sustainable materials, Roberts Tower is leading the way for St. Louis in energy-efficient and environmental design. Indeed, Roberts Tower will combine living well for yourself with living well for others. Its technological innovation will sharpen the cutting edge, ensuring your home will be smarter in the most imaginative ways. Come 2009, Roberts Tower will truly be living above it all.[7]

Roberts Tower is well positioned to take advantage of an affluent and aging Boomer population, eager to live in well-appointed downtown residences, while ensuring minimum environmental impact on our planet.

In this chapter, we draw your attention to five[8] environmental trends that entrepreneurs monitor: demographic, sociocultural, economic, political, and technological. These trends are the drivers that change the nature of competition in an industry or market. While **industry** is the set of suppliers or producers of a particular product or service, **market** is the set of buyers or consumers of the product or service.[9]

For established family firms, it is critical to remain vigilant of environmental trends as they open windows of opportunity for new entrepreneurial undertakings to meet emerging needs in a market. Remember the term **creative destruction**?[10]

---

[5]Barringer, B.R. (2008). *Preparing Effective Business Plans: An Entrepreneurial Approach.* Prentice Hall Entrepreneurship Series, edited by R.D. Ireland and M.M. Morris. Upper Saddle River, NJ: Prentice-Hall.

[6]These towers are scheduled for occupancy in 2009.

[7]http://www.robertstower.com/

[8]Please know that there is no hard-and-fast rule for the number of trends to keep a watch on. The general idea is to be vigilant of key changes in the environment that impact the industry and market in which an entrepreneur is operating or wishes to operate in.

[9]George, G., and Bock, A.J. (2008). *Inventing Entrepreneurs: Technology Innovators and Their Entrepreneurial Journey.* Prentice Hall Entrepreneurship Series, edited by R.D. Ireland and M.M. Morris. Upper Saddle River, NJ: Pearson. p.120.

[10]*Creative Destruction* is a term coined by the Austrian economist Joseph Schumpeter (1942) in his book *Capitalism, Socialism, and Democracy.* It refers to the dynamic flux within capitalism that leads to incessant destruction of old and creation of the new.

While we are driving forward guided by what we see in our rearview mirror, someone else may be redefining our industry. And our products and companies may be the ones destroyed.

Successful entrepreneurs understand the importance of knowing both their current (and potential) customers and competitors well. As they scan their environments, they ask themselves what niche of an industry or market segment they are currently focused on. Is this niche growing or diminishing? What environmental forces are the major influencers of the segments of interest? At what life-cycle stage is their industry or market? An understanding of the following trends is helpful for all entrepreneurial family firms.

Demographic trends are related to the changes in population over time and space. Changes in rate of growth, distribution, household size and structure, education, gender, and so on can all have important implications for the size of the market that is of interest to a firm. The impact of population creeps up in fundamental ways for all business enterprises, because after all it is the needs of people that enterprises are attempting to cater to. If the number of people with specific needs or preferences changes, it has a fundamental effect on the size of the market. For example, with the increase in the number of people over 65 years old, ventures aimed toward catering to the needs of this growing segment are likely to grow in the next two decades.

The United States Census Bureau is a good resource for information on demographic trends. Similar government departments in other nations monitor population trends and make reports available through their Web sites. In addition, books such as *Boom, Bust, & Echo*[11] provide valuable guidance on understanding demographic trends and how an entrepreneur might benefit from them.

Some highlights of the demographic trends in the United States are provided in Table 5.1. What business opportunities can you think of to capitalize on these trends? And, what family businesses are likely to face diminishing segments of customers? How do you think these trends might be the same or different in other countries?

Knowledge of the individual and family life-cycle stages also proves valuable to understand how the changes in population might impact opportunities for business. Just as business owners and their family members are born, age, and die, so are their customers. Successful businesses usually segment their markets. Many family firms benefit from having multiple generations in leadership positions, giving new perspectives to changing demographics in the marketplace. Without careful monitoring, a firm can find itself selling products or services to an ever-shrinking market. The demographic trends also have a significant influence on the labor market including the number and types of employees available and the growth of an enterprise that can reasonably be undertaken. In Table 5.2, we share some industries influenced by demographic trends. Can you think of other industries or industry sectors that are currently being influenced by the key demographic trends in your region?

---

[11]Foot, D.K., and Stoffmann, D. (2001). *Boom, Bust, & Echo: Profiting from the Demographic Shift in the 21st Century.* Toronto, Canada: Stoddart Publishing Company.

TABLE 5.1   Demographic Trends in the United States

- The U.S. population more than tripled from 76 million people in 1900 to 281 million people in 2000 and reached 300 million in 2006
- The population of the western United States grew faster than that of any of the other three regions of the country
- At the beginning of the 20th century, half of the U.S. population was under 22.9 years of age. At the century's end, half of the population was over 35.3 years
- The population of age 65 and over increased tenfold from 3.1 million in 1900 to 35 million in 2000. Rapid growth of this age group will begin in 2011 when the first of the Baby Boom generation reaches 65 years and will continue for many years
- In 1900, the average household consisted of seven or more people; by 2000, there were two persons per household
- In 1970, women represented one of every five heads of household in the United States. By 2000, they were more than one of every three
- Male households represent the greater share of one-person households. In 2000, 50% of the male family householders with no wife present had children present in their households

Sources: http://www.census.gov/prod/2002pubs/censr-4.pdf; http://www.census.gov/population/pop-profile/dynamic/PopDistribution.pdf

Sociocultural trends relate to the social and cultural forces that are influencing the markets and the level of competition. Many of the trends occurring in society at large may be manifested within the venturing family. Increasing diversity, smaller household sizes, higher awareness, and concern for natural environment are some such trends. One major driving trend of the last century is the increased number of women obtaining higher education and joining the workforce. This has led to the need for more services to support the working family such as the increased number of child or senior care services, spas and gyms for women, cleaning services, and lawn care. Moreover, it has propelled the increase of women-led family firms.

The stunning rise of franchising is another significant consequence of this trend. According to the International Franchising Association (IFA), in 2008 there were more than 600,000 franchise operations, spanning more than 75 industries in the United States alone. The combined annual sales from franchise operations was over 800 billion, representing over 40 percent of all retail business in the country.[12] A large proportion of franchise operations are family firms that may eventually face issues of generational succession.

Concern for the natural environment is another important sociocultural trend that is gaining widespread momentum and providing rich avenues for business opportunities on products and services aimed to reduce the negative impact of humans on the planet. With their tighter alignment and concern for their local communities, family firms are well positioned to participate in opportunities developing through this trend. Because of their generally longer history in a

[12]http://www.frannet.com/

community, family firms tend to enjoy higher degrees of trust when they participate in community-building activities and in related products and service offerings. Books like *Natural Capitalism*,[13] *Capitalism at the Crossroads*,[14] and *Small Is Profitable*[15] form great readings for entrepreneurs as the authors provide thought-provoking and practical insights for developing sustainable family business enterprises that are environmentally friendly.

When it comes to sociocultural trends, it is important to distinguish between fads and trends. While fads are narrower in scope and duration, trends extend over long terms and have a broader influence on various segments of the economy. Some fads evolve into trends while others lose energy after some time.[16] An entrepreneurial family firm may position itself to take advantage of opportunities provided by passing fads by using business models that count on fads, such as T-shirt manufacturing for live concerts. Others may feel more comfortable engaging in ventures that are focused on meeting the changing social and cultural needs of a population. An example of a more sustainable trend is the increased number of Hispanics and other minorities in the United States, leading to a need and demand for language training services, increased variety in groceries, diverse range of hair or skin care products, and so on. Regardless of the segment of the population that a venture is focused on serving, it is a good idea to get to know the target customers and their changing needs and thought patterns so as to continue innovations in products or services offerings.

Economic trends and cycles are the recurring expansion and contraction of a national economy.[17] A cycle normally moves from relatively rapid growth of output (expansion) to periods of stagnation or decline (recession) usually followed by recovery (Figure 5.1). A cycle can occur in a single year, but typically covers several years, a decade, or more, and is more characteristic of free enterprise economies than other systems.

Economists, executives, and public officials debate when a nation is in one or another of the cycle stages, but standard measures have been formulated to observe in retrospect when we were in and when we left a particular stage. Gross domestic product, personal income, and unemployment rates are all used to define periods of expansion versus contraction or stagnation. There is some evidence that ventures launched during contraction or stagnation have higher survival rates and outperform companies that start during expansion periods.

The evolution of cycles is influenced by many factors, such as national fiscal and monetary policies, atmospheric conditions and natural disasters, international

[13]Hart, S.L. (2007). *Capitalism at the Crossroads: Aligning Business, Earth, and Humanity*, with a foreword by Al Gore. Upper Saddle River, NJ: Wharton School Publishing.

[14]Lovins, H., Lovins, A., and Hawken, P. (1999). *Natural Capitalism: Creating the Next Industrial Revolution*. Boston, MA: Rocky Mountain Institute.

[15]Datta, E.K., Feiler, T., Lehmann, A., Lovens, A.B., Rabago, K.R., Swisher, J.N., and Wicker, K. (2008). *Small Is Profitable*. Rocky Mountain Institute.

[16]http://www.crazyfads.com/

[17](2007). Economic Cycles. *Encyclopedia of Business and Finance*. http://www.enotes.com/business-finance-encyclopedia/economic-cycles.

FIGURE 5.1   An Economic Cycle

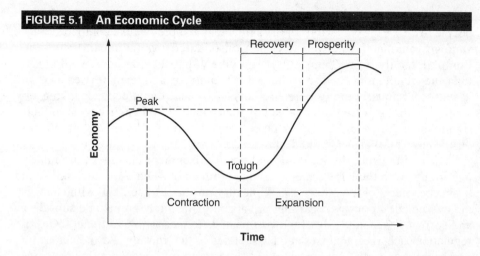

events including wars, and others. While economic cycles cut across all industries, they do not impact all sectors of a nation's economy equally. Some regions may advance as others decline. Some businesses or industries may suffer as others prosper. Industries such as housing or luxury cars are more significantly influenced by economic cycles than other industries such as funeral homes or health care. Downward trends in an economy lead to unexpected growth in some industries. For example, lipstick sales have been observed to boom during times of depression.[18] As it becomes harder to afford jewels or fine clothes, the usage of cheaper means of adorning oneself increases, causing upturns in related sales. Similarly, the sale of beer has been found to increase as the economy dips, while higher-end craft beer or other enhanced beverages are consumed less.

Leaders of entrepreneurial family firms assess and address their own competitive environments, keep abreast of the economic trends, and use this information to strategically launch and exit from businesses. During a recessionary period, such as the one that began in 2008, it would not be surprising to see a family business owner postpone retirement, perhaps to the dismay of the next generation that had anticipated taking charge. On the other hand, economic slowdowns may provide a good opportunity for multiple generations to work together and use the time to understand the desires and abilities of junior-generation family members, and help build their entrepreneurial spirit and business capabilities. There is some evidence that ventures created during recessions actually have higher survival rates than those launched during prosperity. Families might consider helping members start their own firms during economic downturns.

The **political and legal** environment is of significant importance as it can open or close avenues for growth of a family business. For example, when a nation enters into a free trade agreement with another country or a group of countries, domestic firms face both threats and opportunities. Both are reasonably

---

[18]http://www.bankrate.com/brm/news/investingadvice/market-history-a1.asp

predictable because the trade negotiations last a sufficient duration for business-people to assess the conditions of the agreement and the relative competitive advantages among the nations. Recall Consolidated Communications of the Lumpkin family from Chapter 2. It is unlikely that the company would exist today had it not monitored and adjusted to technology and regulatory changes in its industry. Similarly, the Roberts brothers have been very effective in taking advantage of the opportunities enabled by the changing legal environment in their communities. Yet, some firms will be completely surprised as their domestic industries lose market share and decline.

For family firms, the legal and political environment becomes particularly important, given the large scale and scope of regulations on both the family and business systems of the enterprise. While all firms have to contend with changes in governmental policies regarding privatization, taxation, grants and subsidies, and currency exchange rates, family firms have to deal with additional forms of regulation such as estate taxes and laws related to the transfer of ownership from one generation to the next, prenuptial agreements, settlements in divorce cases that might involve the family firm itself, and wealth distribution models between active and nonactive family owners.

International researchers have found considerable variation among countries regarding tax rates and the preservation of wealth across generations.[19] Often, leaders of the most enterprising family firms are well clued into the politicolegal world so as not to be caught by surprise with changes that influence their enterprise. They make use of experts who specialize in detailed knowledge of legal and regulatory actions.

Technological advances and trends have been at the forefront of creative destruction over the last few decades. Technologies refer not only to new products and services derived from intellectual property, but also to advances in transportation, communication, and other activities that affect the ways we live and work. New technologies and technological obsolescence are resulting in shortened life cycles, necessitating the need for continuous innovation in many industries. Schindehutte et al. captured the impact of technology effectively when they observed:

> Technology is a key driver of change—it facilitates interactivity and virtual networks, compresses time and distance, blurs industry boundaries through convergence, and increases the speed of change. Globalization highlights the irrelevance of geography, borders, and hierarchies.[20]

Family firms attached to the past glorious days can find themselves quickly out of tune with the opportunities in their environment. Even in industries such as

[19]Davis, J.A., Swartz, J.B., Chang, E.B., Eyzaguirre, G, J.M., Mattson, R., and Pettker, J.D. (1996). A comparison of four countries' estate laws and their influence on family companies. *Family Business Review*, 9(3): 285–294.

[20]Schindehutte, M., Morris, M.H., and Pitt, L.F. (2009). *Rethinking Marketing: The Entrepreneurial Imperative*. Prentice Hall Entrepreneurship Series, edited by R.D. Ireland and M.M. Morris. Upper Saddle River, NJ: Prentice Hall, p.120.

furniture manufacturing or child care services or antiques, with relatively little technological changes to the core of the business, the impact on the value chain can be significant. In family firms, changes in technology often provide exciting avenues for junior generations to contribute to the established venture.

Changes in technology create new industries, bringing new entrepreneurial stars to the forefront. As an example, the creation of the "Internet social utilities" industry has brought entrepreneurs such as Mark Zuckerberg of Facebook[21] and Brad Greenspan of MySpace[22] to the attention of the business world. Books such as *Inventing Entrepreneurs*[23] and *Wikinomics*[24] provide interesting readings to understand the various influences of technological changes and how leaders of an enterprising family firm might take advantage of them.

In Table 5.2, we highlight some of the industries that have been significantly influenced, either positively or negatively, by changing environmental trends. Can you think of other examples of industry segments emerging or declining today as

TABLE 5.2 Industry Segments Influenced by Environmental Trends[25]	
Demographic trends	**Political-legal trends**
• In-home medical services • Niche gyms • Special needs foods • Smaller portion sizes • Day care and elder care facilities • Family business consultants	• Sarbanes-Oxley compliance consultants • Estate planning experts • Adoption agencies • Assisted living centers
Sociocultural trends	**Technological trends**
• Enhanced beverages • Organic foods • Green apparel • Matchmaking services • Crafts and handmade goods	• Molecular imaging • Technology training and consulting • Alternative energy products • Online dating, gaming, shopping, etc. • Home automation • Media storage
Economic trends	
• Urban high rises and condos • College planning consultants • Management of upscale homes and estates • Executive recruiting • Gently used clothing stores • Bulk grocery stores	

---

[21]http://en.wikipedia.org/wiki/Facebook

[22]http://en.wikipedia.org/wiki/Brad_Greenspan

[23]George, G., and Bock, A.J. (2008). *Inventing Entrepreneurs: Technology Innovators and Their Entrepreneurial Journey*. Prentice Hall Entrepreneurship Series, edited by R.D. Ireland and M.M. Morris. Upper Saddle River, NJ: Prentice-Hall.

[24]Tapscott, D., and Williams, A.D. (2006). *How Mass Collaborations Change Everything*. New York: Portfolio.

[25]Kooser, A., Park, J., Holloway, L., Tiffany, L., and Torres, N.L. (2008). 2008 Hot List. *Entrepreneur Magazine,* December 2007

a consequence of environmental changes? What customer segments are these changes impacting?

Without question, a competitive firm should engage in **environmental scanning** to avoid catastrophes resulting from technology, regulatory, or other changes. Entrepreneurial family firms tend to engage in counterintuitive actions, reversing the patterns of the crowd or acting independently of the cycle. Such behavior can and sometimes does lead to failure, of course, as not all moves are going to be right all the time. However, they continue to move and regenerate. Countercyclical actions should not be taken just for the sake of being different or contrary. This is particularly important for family firms as junior generations take on more responsibilities. In many cases, the shadow of the founder is large and seems omnipresent, compelling juniors toward the desire and need of carving their own space in their enterprise.

Research[26] has indicated that neither the large-scale rebellious rejection of the past nor a blind conservative attachment helps family firms succeed after generational transitions. Instead, it is those who are able to blend progressive attitudes and core foundational values such as hard work and integrity that sustain entrepreneurship across generations of leaders, products, and industry life cycles.

PRODUCT/INDUSTRY CYCLES AND THE FAMILY FIRM

PRODUCT LIFE CYCLE

One of the earliest applications of life-cycle analysis was on product innovation and diffusion.[27] The underlying idea is that products pass through the stages of development, introduction, growth, maturity, and decline as illustrated in Figure 5.2. Of course, the model applies whether we are talking about products or services. The inflection points are defined by changes in the rate of growth of sales.

In another book in this book series, *New Venture Management*, Kuratko and Hornsby[28] provide a depiction of life-cycle stages of various commonly known products (Figure 5.3). According to Christensen and Raynor,[29] more than 60 percent of new product developments never become commercialized. Of those

[26]Miller, D., Steier, L., and Le-Breton Miller, I. (2003). Lost in time: Intergenerational succession, change, and failure in family business. *Journal of Business Venturing,* 18(4): 513–531.

[27]Levitt, T. (1965). Exploit the product life cycle. *Harvard Business Review,* 43(November–December): 81–94; Day, G. (1981). The product life cycle: Analysis and application issues. *Journal of Marketing,* 45: 60–67.

[28]Kuratko, D.F., and Hornsby, J.S. (2009). *New Venture Management: The Entrepreneur's Road Map.* Prentice Hall Entrepreneurship Series, edited by R.D.Ireland and M.M. Morris. Upper Saddle River, NJ: Prentice Hall, p. 21.

[29]Christensen, C.M., and Raynor, M.E. (2003). *The Innovator's Solution: Creating and Sustaining Successful Growth.* Cambridge, MA: Harvard Business School Press.

FIGURE 5.2 A Standard Product Life-Cycle Model

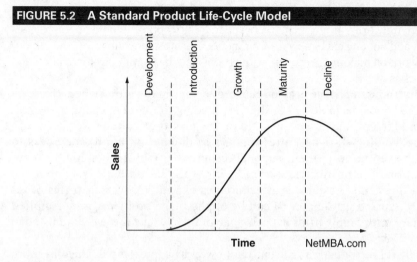

that do reach the market, 40 percent fail to become profitable and are withdrawn. In other words, of every 100 new products developed, only 24 are likely to become commercially profitable. Thus, it is critical for family firm leaders to make intelligent assessments of when and how to introduce new products and when to withdraw or replace them.

There have been many legitimate criticisms of the product life-cycle model such as the variance in duration of each stage across products and industries, and that at times some stages might be skipped completely, and the nature of competition associated with each stage varies across industries. All these are valid arguments, but a foundational understanding of the product life cycle is likely to help family firms

FIGURE 5.3 Life-Cycle Stages of Various Products

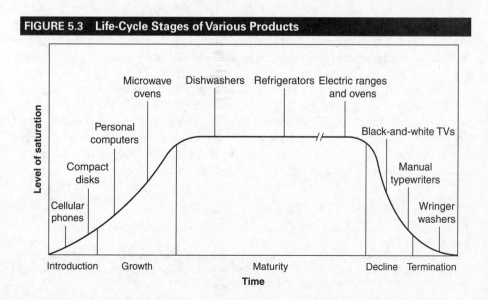

access the trajectory of their current offerings and adopt strategies for renewal. Established family firms are particularly prone to be susceptible to hold on to previous successes and not engage in new developments. The most innovative, of course, continue to work on making their own products obsolete by continuous innovation and new launches.

The introduction stage is characterized by inertia toward newness from the buyers and problems in design or delivery leading to frequent changes, overcapacity, and high production costs.[30] No or low profits are often associated with this stage, leading start-up entrepreneurs to depend on family members to support the venture with their personal resources. Established family firms are well positioned to nurture new product innovations and launches under the umbrella of existing businesses as economies of scale for various forms of resources (discussed in Chapter 6) can be applied. The problems, opportunities, and strategies for family firms in each stage of the product life cycle are listed in Table 5.3.

Successful introduction is usually followed by rapid **growth stage** as more customers begin to adopt the product. Sales to new customers represent a sign of growth that gives way to increased reliance on repeat sales to existing customers as a firm moves into the maturity stage. During the growth stage, as more customers begin to buy a product, competitors favoring imitation strategies join the market with variations of the original product, attempting to capture niches of the market.[31] As the overall size of the market is increasing, there are opportunities for many players to grow. Capacity utilization of facilities increases with a shift toward mass production. The focus on advertising and distribution increases to reach customers in the most efficient manner. Over time, the rate of growth decreases as the relevant group of potential buyers is reached.

The maturity stage is typically defined as the point at which the product becomes commoditized. It is no longer distinctive by customer benefits. Instead, firms find their margins reduced as they engage in more extensive and expensive marketing efforts to promote features that build brand loyalty. For many family firms, continuing to sell such products is not feasible, moving their lines quickly into the decline and death stage.

The decline stage may be triggered when new products and substitutes appear on the market. Family firms guided by the orientation of living in the present (consume) or in the past (cruise) are more likely to resist change than future-oriented progressive firms. Christensen and Raynor[32] also express a warning that is directly in line with these entrenchment concerns. In efforts to improve product lines, senior family business leaders may feel more comfortable relying on individuals with proven track records. Unfortunately, those track records from the past may

[30]Porter, M.E. (1980). *Competitive Strategy: Techniques for Analyzing Industries and Competitors.* New York: The Free Press.

[31]Winter, S.G., and Szulanski, G. (2001). Replication as strategy. *Organization Science,* 12(6): 730–743.

[32]Christensen, C.M., and Raynor, M.E. (2003). *The Innovator's Solution: Creating and Sustaining Successful Growth.* Cambridge, MA: Harvard Business School Press.

TABLE 5.3	Product Life-Cycle Stages		
	Problems	**Opportunities**	**Strategies**
Introduction	• Need to convince customers to try the product • Liabilities of newness in production and delivery processes • Delivering goods/services on time • Resource constraints but high need for timely changes to design and delivery	• Fewer competitors • Possibility of knowing the customers, suppliers, and employees well • Use family members to participate at this time so as to fill in resource needs but also test their interests and abilities	• Bootstrap resources of all kinds • Make customers feel part of the developmental processes • Use advisory board to broaden the reach and experience • Use creative ways to handle resource constraints such as supplier or customer credits
Growth	• Product shortages • Shortage of personnel and supplies • Competitors react more aggressively and imitators join the competition	• Developing production and delivery capabilities • Stable customer base • Marketing strategies • Various pathways to grow, including mergers and acquisitions	• Using family reputation and social capital to gain inroads into market segments and financing • Align guiding values, internal structures, and systems to ensure internal and external fit • Explore growth pathways to follow • Leadership development opportunities
Maturity	• Number of market segments might be declining • Consolidation in the industry • Firm and its leaders may become complacent • Inertia to change given attachment to past success and strategies	• Identify different pathways to grow products and/or markets • Process improvements • Addition of new team members is likely to help infuse energy in others as well	• Understand the causal factors leading to slow or no growth • Renewal measures must be guided by the underlying causes • Depending on the nature of the industry and positioning of the firm, strategic divestment or growth through consolidation

(continued)

TABLE 5.3	*(continued)*		
	Problems	**Opportunities**	**Strategies**
Decline	• Obtaining capital • Attracting and retaining talented nonfamily executives • Policies and procedures may inhibit creativity • Competitors encroachment on markets and employees • High stress on business dimension may cause family stress	• Shed unproductive resources • Move into new products and/or markets • Strengthen family tenacity by sharing low times together • Use the opportunity to train smart divestment skills to the junior generation	• Family firms can access patient capital for renewal • Engage junior generation and use their fresh insights to plan and help renewal • Explore new beginnings using social networks and reputation

not meet the needs of a changing competitive environment. It may be time for a substitute product or some other radical innovation, yet the assignment is given to an individual or team that has achieved success through incremental advancements. Thus, what may appear to be the best selection for revitalizing a product line in decline may result in hastening the product toward failure.

In some instances, there is a need to infuse the firm with new ideas and implement foundational changes. But for established family firms, given their socioemotional attachment to the firm, such changes can be extremely difficult to make. Some family firms, such as Arbill Safety from the last chapter and Consolidated Telephone Company of the Lumpkin family we discussed in Chapter 2, use generational leadership transitions to enter into new product lines and/or geographic expansion. Others, such as the Roberts Companies, seem to progress into innovative directions throughout the career span of the founders. The challenge for such companies will be to see whether the entrepreneurial spirit of the founders has been imbued deep enough into the family and business. An awareness of the limited life span of all products must be kept in mind and new directions sought to ensure sustainable family enterprise.

INDUSTRY LIFE CYCLE

Industries are more than a single product, yet they too have life cycles. For example, in the United States, industries such as black-and-white televisions, manual typewriters, or wringer washers have declined, while others such as dishwashers, electric ovens/ranges, and refrigerators are in a mature state with slow or no growth. Still others such as HDTVs and cell phones are in growth stage, while iPod-type products and Internet social utilities are in the introductory stage of the life cycle (Figure 5.3).

The North American Industry Classification System, (NAICS)[33] developed jointly by the United States, Canada, and Mexico, is a useful way to classify the industry segments that a business is involved in. While there are more than 1,800 coded industries, it is important to point out that many firms are difficult to classify by industry. As the Roberts Companies case demonstrates, a family's firm may be competing in a number of industries. Thus, for such firms, it is important to stay abreast of changes in different industries.

A good way to keep in touch with the developments in an industry is by keeping abreast of the industry-specific magazines, trade publications, and industry reports from sources such as IBISWorld[34] and Standard and Poor's Net-Advantage.[35] Savvy business leaders know the critical importance of maintaining close networks with other key stakeholders in their environment, such as customers, and researchers working on new technological developments. For example, Jim Balsillie and Mike Lazaridis, co-CEOs of Research in Motion (RIM), the manufacturer of Blackberry, are actively involved in the university and research communities of Waterloo in Canada.[36] As stated on the RIM Web site, the primary focus of RIM's philanthropic program is "outreach to students in science, engineering, and business programs." Balsillie and Lazaridis have accomplished this focus by setting up various nonprofit research institutions such as the Centre for International Governance Innovation, Perimeter Institute for Theoretical Physics, and the Institute for Quantum Computing in Waterloo.[37] This strategy helps to keep them attuned to the leading edge research developments. In addition, they are able to locate and hire the best available talent through these networks. This strategy has proven extremely valuable to their continued success and to the progress of their communities as well.

The industrial age brought about the creation of entirely new industries, followed by the knowledge-based economy, which saw the decline of many of those industries and the creation of new ones. As indicated earlier in this chapter, industries are impacted by environmental trends, but not all segments are uniformly affected. In this era of globalization, industries may decline and die in one country or region while simultaneously being born and growing in others. Family firms, especially those in later generations of leadership, are in a good position to take advantage of different industry life stages in various nations. Some firms do this by setting up offices internationally under the leadership of different family members. Governance bodies like family councils, discussed in Chapter 11, are used to develop rules for determining the country assignments for family members. Rotation systems are often utilized to balance the career interests, family-of-attachment needs, life-cycle stages, and talents of each family member.

---

[33] http://www.census.gov/epcd/www/naics.html

[34] http://www.ibisworld.com.au/about/history.aspx

[35] http://www.netadvantage.standardandpoors.com/NASApp/NetAdvantage/index.do

[36] http://www.rim.com/newsroom/media/executive/index.shtml

[37] http://www.rim.com/newsroom/media/executive/index.shtml#mike_lazaridis; http://www.rim.com/newsroom/media/executive/index.shtml#jim_balsillie.

Appendix 5A provides a work sheet to evaluate various forces that influence the broad industry a family firm operates in or wishes to enter. This sheet is part of the "Full Feasibility Analysis" in another book in the Prentice Hall Entrepreneurship Series, *Preparing Effective Business Plans* by Bruce Barringer.[38] The "Industry Attractiveness Assessment Tool" assists in determining the feasibility of entering a given industry. For a more detailed assessment of a particular segment in the industry, the "Target Market Attractiveness Assessment Tool" needs to be completed. By using these analyses, entrepreneurial family firms can strategize future moves for continuous growth of this firm.

NAVIGATING UNCERTAINTY: IMPLICATIONS FOR ENTREPRENEURS AND ENTERPRISING FAMILIES

At the firm level, family involvement with the business can facilitate or hinder a company's ability to negotiate environmental changes and life-cycle transitions of products or industries of interest. Family business founders are often described as intuitive entrepreneurs. They face two challenges in keeping the family firm healthy through their life span as leaders. The first is to avoid losing their entrepreneurial edge by settling into time-honored methods of managing the business. The second, and more problematic, is to convey their tacit knowledge and intuition to the owners and managers who succeed them.

Many family firms have been found to be remarkably tenacious in handling the up-and-down swings in external environments, by maintaining an entrepreneurial spirit across generations of products and leaders.[39] Examples include family firms such as SC Johnson, Corning, Hallmark Cards—which are in public view—but also many lesser-known hidden champions[40] such as Tetra (world leader in tropical fish food), Webasto (world leader in sunroofs and auxiliary heating systems for cars), and Brita (water filters). Such firms engage in continuous innovation to sustain leadership positions in their industries over many decades. How do they gain the tenacity to sustain their entrepreneurial success against the backdrop of changing environments? In this section, we discuss some strategies that have been found effective to navigate the uncertainty for enterprising family firms, both by first-timers and by habitual, experienced entrepreneurs.

Entrepreneurial family firm leaders do not wait for opportunities to come to them. Instead, they maintain an active engagement with their environment, continuously scanning for opportunities and resources. In enterprising families, the

[38]Barringer, B.R. (2008). *Preparing Effective Business Plans: An Entrepreneurial Approach.* Prentice Hall Entrepreneurship Series, edited by R.D. Ireland and M.M. Morris. Upper Saddle River, NJ: Prentice-Hall. pp.70–79.
[39]Miller, D., and Le-Breton Miller, I. (2005). *Managing for the Long Run: Lessons in Competitive Advantage from Great Family Businesses.* Boston, MA: Harvard Business School Press.
[40]Simon, H. (1996). *Hidden Champions: Lessons from 500 of the World's Best Unknown Companies.* Boston, MA: Harvard Business School Press.

preparation of entrepreneurs starts early in life. Intuitively, these families and their members seem to understand what research has revealed—that the first venture is not necessarily going to be successful. Nor is it going to be a failure, as the experiences gained are precious and often integral ingredients for later success. You may recall our observation in an earlier chapter that experiential learning can only come from experience. Entrepreneurs who succeed understand this well and begin practicing entrepreneurship early in their lives.

OPPORTUNITIES AND THREATS

Entrepreneurs create new ventures, products, markets, processes, and so on (Figure 1.1, Chapter 1). Before creating something new to fulfill a need, two things must be understood. First, how well is the need being met at present? Second, what are the forces of change in the environment that are likely to change the need itself? Without such understandings, one might end up reinventing the wheel or inventing a wheel for an automobile that no one wishes to ride anymore.

To become familiarized with the current thinking on governance and management issues, entrepreneurial family firms often require their next-generation members to gain educational training and work experience outside their family firm. We saw this in the cases of Consolidated Telephone Company (Chapter 2), Arbill Safety (Chapter 4), and the Roberts Companies (this chapter). Junior-generation members of established family firms are advised (required in many instances) to gain educational training and outside business experience. As they are going through these preparatory stages, many opportunities to get to know the family business and its environment arise. For example, students in business schools are often required to do projects aimed at understanding the operations of a firm, general environmental trends, or the conditions of an industry. A standard approach to forecast the future is by extrapolating from trends in past and current situations. Such exercises and experiences can provide valuable opportunities to learn the workings and environment of a family business, while thinking of new directions that might be fruitfully undertaken.

STRENGTHS AND WEAKNESSES

Novice entrepreneurs and established family firms face different sets of strengths and challenges. To succeed in the fiercely competitive entrepreneurial arena, it is important to build on existing strengths while knowing the challenges so as to adopt strategies to overcome them.

NOVICE ENTREPRENEURS

We often hear about the many liabilities of newness that novice entrepreneurs face. For example, they are less likely to have established connections with customers, suppliers, bankers, and distributors; they have to establish processes to ensure that products or services are ready on time for delivery; they need to learn the legal requirements to start a venture; and they hire from among family members and friends, as professionally trained individuals are harder to attract.

Are there any assets of newness? If not, why would so many entrepreneurs choose to start new ventures? Fresh ideas and high energy are perhaps the biggest things going in favor of novice entrepreneurs. They need to make decisions about which battles to pick and which ones to avoid. In other words, they must know when competing is worthwhile and when it is better to cooperate with others. Many find that working with family members strengthens their venturing team by adding to the resources and talents needed to launch a venture.

ESTABLISHED FAMILY FIRMS

We often hear of the liabilities of established family firms—how they might become complacent over time, run by plateaued managers who make very few changes to their product or service offerings, customers, employees, and so on. Past successes of entrenched family business owner-managers can squelch proposals for initiatives or turnarounds brought forth by others, retarding entrepreneurial growth of the firm. Over time, firms develop routine responses to problems and patterns of accepted organizational behavior. Standard responses rather than innovative ones reap rewards.[41]

There can be valid reasons why a senior generation might resist efforts by their successors to seek more rapid growth. Poorly implemented growth strategies can lead to undisciplined expansion, financial overextension, excessive debt, and other problems. Done well, however, family shareholders benefit in multiple ways. The solution is achieving the delicate balance of growth and sustainability.[42] Incumbent family firms enjoy significant assets of maturity. Foremost are the connections and relationships that have been built over the years with employees, customers, suppliers, distributors, competitors, and other key players in the firm's internal and external environment. These are valuable assets that are hard to replicate as many of them are subject to slow growth over time. Research has revealed the importance of complementary assets in determining whether an entrepreneurial initiative is likely to succeed or not.[43] **Complementary assets** are capabilities or assets that are needed in conjunction with the new products or services. An example is the significant role of marketing, distribution, after-sales service, and financing, in relation to large-appliance sales or activities such as clinical trials, regulatory management, and drug distribution in the case of the pharmaceutical industry. Depending on the competitive

---

[41]Leaptrot, J. (2005). An institutional theory view of the family business. *Family Business Review*, 18(3): 215–228.

[42]Hutcheson, J.O., and Zimmerman, M.A. (2008). The risk-reward paradigm in family business. In Spector, B. (Ed.). *The Family Business Shareholder's Handbook*. Philadelphia: Family Business Publishing. pp. 106–107.

[43]Rothaermel, F.T. (2001). Incumbent's advantage through exploiting complementary assets via interfirm cooperation. *Strategic Management Journal*, 22: 687–699; Rothearmel, F.T. (2005). Incumbent's advantage. In Hitt, M.A., and Ireland, R.D. (Eds.). *The Blackwell Encyclopedia of Management: Entrepreneurship*. Malden, MA: Blackwell Publishing. pp. 151–152

environment, established incumbents may be better positioned to draw upon complementary assets to bring innovative products to markets more successfully than novice players.

COMBINING ASSETS OF NEWNESS AND MATURITY

Entrepreneurial family firms are well positioned to achieve positive results by forming and launching internal ventures where talented junior-generation family or nonfamily members work in conjunction with senior-generation members to combine the assets of newness and maturity.[44] This strategy helps combine the simultaneous need to change and progress while building on the foundations of past experiences and connections.

Others find innovative ways to combine the assets of newness and maturity. This is done by maintaining close connections with their key stakeholders, such as employees, distributors, suppliers, and customers, during times of prosperity and by reaping the benefits of cooperation during downturns in an economy or industry. In addition, when difficult choices must be made to ensure that the competitive edge of the firm is maintained, entrepreneurial family firms keep the long-term relationships in mind to come up with creative solutions to negotiate the challenges presented by changing environmental conditions.

We return, then, to three recurrent themes in this book. The first is the focus on entrepreneurial family firms that create value through the pursuit of new ventures, products, markets, processes, and so on. Barring catastrophic disasters, such firms are able to avail themselves of opportunities that are invariably presented with changes in environment, regardless of whether these are upturns or downturns. Second, entrepreneurial leaders must not only be visionaries, but also, à la Michael Roberts, be able to communicate their vision, bringing others along as enthusiastic members of their venture teams. Moreover, they need to be complemented with the "functionaire" talents to ensure that the lofty visions are carried through actions. And third, who better to follow your vision than family members who know you well and have seen you deliver on promises in the past? In addition, family members may well accept your leadership even if you have failed in the past because they often have intimate knowledge of the effort you expended or of external circumstances that contributed to the failure.

We must add one caveat. It has been said that there is a fine line between vision and hallucination. As we will see in a later chapter, an insufficiently prepared but confident family leader can articulate visions that may result in conflict or tragedy, both on family and business dimensions. A good understanding of the different types of resources, if managed well, can become assets for an entrepreneurial family firm—a topic we will discuss in the next chapter.

---

[44]Kellermanns, F.W., and Eddleston, K.A. (2006). Corporate entrepreneurship in family firms: A family perspective. *Entrepreneurship Theory & Practice,* 30(6): 809–830.

Summary

- Entrepreneurial family firms that gain success in a short time monitor the trends in their environment and life-cycle changes in products and industries of interest.
- Entrepreneurial family business owners are affected by both external and internal environmental factors that have distinct life cycles.
- Changes in environments present both challenges and opportunities. Entrepreneurs need to be aware of cycle trends but may at times act counter to those trends.
- Monitoring both the product and industry life cycles is essential to long-term firm survival. External factors can unexpectedly shorten the life cycle of an entire industry or only some segments of it.
- The stage of an industry's life cycle may vary from one region to another, leaving open the possibility of extending the life cycle of a product by geographic expansion.
- Most new product ideas are either not brought to market or fail to earn profits when introduced. Even successful products may have life cycles that are shorter than those of the companies producing and selling them, calling for innovative actions to keep the firm healthy.
- Families in business have special threats and opportunities associated with environmental trends, industry, and product stages of development.
- Entrepreneurial family firms combine assets of newness and maturity to retain entrepreneurial spirit across generations.

Discussion Questions

1. When the national economy is in a recession, what actions could a business owner take to grow the firm?
2. Suppose your parents wanted you to join their residential construction company. Given the economic conditions in your community at the time you are reading this book, how would you answer them?
3. Why do you think most new products fail? What do you recommend to reduce the failure rate?
4. What advice would you give to Michael Roberts Jr. in his quest to take the family business to a new level?
5. What differences are there between creating a venture within a family business and a nonfamily business?

Learning Exercises

1. What are the key demographic trends influencing your region? What business opportunities can you think of to capitalize on these trends? And, what businesses are likely to face diminishing segments of customers?
2. Interview the owner of a retail store in your community. Ask what products the store has stocked in the past that have been discontinued and why.

Other Resources

- Christensen, C.M. (1997). *The Innovator's Dilemma.* Cambridge, MA: Harvard Business School Press.
- Datta, E.K., Feiler, T., Lehmann, A., Lovens, A.B., Rabago, K.R., Swisher, J.N., and Wicker, K. (2008). *Small Is Profitable.* Snowmass, CO: Rocky Mountain Institute.
- http://www.entrepreneur.com/
- Foot, D.K., and Stoffmann, D. (2001). *Boom, Bust, & Echo: Profiting from the Demographic Shift in the 21st Century.* Toronto, Canada: Stoddart Publishing Company.
- George, G., and Bock, A.J. (2008). *Inventing Entrepreneurs: Technology Innovators and Their Entrepreneurial Journey.* Prentice Hall Entrepreneurship Series, edited by R.D. Ireland and M.M. Morris. Upper Saddle River, NJ: Prentice-Hall. pp. 120.
- Hart, S.L. (2007). *Capitalism at the Crossroads: Aligning Business, Earth, and Humanity,* with a foreword by Al Gore. Upper Saddle River, NJ: Wharton School Publishing.
- Lovins, H., Lovins, A., and Hawken, P. (1999). *Natural Capitalism: Creating the Next Industrial Revolution.* Boston, MA: Little, Brown & Co.
- Miller, D., and Le-Breton Miller, I. (2005). *Managing for the Long Run: Lessons in Competitive Advantage from Great Family Businesses.* Boston, MA: Harvard Business School Press.
- Porter, M.E. (1990). *The Competitive Advantage of Nations.* New York: Free Press.
- Simon, H. (1996). *Hidden Champions: Lessons from 500 of the World's Best Unknown Companies.* Boston, MA: Harvard Business School Press.

Assessing the Broad Industry Feasibility

	Low Potential	*Moderate Potential*	*High Potential*
1. Number of competitors	Many	Few	None
2. Age of industry	Old	Middle aged	Young
3. Growth rate of industry	Little or no growth	Moderate growth	Strong growth
4. Average net income for firms in the industry	Low	Medium	High
5. Degree of industry concentration	Concentrated	Neither concentrated nor fragmented	Fragmented
6. Stage of industry life cycle	Maturity phase or decline phase	Growth phase	Emergence phase
7. Importance of industry's products and/or services to customers	"Ambivalent"	"Would like to have"	"Must have"
8. Extent to which business and environmental trends are moving in favor of the industry	Low	Medium	High
9. Number of exciting new products and services emerging from the industry	Low	Medium	High
10. Long-term prospects	Weak	Neutral	Strong

Source: Barringer, B.R. (2008). *Preparing Effective Business Plans: An Entrepreneurial Approach.* Prentice Hall Entrepreneurship Series, edited by R. D. Ireland and M.M. Morris. Upper Saddle River, NJ. P. 72. This is one part of the 10-page "Full Feasibility Analysis" for a proposed new business.

RESOURCES FOR STARTING AND MANAGING THE FAMILY FIRM

COLLECTING FAMILY MEMBERS

Many business families have trouble finding the proper balance between home and work concerns when just two or three family members work together in the company. So imagine the challenges facing the Rumpke family at Rumpke Consolidated Companies. The Cincinnati-based waste management business employs dozens of relatives, including all five children of 66-year-old CEO William J. Rumpke. "A few years ago, I tried to count the exact number of relatives in the business, and I gave up when I got to 75," said Rumpke, a son of the company founder. "We have relatives and in-laws spread throughout the company."

Current employees include 20 grandsons of the two brothers who founded the company in the 1930s. Eight granddaughters have husbands who work at Rumpke. Another four female relatives are employed themselves. How were the Rumpkes so successful at recruiting the younger generation? No one is pressured to join, but many young people begin in the business as children, says Jennifer Schnee, a 42-year-old granddaughter of a founder who now works as a customer service manager. "I rode the trucks with my dad from the time I was young," says Schnee. "I started working in the office when I was 16, and I continued working while I went to college. It was in my blood."

Though COO Bill Rumpke Jr. insists that young people are not pressured to join the family business, Rumpke fathers typically introduce their sons and daughters to the company at a young age. Bill began sweeping floors when he was in the seventh grade. After college he joined the recycling business and eventually became head of the unit. Bill says that much of what attracted him to the business was a strong sense of family heritage. "We are proud of this great business that our fathers built up," he says.

The Rumpke system is set up to encourage entrepreneurship among family members. At the heart of the system are garbage truck routes that have been developed over the years. Today, the company has 30 routes, including 28 owned by relatives. Each route is a substantial business, and routes are typically passed from father to son.

As an entrepreneur, the route owner is free to lower a price in order to gain a new customer. After getting enough new customers, the route owner can get a second truck and hire a driver to take over the first vehicle. Rumpke Consolidated owns the trucks and supplies gas, but the route owner is responsible for his labor costs.

Since all the shareholders work at the company, there are no disputes about giving dividends to outsiders or buying out relatives who want to depart from the business. Rumpke has not announced his successor, but he predicts that filling the CEO's chair will not be difficult. "I will be around for awhile," he says, "and after that we have a lot of good young people who are dedicated to maintaining the company and keeping it in family hands."

Source: Luxenberg, S. (2007). A garbage company that collects relatives. *Family Business*, 18(2): 57–60.

Questions

1. Some experts believe that family members should gain experience in other organizations before joining the family business. Do you agree or disagree? Why?
2. What resources do you believe have contributed to the success of Rumpke Consolidated? If you were a cousin considering purchasing a route, what resources would you expect Rumpke Consolidated to provide?

While the Rumpkes have been successful in working together as a family, it would be a mistake to think that all families can work well together. It is a wonderful and prosperous experience when family members collaborate, cooperate, and contribute in a business venture to create value. Few events in life are more tragic, however, than when businesses are at the center of family breakups. It is not difficult to find examples that would frighten anyone out of going into business with relatives. Who among us has not seen bitter arguments that build into lifelong feuds among siblings, cousins, and others over what outsiders often view as the most trivial of issues? Imagine how much worse the conflicts can be when business resources and wealth are involved, as they inevitably are in family firms.

In this chapter, we examine four forms of capital—financial, physical, social, and human—that go into the formation and growth of entrepreneurial family firms.[1] Strategies for increasing levels of stocks of each form of capital are discussed, as are means of leveraging the accumulated capital. We highlight how entrepreneurial family firms effectively transition capital stocks across generations and prepare their next-generation members for enhancing the levels of inherited resources.

OBTAINING, USING, CREATING, LOSING RESOURCES

You may recall from Chapter 3 that *familiness*[2] is the combination of existing stocks of financial, physical, social, and human capital resources in a firm resulting from interactions between family and business systems.[3] The ease of appropriation of resources between family and business systems may lead to either enhanced or reduced stocks of capital for one or both systems, that is, distinctive or constrictive familiness, respectively. Therefore, leaders of entrepreneurial family firms need to possess an understanding of effective resource management. Sirmon et al.[4] explain that effective resource management involves three critical aspects:

- *Structuring*, that is, acquiring, accumulating, and divesting resources so that they are available to the firm when needs and opportunities emerge
- *Bundling* or integrating resources to form capabilities
- *Leveraging*, that is, mobilizing, coordinating, and deploying resources to exploit capabilities to avail advantage of market opportunities.

Not only are entrepreneurs adept at structuring or accumulating resources, they also learn how to realize their value by effective bundling and leveraging so as to serve the needs of their customers, while building wealth for their families and firms.

---

[1]Sirmon, D.G., and Hitt, M.A. (2003). Managing resources: Linking unique resources, management, and wealth creation in family firms. *Entrepreneurship Theory & Practice,* Summer: 339–358.

[2]Habbershon, T.G., and Williams, M. (1999). A resource-based framework for assessing the strategic advantages of family firms. *Family Business Review*, 12(1): 1–25; Habbershon, T.G., Williams, M., and MacMillan, I.C. (2003). A unified systems perspective of family firm performance. *Journal of Business Venturing*, 18: 451–465.

[3]Sharma, P. (2008). Familiness: Capital stocks and flows between family and business. *Entrepreneurship Theory & Practice.* 32(6): 971–977.

[4]Sirmon, D.G., Hitt, M.A., and Ireland, R.D. (2007). Managing firm resources in dynamic environments to create value: Looking inside the black box. *Academy of Management Review,* 32(1): 273–292.

The first step for the entrepreneurial family is to obtain resources—financial, physical, social, and human—to launch the venture. These four forms of start-up capital are likely to come from family members and the family's resource pool. The principal entrepreneur and his or her immediate family members will probably put up their savings, provide space and equipment, make contacts, and actually work in the business to get it off the ground. It is not unusual for the family to invest more of each type of capital to help the venture survive and grow.

If the company succeeds, it begins building its own wealth and using that wealth to leverage other resources for additional growth. Eventually, we see family members seek to extract or consume some of this wealth for their personal use. In the extreme, this can lead to a loss of business resources and ultimate loss of the family's wealth. Entrepreneurial family firms that sustain across generations understand the following:

- Long-term survival of a firm and family is only possible if there is a balanced flow of capital from one direction to the other—excessive in- or outflows of resources over the long term lead to the failure of one or both systems.

- Once the firm begins to generate wealth, it is essential to reinvest some of these resources for the regeneration of the firm.

- Both the cruise—no changes made—or consume—outflow of resources from business to family without regeneration—lead to the failure of the family firm.

As depicted in Figure 6.1, the changes in the levels of stocks of financial, physical, and social capital are moderated by the human capital available to a firm over time. In comparison to others, entrepreneurial family firms that enjoy dedicated support of larger numbers of healthy, technically and socially capable, financially savvy, and psychologically and morally sound individuals are better positioned to manage their financial, social, and physical capital effectively and leverage it to exploit market opportunities. Strategies used by such firms to manage capital resources are discussed next and summarized in Table 6.1.

FIGURE 6.1 Levels of Capital Stocks Over Time

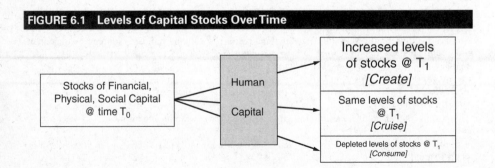

TABLE 6.1 Resource Management Strategies in Entrepreneurial Family Firms

Financial Capital

- Investments by family members in an entrepreneurial venture are treated in the same manner as investments from a professional lender or investor—business plans and written agreement stipulate the terms and conditions of repayment.
- A lawyer is engaged to develop the written agreements involving money transactions among family members.
- The life-cycle stages of individual, family, business, and industry guide whether divestment or generational transfer of the business makes strategic sense.
- Expert help is engaged for planning the transition of ownership from one generation to the next.
- Education, work experience, and charitable giving are used as vehicles to imbue responsible financial ownership and management among family members.

Physical Capital

- When assets of significant value are being shared between family and business systems, written agreements stipulate the terms.
- Family constitutions and councils clarify the rules of engagement and help resolve confrontational issues in advance or provide processes for achieving agreeable resolutions.

Social Capital

- Family members invest strategically in building networks with large numbers of people through active involvement in business associations, social events, and charitable organizations.
- Careful attention is paid to maintaining strong bonds with family members both within the business and outside.
- Senior generation facilitates the inclusion of junior family members in their professional networks by helping the juniors develop social competence and by exposing them to the networks when they are ready for such exposure.
- Junior-generation members invest efforts in developing their social competence and giving before expecting anything in return from the network members.

Human Capital

Physical Dimension

- Families engage in fitness activities together (team spirit, appreciation of each other, and growing older together).
- Parents are involved in children's sports (understanding of health and team spirit) activities.
- Members volunteer for activities in senior centers and hospitals aimed to build compassion and understanding of health issues.
- Adopt norms of fairness in the family and the business.

Intellectual Dimension

- Pursue higher and lifelong education.
- Gain work experience within the business in grade school years.
- Gain work experience outside the business during college and beyond in an industry related to the family firm.

(continued)

TABLE 6.1 *(continued)*

- Participate in professional associations.
- Accept leadership roles in the community and school.
- Clarify and codify rules of entry and promotion in the family firm.
- Prepare legally binding employment contracts, ownership, and intellectual property agreements.

Psychological Dimension

- Imbue pride in the family enterprise by active involvement of family members in the firm at a young age.
- Share historical highs and lows of entrepreneurial experiences with family members so as to provide a close to reality understanding of this career path.
- Provide varied opportunities, within or outside of family firm, to develop general and specific business skills.
- Engage experts to help understand the motivators guiding family members to pursue a career in family business.
- Use experts to help develop a milestone developmental plan to prepare junior family members for positions in the firm that match their talents and career interests.
- Encourage a future-oriented time perspective in family members.

Moral Dimension

- Support and show by example how the principles of integrity, responsibility, compassion, and forgiveness are put into practice.
- Devise family rules that inculcate a sense of responsibility and integrity within the members.
- Demonstrate the courage to engage expert help (religious or otherwise) to reinforce the golden rules.
- Forgive those who might have caused pain or hurt.
- Celebrate and highlight achievements built on the foundations of moral principles.

FINANCIAL CAPITAL

Resources are essential for starting and managing a business. From the beginning, entrepreneurial family firms require financial resources for materials, facilities, equipment, salaries, wages, and other necessary expenses to produce services and products that will generate revenues to sustain the enterprise. Where do entrepreneurs get their start-up funds?

Surveys by the United States Small Business Administration,[5] the National Federation of Independent Business,[6] and others consistently report that personal savings are the primary source of financial capital for about three-quarters of entrepreneurs for launching a new business from scratch or purchasing an existing business. For most new ventures, traditional sources of financing are often not

---

[5]http://www.sba.gov/
[6]http://www.nfib.com/page/home

available. Start-ups lack track records and collateral for obtaining loans with many financial institutions. Equity markets are not open to them. The entrepreneur draws on savings that he or she has accumulated, sometimes mortgaging a home or pulling from pension funds. It is not unusual at this stage for family members to question whether the venture is the best use of those funds. There are opportunity costs with any investment, and some family members might prefer that the money be applied to something less risky.

When you have exhausted your own resources, you are likely to turn to those who care about you and know you best—family! Family can be a source of financial capital in a variety of ways. Examples include the working spouse who provides a stream of income while company revenues are reinvested, parents who mortgage a home or dip into retirement funds to help purchase equipment or provide working capital, and a sibling CEO who supports the new venture as a spin-off from an established family enterprise.

We joke about bankers as being those who lend money to people who do not need it. Prospective entrepreneurs often get advised not to bother with banks because they will not make loans to start-ups. Many family business founders, however, find banks to be sources of funds from the very beginning. A founding entrepreneur might have a relative (typically a parent) who has a solid credit record and may be willing to cosign a note. Family members may be able to combine assets and provide sufficient collateral for an initial loan. A critical fact to keep in mind when dealing with banks is that they must safeguard their assets and answer to their depositors. Thus, they cannot and will not make risky loans without a reasonable assurance of being repaid.

Before asking any family member for financial support, the thoughtful entrepreneur will prepare a well-thought-through business plan. While there are a large number of good resources that provide help in preparing business plans, two books in this Series, *New Venture Management*[7] and *Preparing Effective Business Plans*,[8] are particularly useful for related guidance. The business plan is shared with members of the family from whom financial help is being sought. And every good business plan contains an exit strategy. What happens if the venture fails? What happens if retirement savings are lost? What happens if the children's college funds have been exhausted? There have been cases of lawsuits and worse, especially if the relatives who lost money believe that it resulted from incompetence or malfeasance. It is incumbent on the entrepreneur to help the family think through such eventualities in advance.

A written agreement stipulates the terms and conditions when the loan will be repaid and the interest rate that will be used to calculate repayment amounts.

---

[7]Kuratko, D.F., and Hornsby, J.S. (2009). *New Venture Management: The Entrepreneur's Road Map.* Prentice Hall Entrepreneurship Series, edited by R.D. Ireland and M.M. Morris. Upper Saddle River, NJ: Prentice-Hall.

[8]Barringer, B.R. (2009). *Preparing Effective Business Plans: An Entrepreneurial Approach.* Prentice Hall Entrepreneurship Series, edited by R.D. Ireland and M.M. Morris. Upper Saddle River, NJ: Prentice-Hall.

Family investors should know from the business plan under what circumstances they can expect a return on their investment or an exit from the firm. If the company encounters problems and cannot repay the loan, the terms should be formally renegotiated. Investors should be kept informed of the firm's condition, with no surprises in case their investments are in jeopardy. In families, we sometimes attempt to shield one another from bad news. There is no place in a professional relationship for withholding information.

As the business prospers, it is reasonable to expect family members to want to have loans repaid, to receive returns on their investments, or just to be given what they believe is rightfully theirs because they are relatives. When mixing personal relationships and ownership of a business, important issues must be dealt with by the entrepreneur. What if trouble emerges in the family system? Against the backdrop of high divorce and separation rates, written agreements often come in handy when engaging in money transactions with family members. As the laws governing such transactions vary from place to place, it is prudent to engage a qualified lawyer for drafting such agreements, an expense well worth the investment in a relationship that influences both work and personal lives. For family firms that successfully accumulate financial capital in one generation, adequate attention needs to be paid to transfer stocks across generations and train the receiving generation for responsible management of the financial capital.

Before the mechanics of a stock transfer can be worked out, it becomes important to consider a large number of individual, family, business, and macroenvironmental variables. The life-cycle stages of individuals, family, business, product, and industry need to be considered before determining whether divestment or continuance of the business as a family-owned entity makes the most sense. If it is determined that the business is indeed an entity with high growth potential and there are capable family members eager to pursue their career in the family firm, the long- and short-term financial needs of both generations and the business must be taken into account in planning ownership transfer. Successful family firms understand both the complexity and the importance of these issues. Moreover, they are cognizant of the emotional blinders that can deter family members from making the best decisions for the long-term prosperity of the firm. Thus, they engage experts to help them in dealing with ownership transition in a proactive and timely manner.

PHYSICAL CAPITAL

There are many similarities between physical capital and financial capital. Financial capital is often used to acquire physical assets. Support provided by relatives can take the form of physical capital rather than a monetary investment. Many an entrepreneur has started a venture out of the garage or basement of his or her parents' home or that of other relative. If a family business already exists and a family member is in the process of starting or growing a new venture, the existing business may serve as an incubator, providing not only space but also equipment, office materials, staff time, or other in-kind support.

This often occurs with habitual entrepreneuring families. Parents may encourage such venture spin-offs when they have multiple children with entrepreneurial aspirations, but room for only one at the top of the existing firm.

A good example of an entrepreneurial family firm that has successfully followed this strategy is the Kennards from Australia. Since 1948, the family has been well known for its "equipment hire" business as Walter and his wife, Theo, offered sanders, spray painters, box trailers, and so on for hire to interested customers. Their children—Neville, Joan, and Andrew—helped them clean, repair, and load equipment. Over time, the two sons, Neville and Andrew, took the business and grew it to a significantly larger level and started the "self-storage" business. Today,[9] the two branches of the family—Neville and his son Sam, and Andrew and his son Angus—fully own and manage Kennards Self-Storage and Kennards Hire, respectively. The family remains close, and both branches are leading players in their respective industry segments.

The physical assets of family members may be used to collateralize loans. Although an example was given above of mortgaging a home to provide start-up funds, with physical capital we are referring to assets that are used first and foremost to generate the products and services sold by the company, but may also be pledged to a financial institution for cash to be used for other business purposes. This could also take the form of a sale and leaseback, by which the owner sells the equipment or property to another family member, presumably one in another business; takes a lump sum of cash to fund operations; and then pays a lease fee to the new owner of the property under a contracted relationship.

As a firm grows, acquires resources, builds wealth, and has its own physical resources, a family must take care not to abuse those resources. Sometimes, family members fail to distinguish between personal property and company property. Family members have been known to take some of the physical resources of the business—a motor vehicle, a computer, a cell phone, and so on—and treat them as their own. Not only are there legal and tax implications, but also such actions can affect the morale of nonfamily employees. This behavior rarely goes unnoticed.

As with financial transactions between family members, if an asset of significant value is involved, it is helpful to draw out a written agreement stipulating the terms of usage. Many successful family enterprises have used councils, constitutions, and other mechanisms to establish rules of engagement. These policies and procedures can either resolve confrontational issues in advance or provide processes for achieving agreeable resolutions.

SOCIAL CAPITAL

Organizations are nothing if not networks of people interacting to achieve common goals. Thus, from their origins, family firms consist of social interactions between the founder(s) and others who commit to the ventures. **Social capital**

---

[9]http://www.kennards.com.au/; http://www.kss.com.au/

refers to the benefits the entrepreneur and the venture derive from a network of relationships.[10] Research shows us that social capital is one of the most valuable intangible assets an entrepreneur can create and possess.[11] We all know the cliché that it is not what you know, but who you know that matters in business and careers in general.

It has long been known that successful entrepreneurs are characterized more by many shallow rather than a few deep interpersonal relationships.[12] The shallow relationships, also known as *bridges,* are the direct and indirect links of an entrepreneur with others. They facilitate informational benefits that enable the identification of fruitful opportunities. Entrepreneurs meet people through business associations, social events, charitable organizations, and in many other ways. These bridges of networks may lead in many and often unexpected directions. They may be sources of new opportunities, of financing, of customers, and of other desirable outcomes.

Bonds, on the other hand, are the deep-set relationships between individuals. While fewer in number, they help in the building of cohesiveness and solidarity within a family or business. Investment in such ties enables the establishment of trust and discouragement of malfeasance. However, maintenance of both shallow bridges and deep bonds requires time, an extremely scarce resource for most entrepreneurial family firm leaders. As excessive focus on bonds can cause risky shortages in bridges, and vice versa, it becomes necessary to adequately balance investments of time to build and maintain both types of relationships.

A key to acquiring social capital is not just in being known, but also in having a positive reputation. Social capital is considered to be reciprocal. You do not just take from your network. You establish and maintain your connections both within the family business and with externals. Bankable social capital is more than simply building an inventory of business cards. **Social competence** is critical. By social competence, we mean the ability to interact with others effectively, to make a good first impression, to be persuasive, and to be emotionally sensitive.[13]

A major issue for families in business is whether or not relatives can transfer social capital among themselves.[14] The entrepreneurial founder may have long-standing relationships with customers, bankers, suppliers, and others. Can these be passed along to the next generation of leaders? You may carry the same name, but have you become acquainted with these individuals? Do they have the same respect for you that they did for your parents? How can you work to gain

---

[10]Nahapiet, J., and Ghoshal, S. (1998). Social capital, intellectual capital, and the organizational advantage. *Academy of Management Review,* 23(2): 242–266.

[11]Davidsson, P., and Honig, B. (2003). The role of social and human capital among nascent entrepreneurs. *Journal of Business Venturing,* 18: 301–333.

[12]Granovetter, M.S. (1973). The strength of weak ties. *American Journal of Sociology,* 78: 1360–1380.

[13]Baron, R.A. (2005). Social capital. In Hitt, M.A., and Ireland, R.D. (Eds.). *The Blackwell Encyclopedia of Management: Entrepreneurship.* Malden, MA: Blackwell Publishing. pp. 224–226.

[14]Steier, L. (2001). Next-generation entrepreneurs and succession: An exploratory study of modes and means of managing social capital. *Family Business Review,* 14(3): 259–276.

that respect? Compagno et al. offered the following advice for transferring social capital from one family member to another:

- The successor must recognize that ties exist linking members of an organizational network.
- Both parties need to recognize the content of relationships: business advice, financial resources, reputation, friendship, emotional support, and so on.
- The successor must gain legitimacy.
- The family members should collaborate in seeking to maintain or rebuild relationships.
- All parties must understand that it is difficult to transfer tacit knowledge.[15]

Regarding point 5, despite the difficulties, it is evident that the family is a repository of tacit knowledge. Family members, through relationships and the tacit knowledge gained through the years of interaction, can integrate knowledge more rapidly and effectively than nonfamily firms in order to engage in dynamic adaptation of capabilities. What business owners must recognize is that the transfer of such knowledge is not automatic.[16]

Some family business inheritors make the mistake of assuming that social capital is invested in the business. It is not. It is highly personal to the individual. If the succeeding generation does not put in the face time that the founder did, social capital can dissipate rapidly.

HUMAN CAPITAL

The fuel of entrepreneurial fire is lit by the individuals involved in the venture. **Entrepreneurial human capital** has often been described as the set of knowledge and skills that individuals bring to bear to create and exploit market opportunities.[17] We refer to this as the *intellectual dimension* of human capital. While physical labor is generally treated as an undifferentiated commodity, to avoid undue stress it is prudent for leaders of entrepreneurial family firms to take into consideration their ventures' needs and available stocks of *physical dimensions* of human capital.

Against a backdrop of serious unethical allegations in the last few decades such as the infamous examples of Enron, WorldCom, Arthur Anderson, and family firms such as Adelphia Communications,[18] the importance of business being

---

[15]Compagno, C., Francesca, V., and Daniel, P. (2002). Rebuilding social capital during the succession process. In Matti, K., and Nina, K. (Eds.). The Future of Family Business: Values and Social Responsibility, Proceedings of the Family Business Network World Conference, Helsinki.

[16]Chirico, F., and Salvato, C. (2008). Knowledge integration and dynamic organizational adaptation in family firms. *Family Business Review*, 21(2): 169–181.

[17]Coff, R. (2005). Entrepreneurial human capital. In Hitt, M.A., and Ireland, R.D. (Eds.). *The Blackwell Encyclopedia of Management: Entrepreneurship*. Malden, MA: Blackwell Publishing. pp. 82–84.

[18]Former Adelphia Communications CEO, John Rigas, and his son Timothy were convinced of hiding more than $2 billion in debt when embezzling cash for numerous extravagances (from Doug Lennick and Fred Kiel's book *Moral Intelligence,* p.17)

guided by moral principles has been brought to the forefront.[19] Long-lasting successful firms—family[20] and nonfamily firms,[21] well known or not[22]—have been repeatedly found to be guided by moral principles that transcend across cultures, religions, and geographic boundaries. This suggests the importance of reflecting on the *moral dimension* of human capital for entrepreneurs in family firms.

In this section, we focus on all four dimensions of human capital—physical, intellectual, psychological, and moral—as we contend that inadequate supplies of any of these dimensions can lead to disappointing results for entrepreneurs who are eager to create transgenerational value and wealth in family firms.

- Physical dimension—health issues (what can we do?)
- Intellectual dimension—knowledge and skills (what do we know?)
- Psychological dimension—commitment and emotions (what do we want to do?)
- Moral dimension—ethical issues (what is the right thing to do?)

PHYSICAL DIMENSION OF HUMAN CAPITAL

Let us start with the most basic—labor or the physical dimension of human capital. Entrepreneurs seldom take into account the tremendous physical and time demands their businesses will impose. Oh, certainly, every prospective business owner talks about how she or he is prepared to work as hard as needed to get the company off the ground. The truth is that there really are only 24 hours in a day and 7 days in a week, and that our bodies still require food and sleep. Yes, entrepreneurs know they are exaggerating when they say they will work "24/7," but what few understand is that there will be occasions when the survival of the firm demands more than they can give. What happens when your store is burglarized, and you must file police reports, and there is yellow tape around your facility, but you still have to sell merchandise to get cash to pay your bills? Who will fill in for you when you have to be at the police station and at the store at the same time? Do you think you will never get sick or be injured? Who will deliver the goods when you cannot get up from your bed? There are countless other examples we could present, demonstrating that you cannot be in two or more places at once.

It is during these critical moments that we call upon those who care most about us, those who will make the sacrifices to see us through a crisis. We know from the three-circle model that family businesses may have relatives involved in a firm as employees, owners, or in both roles (Figures 4.2, 4.3, Chapter 4). Even

[19]Lennick, D., and Kiel, F. (2008). *Moral Intelligence: Enhancing Business Performance & Leadership Success.* Upper Saddle River, NJ: Wharton School Publishing.

[20]Miller, D., and Le-Breton Miller, I. (2005). *Managing for the Long Run: Lessons in Competitive Advantage from Great Family Businesses.* Boston, MA: Harvard Business School Press.

[21]Collins, J.C., and Porras, J.I. (2002). *Built to Last: Successful Habits of Visionary Companies.* New York: HarperBusiness Essentials.

[22]Simon, H. (1996). *Hidden Champions: Lessons from 500 of the World's Best Unknown Companies.* Boston, MA: Harvard Business School Press.

those family members, not directly affiliated with the business, will come to our aid in emergencies. This is particularly true in the very early stages of the life of the venture.[23] As a business grows and matures, financial or physical resources may substitute for human resources. That is not likely to be the case for the start-up. Limits on human capacity can generate conflict and instigate other problems in a family firm. Excessive time demands on those working in the business can strain marital, parent-child, or sibling relationships. Many families have found it difficult or impossible to avoid carrying the family hierarchy of relationships into the business-reporting relationships.

INTELLECTUAL DIMENSION OF HUMAN CAPITAL

The intellectual dimension of entrepreneurial human capital consists of the KSAs—knowledge, skills (technical and social), and abilities of a person that allow for unique and novel actions.[24] The competitive strength of an entrepreneurial family firm may be based in the **tacit knowledge** shared by people within the organization through their mutual experiences. Tacit knowledge is the nonverbal, noncodified knowledge that is difficult and sometimes impossible to communicate among individuals.[25] Tacit knowledge is contrasted from explicit knowledge that can be codified and transmitted in formal and systematic language.[26] Family members absorb this knowledge from one another through their lifetime of interactions. This can represent a competitive advantage, because one family member will often be able to predict how the other is likely to react. Similarly, they may be more accurate in nonverbal communication, innately understanding messages that they are conveying to one another. There is also reason to believe that the tacit knowledge possessed by family members can make for easier and more successful transitions in management and ownership.

How can one acquire knowledge—explicit and tacit, general business skills and those specific to a firm, and capabilities that are likely to be useful for value creation in entrepreneurial family firms? Education, training, and work experience, both within and beyond one's family firm, have been suggested to be important preparation for family members eager to succeed in transgenerational value creation. However, the specific type of education, training, or experience likely to be most useful for developing entrepreneurial skills in individuals varies from one firm to another as the ingredients for success vary in different contexts.[27]

---

[23]Aldrich, H.E., and Cliff, J.E. (2003). The pervasive effects of family on entrepreneurship: Toward a family embeddedness perspective. *Journal of Business Venturing,* 18(5): 573–596.

[24]Sirmon, D.G., and Hitt, M.A. (2003). Managing resources: Linking unique resources, management, and wealth creation in family firms. *Entrepreneurship Theory & Practice,* Summer: 339–358.

[25]Polayni, M. (1962). *Personal Knowledge: Towards a Post-Critical Philosophy.* Chicago: University of Chicago Press.

[26]Inkpen, A.C. (2005). Knowledge life cycles and entrepreneurial ventures. In Hitt, M.A., and Ireland, R.D. (Eds.). *The Blackwell Encyclopedia of Management: Entrepreneurship.* Malden, MA: Blackwell Publishing. pp. 163–167.

[27]Coff, R. (2005). Entrepreneurial human capital. In Hitt, M.A., and Ireland, R.D. (Eds.). *The Blackwell Encyclopedia of Management: Entrepreneurship.* Malden, MA: Blackwell Publishing. pp. 82–84.

Entrepreneurial family firms know the importance of clarifying and codifying expectations for the preparation and involvement of family members in business. A useful format of stating the expectations in the form of **"Rules of Entry"** has been developed by Patricia and Paul Frishkoff and is provided at the end of this chapter (Appendix 6A). As you may recall from Julie Copeland's comments in the opening vignette of Chapter 4, their family firm, Arbill Safety, required junior-generation members to gain work experience outside the family firm before they could join the company. Others such as Rumpke Consolidated do not wait until the juniors are of age to take on full employment. Instead, they introduce them to work lives in the family firm at young ages as children shadow their parents and experience different aspects of their family firm. In addition to initiating members of junior generation in the business, this strategy helps in transfer of tacit knowledge from senior- to junior-generation family members.[28]

One of the challenges faced by family firms is to attract talented nonfamily employees especially at senior levels, as such positions are often reserved (or perceived as such) for family members.[29] However, by developing a clear set of rules for entry and progression in a firm, successful family firms ensure that individuals, family, and nonfamily members who possess the intellectual capital needed to create value for a firm are employed and placed in leadership positions. Although such firms are careful to employ capability-based criteria for positioning individuals (family or nonfamily) in business, as we have seen in the case of Rumpke Consolidated, they go to great lengths to develop and utilize the talents of all family members regardless of the gender, age, generation, birth order, or blood relationship. This trend has been reported in progressive family firms around the world as the norm of primogeniture (eldest son leads the firm) seems to be fading in favor of capability-based appointments.[30]

PSYCHOLOGICAL DIMENSION OF HUMAN CAPITAL

Psychological dimension of human capital is reflected in an individual's stance toward entrepreneurship. It is characterized by the levels of self-efficacy or confidence in one's abilities to undertake and succeed in a task, resilience to bounce back when beset by problems and adversity, and perseverance to accomplish goals, including redirecting paths where necessary.[31] The combined individual

---

[28]Sirmon, D.G., and Hitt, M.A. (2003). Managing resources: Linking unique resources, management, and wealth creation in family firms. *Entrepreneurship Theory & Practice,* Summer: 339–358.

[29]Dunn, B. (1995). Success themes in Scottish family enterprises: Philosophies and practices through the generations. *Family Business Review,* 8: 17–28.

[30]Chrisman, J.J., Chua, J.H., and Sharma, P. (1998). Important attributes of successors in family businesses: An exploratory study. *Family Business Review,* 11(1): 19–34; Dana, L., Smyrnios, K., and Romano, C. (2000). Succession matters: A comparison of views of owners, spouses, and their adult children—Attributes of successors and succession issues considered important by families in business. Paper presented at the Family Business Australia conference; Sharma, P., and Rao, S. A. (2000). Successor attributes in Indian and Canadian family firms: A comparative study. *Family Business Review,* 13(4): 313–330.

[31]Luthans, F., Youssef, C.M., and Avolio, B.J. (2007). *Psychological Capital: Developing the Human Competitive Edge.* Oxford, UK: Oxford University Press.

attributes of self-efficacy, optimism, hope, resilience, and perseverance permeate an entrepreneurial family firm, leading to value creation and improved performance.

As noted in Chapter 3, the foremost host for nurturing these characteristics is the family of origin[32] that imbues beliefs, values, and attitudes toward entrepreneurship; inculcates a future-oriented time perspective as a norm in family members; and provides opportunities for participating in the family incubator to acquire tacit knowledge about the family firm and skills that can be transferred to other career pursuits.

The Rumpke family appears to be high in this dimension. While the parents do not force their children to join Rumpke Consolidated, a positive attitude toward the business is infused in them at a young age, fostering pride in the enterprise and a desire to contribute to its growth. The optimism for a life-long pursuit of value creation through Rumpke Consolidated seems to trickle down across generations, fostering an attitude to build their futures within the extended family firm.

Research on commitment suggests that motivators of desire, obligation, greed, or need can propel family members to pursue careers in their family firms.[33] It is important to keep in mind that the pursuit of a career in a family enterprise has opportunity costs attached to it. Family members who join their firm guided by feelings of a desire to contribute to its future development and growth engage in discretionary activities, making them better performers and leaders of their firm.[34] As they reach later stages of their life cycle, they have been found to devote adequate efforts to ensure that a capable successor is in place and pass the leadership baton in a timely manner. Others, whose careers in family firms are anchored by feelings of obligation or cost avoidance remain mediocre performers during their career spans and have difficulty in orchestrating a smooth succession.[35]

Although age-appropriate opportunities are provided to all family members to build self-confidence, leaders of entrepreneurial family firms are cognizant of the varied bases of commitment that may draw family members toward the firm. They use experts to understand the motivators drawing family members toward the firm and ensure that only those guided by a desire to make positive contributions are involved actively in the business. Careful planning is done to help build the self-efficacy of such affectively committed family members. To provide you with a preliminary indication of the basis of commitment that is driving the decision of an individual to join a family firm, a brief assessment tool is provided in Appendix 6B. However, expert advice should be sought for a complete assessment. For a list of professional family business advisers in your region, we encourage

---

[32]Family of origin is the family in which we are born or adopted into and spend the preadulthood and part of provisional adulthood years of our life.

[33]Sharma, P., and Irving, G. (2005). Four bases of family business successor commitment: Antecedents and consequences. *Entrepreneurship Theory and Practice*, 29(1): 13–33.

[34]Irving, P.G., Marcus, J., and Sharma, P. (2007). Predictors and Behavioural Consequences of Family Business Successors' Commitment. Presented at the Academy of Management meetings, Philadelphia.

[35]Gagne, M., and Brun de Pontet, S. (2008). Subjective well-being among family business leaders nearing succession: The role of goal adjustment and work motivation. Presented at the Family Enterprise Research Conference, Milwaukee.

you to consult the Family Firm Institute,[36] which is an international professional association of family business advisors and educators.

MORAL DIMENSION OF HUMAN CAPITAL

Moral dimension of human capital refers to the mental capacity of an individual to determine how universal principles or golden rules of integrity, responsibility, compassion, and forgiveness should be applied in personal and professional conduct. In their book *Moral Intelligence,* Lennick and Kiel explain the four principles as follows:

> *Integrity* is the hallmark of the morally intelligent person. When we act with integrity, we harmonize our behavior to conform to universal human principles. We do what we know is right; we act in line with our principles and beliefs.
>
> Only a person willing to take *responsibility* for her actions—and the consequences of those actions—will be able to ensure that her actions conform to universal human principles.
>
> *Compassion* is vital because caring about others not only communicates our respect for others, but creates a climate in which others will be compassionate toward us when we need it most.
>
> *Forgiveness* is crucial because without tolerance for mistakes and the knowledge of our own imperfection, we are likely to be rigid, inflexible, and unable to engage with others in ways that promote our mutual good. (p7)

Leaders of successful family firms point toward integrity as the most desirable attribute in the next-generation family members[37] and rate it as being even more important than commitment, competence, education, or experience. Sharma et al. observed that "integrity and commitment are the most important successor attributes sought by family firms. Competence ranks lower because competence without integrity and commitment is unlikely, to help most families realize their visions for the business and the family."[38]

The power of forgiveness and its integral role in the business and family lives have been noted by many authors such as Frederic Luskin in *Forgive for Good* and D. Patrick Miller in *Little Book of Forgiveness.* Family business consultant Hubler found the power of this virtue so compelling that he has developed "The Family Forgiveness Ritual"[39] to help his clients realize that hurt is a normal part

---

[36]http://www.ffi.org/otnDir.asp

[37]Chrisman, J.J., Chua, J.H., and Sharma, P. (1998). Important attributes of successors in family businesses: An exploratory study. *Family Business Review,* 11(1): 19–34.

[38]Sharma, P., Chua, J.H., and Chrisman, J.J. (2005). Succession planning. In Hitt, M.A., and Ireland, R.D. (Eds.). *The Blackwell Encyclopedia of Management: Entrepreneurship.* Malden, MA: Blackwell Publishing. pp. 231–233.

[39]Hubler, T.M. (2005). Forgiveness as an intervention in family-owned business: A new beginning. *Family Business Review,* 18(2): 95–103. Briefly, the stages of the ritual involve—presentation by clergy person on the religious philosophy of forgiveness, a process that allows family members to share what they want to forgive other for or be forgiven for; an absolution ritual performed by clergyperson that helps wash away the hurt; followed by a celebratory meal.

of life. Involving a clergyperson, this ritual has been found valuable to help family firms forgive each other and either rejoin a relationship or never speak again to the person. Regardless of the chosen pathway, outcomes of individual peace and improved performance of the family and its firm have been found.

Although entrepreneurial family firms are rarely launched with an explicit moral focus, the most costly mistakes made are frequently moral rather than strategic or operational.[40] While these universal golden rules are straightforward, their implementation can be quite challenging over the long term as it is easy and sometimes exciting to stray from these paths. Family firms that enjoy sustained competitive advantages have been built on secure foundations of ethical and moral grounds.[41] The importance of these principles as a way of life is well understood by entrepreneurial family firm leaders who make conscious efforts to imbue these values in the early childhood years through role modeling, encouraging appropriate behaviors, and reinforcing these morals through school, religion, sports, and other opportunities presented to parents or grandparents in these tender years. A similar approach of reinforcing golden rules of behavior through varied opportunities is used in the context of the family firm as well. Books by Truett Cathy, the founder of Chick-fil-A, provide several pragmatic examples of how values can be imbued in entrepreneurial family firms.[42]

RESOURCES FOR ENTREPRENEURIAL FAMILY FIRMS

A key distinction between family and nonfamily businesses is the resource base that families provide. Family members, inside and outside the firm, have the potential to contribute in all four categories of capital described above. We ask you to keep in mind that resource application to the venture can vary from stage to stage in life cycles. In Part A of this book, we introduced you to multiple life cycles: individual, family, business, product, industry, and economy. By now, the complexity of the interactions among these life cycles may be disconcerting and confusing to you. But imagine the problems that family business owners experience when they ignore those interactions.

At this point, we want you to focus on the assets families bring to the venture in the resource categories. In the birth stage of an individual's life, family is everything— the source of sustenance, of education, and of values. In the birth stage of the venture, the family provides financial and human capital that the entrepreneur has trouble

---

[40]Lennick, D., and Kiel, F. (2008). *Moral Intelligence: Enhancing Business Performance & Leadership Success.* Upper Saddle River, NJ: Wharton School Publishing.

[41]Miller, D., and Le-Breton Miller, I. (2005). *Managing for the Long Run: Lessons in Competitive Advantage from Great Family Businesses.* Boston, MA: Harvard Business School Press.

[42]Cathy, S.T. (1989). *It's Easier to Succeed Than to Fail.* Nashville: Thomas Nelson Publishers; Blanchard, K., and Cathy, S.T. (2002). *The Generosity Factor: Discover the Joy of Giving Your Time, Talent, and Treasure.* Grand Rapids, MI: Zondervan; Cathy, S.T. (2002). *Eat More Chikin: Inspire More People.* Hapeville, GA: Looking Glass Books.

obtaining from nonrelations. Family members may help in identifying and obtaining products that have rapid growth potential. When the industry in which a business competes matures, family members may help open new markets, perhaps internationally through their own involvement or through their contacts.

Looking ahead to Part B of the book, we turn our attention to each stage of the life cycle to assess where there may be compatibility and where there may be conflict. You will read positive and negative examples regarding families in business. It is our intent that you learn from both in order to manage the family firm successfully.

Summary

- All entrepreneurs must learn how to effectively and efficiently manage their resource portfolio to ensure that the stocks of capital increase over time (through creation activities) rather than staying constant (through cruising) or depleting (through consuming).
- The successful family business obtains and deploys several types of capital:
  o Financial capital, the money that is the lifeblood of the firm
  o Physical capital, the assets that generate revenue for the venture
  o Social capital, the "who you know" contacts that open doors for family and business
  o Human capital, the "what you know" of the enterprise, the skills of people in the business that keep it operating and competitive.
- The changes in levels of stocks of financial, physical, and social capital are moderated by the human capital available to a firm over time.
- Social capital is highly personal to an individual. Social competence of the next generation and cooperation of the senior generation are necessary to transfer the accumulated stocks of capital across generations of family firm leaders.
- Entrepreneurial family firms that enjoy dedicated support of a larger number of healthy, technically competent, socially skilled, financially savvy, affectively committed, and morally sound individuals are well positioned to effectively manage their financial, social, and physical capital and to leverage these to exploit market opportunities.
- The specific type of education, training, or experience likely to be most useful for developing entrepreneurial skills in individuals varies from one firm to another as the ingredients for success vary in different contexts.
- Family firms benefit from developing clear rules of entry and promotion in their firms that apply both to family and nonfamily members.
- Transferring the accumulated capital from one generation to the next and preparing juniors to further build and leverage on their inherited capital endowments provide challenges and opportunities for family firms.
- The three-circle model and stakeholder maps of family, ownership, and business help to visualize and portray different levels of family involvement in business, comprehend why conflicts arise over capital, and aid in determining how resources can be used to resolve conflicts while making organizations more effective.

Discussion Questions

1. What advantages does a family business have over a nonfamily business regarding human capital? (HINT: Remember to think of the different dimensions of human capital discussed in this chapter.)
2. If you were in business with your spouse, what kinds of arguments do you think you might have over financial capital? Would arguments be different in nature if you were in business with your brother or sister? How about when in business with a friend and falling in love with her husband or his wife? What proactive strategies might be useful to manage potential conflicts over resources in each of these situations?
3. Think of an individual whom you feel has high stocks of social capital. What factors have contributed to his success?
4. Describe and compare how someone you know exhibits affective (desire based), normative (obligation based), and continual (need or greed based) commitment toward his or her career choice.
5. Think of an individual well known for integrity. What visible behaviors does he or she exhibit that lead to such perceptions about him or her?
6. Do you think forgiveness can be taught? If so, how? If not, why not?

Learning Exercises

1. Identify a family business that will share information about both the business and the family. List the names of family members and key employees. Develop a stakeholder map for this family business. What does this information tell you about the resource challenges and opportunities enjoyed by this firm?
2. Can you think of a movie or classic novel that provides evidence of family-business interface? What issues are brought to light in this work? How can these issues be understood through stakeholder maps and varied perspectives on resources?
3. Can you think of a television show, movie, or classic novel that provides evidence of family-business interface? What issues are brought to light in this work? How can these issues be understood through stakeholder maps and varied perspectives on resources?
   HINT: The following list is based on suggestions by Professors Mattias Nordqvist from Jonkoping International Business School, Sweden; Ken Moores from Bond University, Australia; and Reg Litz from the University of Manitoba, Canada. It may provide a useful start:

Television Shows:

Arrested Development (Mitchell Hurwitz)
Brothers & Sisters (Jon Robin Baitz)
Cane (Cynthia Cidre)
Dallas (David Jacobs)
Dynasty (Richard & Esther Shapiro)

Falcon Crest (Earl Hamner)
Six Feet Under (Alan Ball)
The Sopranos (David Chase)

Movies:

Cat on a Hot Tin Roof (director: Richard Brooks)
Executive Suite (director: Robert Wise)
Kinky Boots (director: Julian Jarrold)
Life as a House (director: Irwin Winkler)
Sabrina (director: Billy Wilder)
The Giant (director: George Stevens)
The Godfather (director: Francis Ford Coppola)
The House of Rothschilds (director: Alfred L. Werker)
The Inheritance (director: Per Fly)
Tucker: The Man and His Dream (director: Francis Ford Coppola)

Novels/Plays:

All My Sons (Arthur Miller)
Fathers and Sons (Ivan Turgenjev)
The House of Buddenbrooks (Thomas Mann)
Dombey and Son (Charles Dickens)
The Rise of Silas Lapham (William Dean Howells)
Martin Dressler (Steven Millhauser)
The Head of the Firm (Hjalmar Bergman)

For useful videos and other resources for entrepreneurial family firms, check out the Resources section of the Canadian Association of Family Enterprises Web site: http://www.cafecanada.ca/

4. Using Appendix 6A as a guide, develop the *Rules of Entry* for a family business that you are familiar with. You may find it interesting to develop these rules in working with members of different generations of this family firm. To what extent do their perspectives differ? Are they in different segments of the stakeholder map (Figure 4.2, Chapter 4)?

5. Interview a junior-generation family member involved in a family business asking her or him the factors that led to her or his decision to pursue a career in the family firm. Using the preliminary assessment tool in Appendix 6B, gauge the nature of commitment that is the key driver of her or his career choice. How well do the story and the tool align? Why do you think you find this level of alignment in this case?

Other Resources

- Blanchard, K., and Cathy, S.T. (2002). *The Generosity Factor: Discover the Joy of Giving Your Time, Talent, and Treasure.* Grand Rapids, MI: Zondervan.
- Cathy, S.T. (1989). *It's Easier to Succeed Than to Fail.* Nashville: Thomas Nelson Publishers.

- Cathy, S.T. (2002). *Eat More Chikin: Inspire More People.* Decatur, GA: Looking Glass Books.
- Clemens, J.K., and Wolf, M. (2000). *Movies to Manage By: Lessons in Leadership from Great Films.* New York: McGraw-Hill Professional.
- Goleman, D. (1995). *Emotional Intelligence: Why It Can Matter More Than IQ?* New York: Bantam.
- Goleman, D. (1998). *Working with Emotional Intelligence.* New York: Bantam; Goleman, D., Boyatzis, R., and McKee, A. (2002). *Primal Leadership: Realizing the Power of Emotional Intelligence.* Boston, MA: Harvard Business School Press.
- Hubler, T.M. (2005). Forgiveness as an intervention in family-owned business: A new beginning. *Family Business Review,* 18(2): 95–103.
- Lennick, D., and Kiel, F. (2008). *Moral Intelligence: Enhancing Business Performance & Leadership Success.* Saddle River, NJ: Wharton School Publishing.
- Luthans, F., Youssef, C.M., and Avolio, B.J. (2007). *Psychological Capital: Developing the Human Competitive Edge.* Oxford, UK: Oxford University Press.
- Lennick, D., and Kiel, F. (2008). *Moral Intelligence: Enhancing Business Performance & Leadership Success.* Saddle River, NJ: Wharton School Publishing.

Resources for Family Business Owners

- Canadian Association of Family Enterprises — http://www.cafecanada.ca/
- Family Firm Institute — http://www.ffi.org/
- Leadership in Family Enterprise — http://www.patandpaul.com/
- National Federation of Independent Business — www.nfib.com.
- Rural Minnesota Life, Department of Family Social Science, University of Minnesota — http://fsos.cehd.umn.edu/projects/mnlife.html
- United States Small Business Administration — http://www.sba.gov/

Rules for Entry into the Family Business[43]

By Drs. Patricia and Paul Frishkoff
http://www.patandpaul.com/

Business conditions dictate that the next generation of leaders in family business-es be more experienced, knowledgeable, and flexible than their bosses, ready to run leaner and more productive enterprises. They need to prepare. Just being born with the right last name is NOT adequate preparation. The senior genera-tion must clarify and codify expectations. What does it take to be ready to run this family business?

Establishing a formal set of rules for entry informs young family members about what to expect and how to prepare. Such rules should be in place before younger family members begin educational choices, and may need to be appro-priately "grandfathered" in.

Issue: Eligibility

Considerations: Will the presidency go to a blood relative? What about in-laws, stepchildren, and significant others, including live-ins? Will top positions go to nonfamily members?

Sample Rule: A *four-year college degree is required in a field that is useful or related to our company.*

Issue: Education

Considerations: Is education beyond high school needed? If so, how much? Does major matter?

Sample Rule: A *four-year college degree is required in a field that is useful or related to our company.*

Issue: Outside Experience

Considerations: Would outside experience help build capability and self-esteem? How could the individual and business gain from such? What type of work experience or industry is desirable?

Sample Rule: A *minimum of three years of employment in a complementary position in a larger firm. Individual finds own position. At least one promotion is required.*

---

[43]Copyright 2008 *Leadership in Family Enterprise.* Used with permission of Patricia Frishkoff.

Issue: Coming and Going

Considerations: What does coming and going say about commitment? How often can it happen? Will it impact the morale of other candidates?

Sample Rule: If you choose to leave long-term employment, for other than medical or educational purposes, chances for rehire will be impaired. You will be bound by the buy-sell agreement in force.

Issue: Age Limits

Considerations: How long can you wait for the next generation to make their career choices? Will there always be a position for them?

Sample Rule: Next generation interested in long-term employment must complete education and experience and commence work by age 35.

Issue: Compensation

Considerations: Will all family members be paid the same or will their compensation be based on market? What perks can they expect?

Sample Rule: Family members will be paid market-based salaries and will be given perks appropriate to their position. They should not expect more than nonfamily counterparts.

Issue: Performance Review

Considerations: Who supervises them? How will they know how well they are doing? What if they are not cutting it?

Sample Rule: Family members will report to a supervisor who is not a parent and who has the authority to terminate. Performance reviews will occur every six months, highlighting positive and negative aspects. Continued employment will be dependent on excellent performance.

Issue: Role and Relationship

Considerations: Will new hires be treated more as employees or as partners? How much say will they have in decisions?

Sample Rule: You will be assigned a job for which you are qualified, and be given the authority to perform that job. Family members may enter either management or line positions. Only managers will be on the management team. Teamwork among family members is expected; lack of such is condition for dismissal.

Issue: Ownership

Considerations: When will ownership be transferred? To whom? Under what conditions?

Sample Rule: Majority ownership of voting common stock will eventually rest with the family members employed by the company. Other family members may be given the opportunity for ownership, but without a voting position.

Commitment Index: A Preliminary Assessment Tool
Developed by Pramodita Sharma

Using the five-point scale below, please indicate the extent of your agreement with the following:

	1	2	3	4	5
Strongly Disagree			*Strongly Agree*		
1. I feel a sense of belonging to my family business.	1	2	3	4	5
2. Even if it were to my advantage, I do not feel it would be right to leave my family business.	1	2	3	4	5
3. Right now, pursuing a career in my family business is as much a matter of necessity as it is of desire.	1	2	3	4	5
4. I feel that I have too few options to consider a career outside my family business.	1	2	3	4	5
5. I would be very happy to spend the rest of my career with my family business.	1	2	3	4	5
6. I would feel guilty if I did not pursue a career with my family business.	1	2	3	4	5
7. Too much of my life would be disrupted if I decided I did not want to pursue a career with my family business.	1	2	3	4	5
8. One of the few negative consequences of leaving my family business would be the scarcity of available resources.	1	2	3	4	5

YOUR COMMITMENT INDEX

ADD YOUR SCORES FOR:

1 +5 = _____ (Desire score out of 10)

2 + 6 = _____ (Obligation score out of 10)

3 +7 = _____ (Cost avoidance score out of 10)

4 + 8 = _____ (Need based score out 10)

PART B

ENTREPRENEURSHIP THROUGH THE STAGES

Part A of this book introduced you to life-cycle stages of an individual, family, organization, and the environment in which a venture operates. We found that each life-cycle stage is rampant with challenges as well as opportunities. Leaders of entrepreneurial family firms continue to find resources to create value for themselves, their ventures, family members, and community. Instead of being discouraged by the challenges posed by the overlaps between the family and business, these individuals strategically adopt structures and strategies to harness the opportunities in each stage of their firm's life cycle, while keeping the challenges in check.

In Part B (Chapters 7–10), we take a closer look at each stage in the life cycle of a firm. A chapter each is devoted to the four stages in the standard life-cycle model presented in Part A: start-up (Chapter 7), growth (Chapter 8), maturity (Chapter 9), and decline—degeneration or regeneration? (Chapter 10). In each chapter in Part B, we discuss the features of each stage of a venture's life and elaborate on how these features influence and are influenced by the life-cycle stages of the individual, family, and environment in which the firm operates. The nature of resource exchanges between the family and business system at each stage of the firm's life cycle is elaborated upon. The problems faced and opportunities available are highlighted. Using examples of entrepreneurial family firms from around the world, we cull some of the winning strategies that leaders of such firms use to effectively govern and manage their firms in the life-cycle stage. As you go through each chapter, notice how entrepreneurial actions and conditions for entrepreneurship vary at each stage of a venture's life. We encourage you to pay attention to the governance mechanisms that prove useful in firms with varying levels and modes of family involvement in business.

CHAPTER 7

STARTING THE VENTURE: OVEREXTENDED, UNDERCAPITALIZED

PLAYING TO STRENGTHS

Walt (Disney) was the . . . front man, but without his brother Roy by his side from Day One in 1923, the Disney name wouldn't be the iconic brand the whole world knows today. "If it hadn't been for my big brother," Walt once joked, "I swear I'd have been in jail several times for check bouncing"—and that wisecrack contained a grain or two of truth.

Walt was a creative genius and a mercurial visionary. Before he turned 20, he was making crude animated cartoons in a makeshift studio in his family's garage in Kansas City and selling them to a local theater. Over the next five decades until his death in 1966 he won 32 Academy Awards—by far the most ever awarded to an individual. (The runner-up is MGM art director Cedric Gibbons, with 11.) Walt had an uncanny connection to the entertainment desires of the American family, but he wasn't an accomplished businessperson.

In the early 1920s, Walt founded a short-lived commercial art partnership and an animation company that quickly went bankrupt. It was only at Roy's suggestion that he moved to Hollywood. Roy, who was recovering from tuberculosis at the time, was eight years older than Walt, but they were close even as children. "We had to sleep in the same bed," Roy would say. "Walt was just a little guy, and he was always wetting the bed. And he's been peeing on me ever since." That comment reflects in some small way the intensity of the Disney brothers' sibling rivalry—a relationship based on equal parts of respect and resentment.

Walt tried to find work as a director, without success. Then, with Roy's encouragement, he returned to his entrepreneurial roots and pursued animation once more. In October 1923, Walt received an offer from a New York distributor willing to buy a series of short cartoons. This time, he turned to Roy as a partner. Together they founded Disney Brothers Studio, the first incarnation of today's media giant.

Roy, a straight-talking, steady-tempered son of the Midwest who had worked in a bank back in Kansas City, handled what Walt called "the business end." He raised the money to launch the venture out of his own savings and from family and friends. His managerial skills left Walt free to do what he did best, throwing himself into the production of a series of innovative and popular short films that placed a real-life child actress named Alice in an animated story—a distant ancestor of the company's 1988 hit *Who Framed Roger Rabbit*.

Seemingly without conscious forethought, the Disney brothers had adopted a division of labor that played to their individual strengths. The Disney Company needed Roy's business acumen as much as it needed Walt's creative vision, and the synergies between those natural talents wielded a huge impact on their company's development.

Source: Kinni, T. (2004). The Disney Brothers' Dilemma. *Family Business*, 15(2): 32–35.

Questions

1. Which of your relatives would you invest in if they came to you to help start a new company? Why?
2. Which of your relatives would you go to for help in starting your own business? Why?

Theodore Kinni makes a profound statement in the excerpt above from his article about Roy and Walt Disney—"Seemingly *without conscious forethought*, the Disney brothers had *adopted a division of labor* that played to their individual strengths" (italics added). As entrepreneurs launch their ventures, they generally find themselves short on key resources we discussed in the last chapter—financial, social, physical, and human. This shortage makes them prone to using help from wherever they can find it, without necessarily giving due thought to the long-term consequences of using readily available help. Given the ease of appropriation between family and business systems, family resources are often called upon to help entrepreneurs develop their ideas and launch their ventures. Walt Disney's using brother Roy's support is no exception.

In hindsight, the strategically smart adoption of the division of labor that harnessed the individual talents of the Disney brothers seems to have laid a strong foundation for the remarkable success of this family enterprise. But, before they serendipitously fell into this complementary division of labor, they had had their share of failures and frustrations. Imagine how many problems could be avoided if the family members gave conscious forethought to their relative strengths and weaknesses when designing their businesses.

COOPERATION AND CONFLICT FROM THE BEGINNING

We call your attention to the title of Kinni's article: "The Disney Brothers' Dilemma." The remainder of this article that was published in *Family Business Magazine* explores areas of contention and conflict between the brothers. Do not ever think that conflict in the family firm or any organization can be avoided. If you follow every prescription that we offer in this book, there will still be conflict in your family. Family members know each other too well, especially how to push each other's hot buttons. As we discussed in Chapter 2 on individual life cycles, there are often significant differences in thinking and preferences among family members of different generations. In Chapter 3, we learned that sibling conflicts and rivalries are an inherent part of family life, as siblings compete with each other for the precious resource of parental attention.[1] In fact, if you find that there is no conflict among family members, you can be assured that it is being suppressed in some way that will only make it worse when it arises.[2]

Entrepreneurial family firm leaders understand the fundamental difference between management and governance of a firm. As you may recall from Chapter 1, while management provides leadership of operations to ensure that a firm's work is completed, governance establishes and monitors the firm's overall direction, including the extent and mode of family involvement in different stages of a firm's life. Leaders of enterprising family firms are aware of the need to monitor the **familiness** of the firm so as to maintain a balanced flow of resources between family and business systems. They keep in mind that regardless of the identity of the giver and receiver (family or nonfamily member), each gift of time or money has an implicit cost and must be repaid in some form or shape.[3] The culture of disciplined governance is imbued in an enterprise at its formative stages by adopting mechanisms to enable proactive voicing of perspectives before disagreements become conflicts or brew as resentments.

Since the early academic writings on family businesses, such as *Keeping the Family Business Healthy* by John Ward[4] and *Cultural Change in Family Firms* by Gibb Dyer Jr.,[5] the tenacious influence of the founding generation on the company and family culture has been observed. The values held sacrosanct by the founding family at the start-up stage in terms of the mode and extent of

[1]Sulloway, F.J. (1996). *Born to Rebel: Birth Order, Family Dynamics, and Creative Lives.* New York: Pantheon; Kluger, J. (2007). The power of birth order. *Time,* October 29: 43–48.

[2]Sorenson, R.L. (1999). Conflict management strategies used by successful family businesses. *Family Business Review,* 12(4): 325–339.

[3]Mauss, M. (1990). *The Gift: Forms and Functions of Exchange in Archaic Societies.* London: Routledge.

[4]Ward, J.L. (1987). *Keeping the Family Business Healthy: How to Plan for Continuing Growth, Profitability, and Family Leadership.* San Francisco: Jossey–Bass Publisher.

[5]Dyer Jr., W.G. (1986). *Cultural Change in Family Firms: Anticipating and Managing Business and Family Transitions.* San Francisco: Jossey–Bass Publisher.

family involvement in business have a deep-rooted influence on the trajectory of the firm's growth over generations. These values, in turn, sow the seeds for appropriate governance of the firm, influencing performance on family and business dimensions.[6]

As we noted previously, the purpose of this book is to prepare you to lead and succeed in creating and building one or more entrepreneurial family firms in your career. Toward this end, it is important not only to identify opportunities for a firm at different stages of its life cycle, but also to mobilize and effectively manage resources and exploit their potential. Proactive adoption of appropriate governance mechanisms to manage and resolve conflicts that will inevitably arise over the life cycle of a firm can help the growth and development of an entrepreneurial family firm.[7] Recent research suggests that in comparison to others, family firms with healthier relationships within the family system perform better than their competitors.[8] On the basis of a study of 732 large Spanish family firms with an average of 110 employees, scholars Basco and Rodríguez concluded that

> family enterprises which give emphasis to both family and business, but relatively more to family, have better family results and similar business results compared to those enterprises which eliminate family from their management and governance decisions.[9]

In this chapter, we explore the pre-start-up and start-up stages of the family enterprise. These stages surround the entrepreneurial event of new venture creation. It is in these early stages that the land is prepared for sowing the seeds of disciplined governance of the venture over time. Business ideas are generated and screened. Roles of family and nonfamily members in selecting and exploiting opportunities to pursue are determined. Questions about sources of funding before a venture starts selling products and services are addressed. The players and their respective roles in the start-up team are determined.

What problems and opportunities are normally associated with these stages? What strategies tend to work to build a strong foundation for an entrepreneurial family firm? As explained in earlier chapters, the choices made by each entrepreneur are likely to be unique as these are influenced by the life-cycle stages of individual, family, and environment. How do successful entrepreneurs resolve conflicts in life cycles as they create entrepreneurial family firms? This chapter explains these issues that an entrepreneur must address at the inception of a business.

---

[6]Sharma, P., and Nordqvist, M. (2008). A classification scheme for family firms: From family values to effective governance to firm performance. In Tapies, J., and Ward, J.L. (Eds.). *Family Values and Value Creation: How Do Family-Owned Businesses Foster Enduring Values.* New York: Palgrave Macmillan. pp.71–101. http://www.palgrave.com/products/title.aspx?PID=300866

[7]Harvey, M., and Evans, R.E. (1994). Family business and multiple levels of conflict. *Family Business Review,* 7(4): 331–348.

[8]2008 Laird Norton Tyee Northwest Family Business Survey, http://www.familybusinesssurvey.com/thanks.aspx

[9]Basco, R., and Peréz Rodríguez, M. (2009). Studying the family enterprise holistically: Evidence for integrated family and business systems. *Family Business Review,* March issue.

START-UP QUESTIONS: WHY, WHAT, HOW, WHO?

In recent years, there has been increased attention given to the topic of **nascent entrepreneurs**.[10] These are individuals who are actively involved in thinking about creating new ventures. Not all nascent entrepreneurs will actually launch a company, but these are persons who are writing business plans, soliciting funding, putting together a venture team, or in some other way moving forward with the expectation of creating something new. The study of nascent entrepreneurs is of particular interest to economic development specialists who examine the macroconditions that foster business creation and growth, positively impacting economies.

As explained in Chapter 1, an entrepreneurial venture can either be created independently by a *lone entrepreneur* or by an ***entrepreneurial team*** in which the team can either be family or nonfamily members (Figure 1.1). Research suggests that 77 percent of new ventures established in the United States are born as family firms, while another 3 percent become family firms within the first two years of their founding.[11] A nascent entrepreneur whose family of origin or family of attachment owns businesses must decide whether to launch an entrepreneurial firm under the umbrella of his/her family's business or as an independent entity. Thus, nascent entrepreneurs must address some fundamental questions such as—*Why* bother with an entrepreneurial career when there are so many alternate career paths to choose from? If an individual decides to spend time and energy on an entrepreneurial creation, a need arises to address questions such as the following: *What* products or services should this venture provide to create value for the individual, his/her family, and society? *Who* should be involved in the enterprise? What should be the role of family members in the entrepreneurial venture? *How* should the factors of production or resources be brought together to make the venture a reality? Should resources from family be used in the new venture? If so, what should be the conditions of the usage of these resources? Let us reflect on each question below:

WHY BOTHER?

Nascent entrepreneurs must address the reason why they should engage in a new creation, be it a new venture, product, or market/service. A combination of individual, contextual, and macroenvironmental factors contributes to the decision to launch a venture. The **push-pull theory** of motivation for an entrepreneurial career path suggests that broadly speaking, individuals are either drawn or pulled toward entrepreneurship by the positive forces, or thrust into an entrepreneurial pathway

---

[10]Delmar, F., and Davidsson, P. (2000). Where do they come from? Prevalence and characteristics of nascent entrepreneurs. *Entrepreneurship and Regional Development,* 12: 1–23.

[11]Chua, J.H., Chrisman, J.J., and Chang, E.P.C. (2004). Are family firms born or made? An exploratory investigation, *Family Business Review,* 17(1): 37–54.

TABLE 7.1 Pull and Push Factors Driving Individuals toward New Creations	
Pull Factors Opportunistic Entrepreneurs	*Push Factors* Necessity Entrepreneurs
• Recognition of an opportunity to create value through personal or work experiences • Passion for creativity • Desire to make own mark in a family enterprise • Family culture of innovation and creativity • Inspired by entrepreneurial role models in family, close relatives, or friends	• Inability to obtain employment due to the lack of demand of individual's talents or abilities, and/or some form of discrimination • Perceived opportunity cost of losing income by not joining one's family enterprise • Family norms such as primogeniture that require the eldest son to take over the leadership of a family firm, regardless of his abilities or desires

by the push of negative forces in their environment.[12] Those drawn by pull factors are referred to as "opportunistic entrepreneurs or ventures" while those propelled by push factors are called "necessity entrepreneurs or ventures" (Table 7.1).

Opportunistic entrepreneurs are individuals who intentionally want to be in business for themselves. They may be driven by an opportunity that they or others have recognized. Examples include the launch of social networking Web sites such as MySpace[13] or Facebook.[14] Opportunities may be revealed or inspired through work or personal experiences and exploited by teaming up with family or nonfamily members. For example, Sam Walton's experience at J. C. Penney and Ben Franklin enabled him to understand the retail market, pulling him to establish Wal-Mart by teaming up with his brother Bud. Another example is the 1991 launch of It's Just Lunch (IJL),[15] a lunch dating service for business professionals. Now with more than 100 offices worldwide, IJL was founded by a Chicago woman when she experienced the need for such service after her engagement was called off.

Others may be drawn toward innovative actions by their passion for creativity in a particular domain. Jørn Utzon's creation of the Sydney Opera House[16] is one such example. In the context of family firms, a desire by the junior generation to make a distinct mark on their family enterprises often leads to new creations. As an example, driven by a collective desire to make their mark, six fourth-generation cousins of Australian winemakers, the Brown Brothers family, created a new brand of wines, "Kid You Not."[17] These wines are targeted to meet the needs and desires

---

[12]Bird, B. J. (1989). *Entrepreneurial Behavior.* Glenview, IL: Scott, Foresman and Company; Shapiro, A. (1975). The displaced uncomfortable entrepreneur. *Psychology Today*, 9 (November): 83–88.

[13]http://en.wikipedia.org/wiki/MySpace

[14]http://en.wikipedia.org/wiki/Facebook

[15]http://www.itsjustlunch.com/

[16]http://www.sydneyoperahouse.com/about/house_history_landing.aspx

[17]http://www.wineandfoodtube.com/tube/view/0/the-wine-story-kid-you-not-4646/

of individuals who fall in the same age bracket as the cousins, 20- to 35-year-olds. In comparison to the wines traditionally blended and sold by the Brown Brothers since the founding of this firm in 1889,[18] the Kid You Not wines are quite distinct in terms of blends, taste, design labels, distribution, and marketing channels used to reach their target customers. This is evident from their creative Web site www .kidyounot.com.au. Although distinctive in many ways, the Kid You Not wines express the core values of the Brown Brothers—passion, innovation, and unpretentiousness. These are values that the entire Brown family is proud of.

In contrast to the opportunistic entrepreneurs, the **necessity entrepreneurs** start businesses because they are pushed into such careers by need. Examples are an inability to obtain employment due to the lack of marketable skills and talents, or having migrated to another country where they are unable to find work due to language deficiency or because of some form of discrimination. In family firms, individuals may be pushed toward pursuing a career in their family firms due to their perception that they are likely to lose in terms of earnings or benefits from the firm if they do not take an active role in it. Alternatively, there are cases of familial norms, such as primogeniture, where the eldest son is expected to take charge of the family firm, placing an obligation on the firstborn son to pursue such a career.[19]

THE "WHAT" FACTORS

Regardless of whether an individual chooses to embark on an entrepreneurial career path propelled by push or pull factors, the opportunity search process begins with an intentional decision regarding the "degree of newness" of the new creation. Two related questions need to be addressed as the entrepreneur tries to identify and sort through various opportunities: (1) What products or services should the venture focus on, and (2) what should be the market scope? Entrepreneurs with family members already involved in a business must decide whether to go into **related** or **unrelated ventures**, that is, what should be the degree of differentiation in terms of product/service and market scope of the new venture from existing family firms.

As you will recall from Chapter 4 (Figure 4.2), an entrepreneur may choose a venture focused on developing new products/services or on expanding existing offerings either in the same or in new markets. Furthermore, she may work with individuals she has worked with and knows well from before (an existing team of family or nonfamily members) or form a new team with family or nonfamily members. The resources needed and risk factors vary with the degrees of newness of an entrepreneurial action, as well as the degree of relatedness with existing family firms. Therefore, decisions on several fronts must be made at the critical start-up stages. This does not mean that decisions made at these early stages of

---

[18]http://en.wikipedia.org/wiki/Brown_Brothers_Milawa_Vineyard
[19]Sharma, P., and Irving, P.G. (2005). Four bases of family business successor commitment: Antecedents and consequences. *Entrepreneurship Theory and Practice*, 29(1): 13–33.

the venture cannot be changed later. As you may imagine, many are. However, such changes consume precious resources of an entrepreneur. Savvy entrepreneurs know the importance of these first decisions as they intuitively keep in mind the title of one of Truett Cathy's (from Chick-fil-A fame) books, *It's Easier to Build Boys than Mend Men.*

Family members can instigate, support, inhibit, or reject foundational decisions made by an entrepreneur. As we noted in Chapter 3, research suggests the significant influence of the family of origin and family of attachment on entrepreneurial pursuits of family members. It has been found that entrepreneurs frequently have close relatives who have been or are independent business owners. As entrepreneurial skills must be proactively developed and practiced, it is often under the rubric of firms run by family and friends that the entrepreneurial spirit and capabilities of family members are developed—either through formal employment or by informally "helping out" in the family firm. These experiences help nurture opportunity recognition and the confidence to embark on an entrepreneurial career path.

But simply the confidence to start a new venture is not a sufficient condition for its success. A study of more than 37,700 U.S. firms reveals that while more than half of business founders had self-employed family members before starting their businesses, the success of the businesses was only weakly related to having a self-employed family member. Instead, success was strongly related to prior work experience in the businesses of those family members. This study suggests the importance of acquiring general and business-specific human capital in preparation for launching an enterprise that is likely to succeed. Savvy next-generation family members are proactive in terms of their own skill development. They do not necessarily wait for their senior-generation members to ask them to join the family firm. Instead, they seek active employment and challenging assignments in entrepreneurial firms—their own family's firm or others. They start doing this at a young age so as to build their entrepreneurial resume and skills.

Nascent entrepreneurs eager to launch ventures that are unrelated to their family firms often face the family firm shadow as their new creation is compared with the successful existing ventures run by family members. Worried about the fear of failure or not being as successful as the previous generations, these entrepreneurs may scan so many opportunities that they exhaust themselves and never start, or become confused by the comparisons and bypass good ideas in search for the perfect one. Such a state is sometimes referred to as **paralysis by analysis**.

While branching out in new directions under the shadow of family firms can be challenging, it is important to note that studies of long-lasting family firms reveal that in such firms opportunity recognition and exploitation are at the core of these firms across generations.[20] They understand that sustainability of their family firm depends on the abilities of the next generation to innovate

---

[20]Miller, D., and Le-Breton Miller, I. (2005). *Managing for the Long Run: Lessons in Competitive Advantage from Great Family Businesses.* Boston, MA: Harvard Business School Press.

and accept risk. In some of the most successful family firms, each generation either regenerates the existing firm and its offerings or creates a spin-off from the family firm or an entirely new venture. In seeking to create value across generations, such enterprising firms engage in continuous innovation in all stages including pre-start-up and start-up. However, leaders of such entrepreneurial family firms keep in mind that entrepreneurial skills are developed over time and require practice. They provide avenues for junior-generation members to work independently on smaller entrepreneurial initiatives to hone their skills.

As family members inevitably end up providing physical, financial, social, and human resources to new creations, it is prudent for an entrepreneur to keep in mind the relative life-cycle stages of family members when deciding on the extent of newness to embark upon. For example, in the context of an ailing family member, the familial resources are likely to be consumed in caring for this member, and it would be best not to engage in expensive, high-risk venturing. At such stages of family life, the entrepreneurial spirit can continue to be pursued through initiatives with lower degrees of newness, requiring fewer resources. On the other hand, when more resources are available, entrepreneurial initiatives of higher degrees of newness can be undertaken.

Opportunity recognition occurs more readily when structured and carried out with discipline. When choosing an entrepreneurial venture to embark upon, we encourage you to develop a business plan to guide your thought processes regarding the extent of relatedness with existing ventures in your family. Toward this end, the book in this Series on *Business Plans* by Barringer provides valuable guidance.[21] Templates are provided to help you screen opportunities systematically through preliminary feasibility analysis so as to separate interesting ideas with high or low potential of being developed into a viable value-creating venture. When such an opportunity is identified, next to arise are the "how to" questions: How to exploit the opportunity and make it work? How should the factors of production or resources be brought together to make the venture a reality?

THE "HOW TO" QUESTIONS

Exploitation of an opportunity requires financial, social, physical, and human resources. The start-up stage is characterized by stretched resources and unpredictable highs and lows in activity, often straining entrepreneurs to the breaking point.[22] Balancing resource inflows and outflows remains a major challenge for most entrepreneurs. Those in the necessity category may be without income and may be scrambling for funds to maintain themselves and their families while simultaneously incurring the expenses of trying to start a venture. The ease of transferability of resources between family and business systems places family

[21]Barringer, B.R. (2008). *Preparing Effective Business Plans: An Entrepreneurial Approach.* Prentice Hall Entrepreneurship Series, edited by R.D. Ireland and M.M. Morris. Upper Saddle River, NJ: Prentice-Hall.

[22]Aldrich, H.E., and Cliff, J.E. (2003). The pervasive effects of family on entrepreneurship: Toward a family embeddedness perspective. *Journal of Business Venturing,* 18(5): 573–596.

members in a position of significant influence where they can act as either a source of support or the cause of failure of the venture.

Let us first talk about financial resources. An entrepreneur must incur expenses before the first sale is made. Obvious ones involve registration and licensing, and obtaining a location and appropriate equipment and furnishings, inventory, and office supplies. But there are also the nonobvious expenses of travel to shop for competitors and scout locations, compiling data about markets, contacting and perhaps entertaining prospective suppliers, interviewing and screening potential employees, and many more.

On the inflow side, timing of a first sale is an issue to contend with. Customers may be hesitant to buy from a new start-up, placing the entrepreneur under significant pressure to deliver high service and merchandise to those who patronize his or her firm. Dissatisfied customers can lead to closure of the venture. Suppose, however, that the start-up is able to satisfy current customers but desperately needs more products and more capital to satisfy the expanding customer base. New companies are mistrusted by suppliers and creditors. Will your firm really survive long enough to pay your bills or repay loans? Thus, the fledgling entrepreneur is at the mercy of these suppliers and creditors and may have difficulty accessing either or both with reasonable terms. If the company must pay cash on delivery, but extends credit terms to buyers, the business may find itself forced into bankruptcy as a by-product of its success. It is obvious, but also verified by research, that most of these expenses are paid from your own pocket.[23] Where do you turn when the pocket is empty? To family.

As we saw in the case of Disney brothers and other examples we have shared in this book, family members come to the support of aspiring entrepreneurs by providing the resources that the entrepreneur falls short on and they are in a position to supply. The capital can come in many forms. It may be direct infusion of cash through investments, loans, or even gifts. It may result from cosigning loans, pledging assets, or drawing from savings, including pension funds. Entrepreneurs have to be creative not only with opportunity recognition, but also with finding start-up or seed capital needed to sustain the business until it begins to generate funds or becomes attractive enough to obtain funding from other sources.[24]

The list of ways relatives have helped entrepreneurs is virtually endless. Often, a family's social connections help launch new ventures. In addition to first funding, it is not uncommon for entrepreneurs to get their first customer or donations of furniture and equipment through their family members. The start-up stage is characterized by unpredictable highs and lows of activity. Family members help absorb the ups and downs of resource needs at this stage. Sometimes, all an entrepreneur needs is encouragement, as launching a new venture tends to be an emotional rollercoaster. There may be moments of nervous pauses in activity such as the seemingly long wait for the first sale order to arrive against

---

[23]Vesper, K.H. (1996). *New Venture Experience.* Seattle, WA: Vector Books.
[24]http://en.wikipedia.org/wiki/Seed_money

the backdrop of piling expenses. Family members are well positioned to provide emotional support. At other times, they can come to the rescue through contributing their time and personal efforts. They may pitch in when nonfamily employees fall ill or walk off the job. Or, they may help with construction or renovation of facilities.

As an example, when 17-year-old Fred DeLuca started the first Subway Restaurant,[25] a family friend, Dr. Peter Buck, provided him with $1,000 needed to open the store. The two became business partners and used all the equipment they could find from their families to launch their first store. Fred's fiancée (now his wife) and mother provided the human and emotional support, while a colleague of his father designed the logo and painted the first Subway sign. Today, with more than 30,000 stores in 87 countries, it seems hard to imagine that just about 40 years ago, this entrepreneurial venture started with a lot of help from family and friends.

Savvy entrepreneurs know not to take family members support for granted. In some instances, family members may be opposed to the start-up from the beginning. One reason for such opposition can be a concern that the venture will consume the founder's time and family savings when these are needed for other purposes. Or, the opposition may be based on the family's assessment of the level of preparedness and ability of the entrepreneur to be successful in the chosen venture. At other times, members just get worn down and frustrated, giving up on the venture and the founder.

Discouraging comments from those you love and those you live with can sap your energy and enthusiasm. Family can sabotage your business building efforts intentionally and unintentionally. If they believe you are devoting too much time and effort to the company and too little to your spouse, children and others, they may plant feelings of guilt in your mind or demand your presence at more family functions. Relatives who have provided equity capital or loans may have personal requirements for their funds and express the need for payment or reimbursement at inopportune moments. To avoid such situations, savvy entrepreneurs understand the necessity of ensuring that they have prepared their family members for the highs and lows of creating an entrepreneurial venture and have their support and cooperation in doing so.

At the start-up stage, resources generally flow from family to business. The unstated assumption is that when the business begins to generate a profit, the investments of family members will be repaid in some form. As family members are generally not used to writing down their agreements, hidden expectations of how and when they can expect to get returns from the invested seed money or investment of time and effort can lead to resentment, disagreements, and conflicts at a later stage. Seasoned entrepreneurs understand the importance of written agreement to ensure that clarity of thoughts is achieved and settlements negotiated with all those involved in the venture—family or nonfamily members.

---

[25]http://www.subway.com/subwayroot/AboutSubway/history/subwayHistory.aspx

THE "WHO" QUESTIONS

The next important question for an entrepreneur to decide is, Who should be involved in the venture team and what role should each of these individuals play? In particular, what should be the extent and mode of family involvement in the business? Every entrepreneur is part of a team, regardless of whether or not there are any employees when the new venture is started. Scholars have noted that "the myth of the lonely only entrepreneur can and should be laid to rest."[26] A longitudinal study of Z.I. Probes (ZIP) from its founding in 1987 to the first public offering captures the critical role of the family in entrepreneurial ventures. ZIP was created by Don Clarke and Tokunsuke (Toku) to serve the oil and gas industry in Alberta, Canada.[27] Steier notes the important, albeit unstated, role of family members in opportunity recognition, decision to proceed, and assembling of resources. Not only did family members of the founders provide the "first mover investments or seed money for the venture," they were also instrumental in helping the founders build a network of financial investors that enabled the growth of this venture. On the basis of this study, Steier concludes that "familial relationships as well as familial activities provide important conditions necessary to incubate new businesses."[28]

You may start your business because you have a friend or associate who has committed to be your first customer or supplier. You begin by building your supply chain, with that customer or supplier being perhaps a source of credit or at least advice. You may have a banker, an accountant, an attorney, or other professional intimately involved with the venture. And you may need partners or key employees from the beginning. We all want to be associated with talented, committed, hardworking people, both at home and in the workplace. Every entrepreneur expects to have a competent team of individuals to help make the company a success. Where are those competent, hardworking individuals? If they are as good as we want them to be, no doubt they are fully employed and well compensated. Why will they leave their current occupations to join your high-risk start-up? Who is likely to believe in your vision and put themselves at risk when you call? Once again, family.

However, are your relatives the best qualified for the work that will be required in the start-up stage? And, are they likely to grow and adapt to the needs of the venture as it evolves through different stages of its life? As we saw in the opening vignette, the Disney brothers had the complementary skills to make a go of it. Evidently, they were lucky. Can you count on the same luck, or can you make a conscious effort to form the right team? How can an entrepreneur ensure

---

[26]Schoonoven, C.B., and Romanelli, E. (2001). Emergent themes and the next waves of entrepreneurship research. In Schoonoven, C.B., and Romanelli, E. (Eds.). *The Entrepreneurship Dynamic: Origins of Entrepreneurship and the Evolution of Industries*. Stanford, CA: Stanford University Press. pp. 383–400. Quote on page 387.

[27]http://www.zipcanada.com/agriculture/company/z-i-probes-inc-160/summary.html

[28]Steier, L. (2007). New venture creation and organization: A familial sub-narrative. *Journal of Business Research,* 60: 1099–1107. Quote on page 1104.

that he gets the help needed to launch a venture, but is also well prepared to shed and add team members to ensure the growth of an enterprise over different life-cycle stages.

How can an entrepreneur ensure that the life support needed at the start-up stage of a venture from family members does not become an impediment to the growth of the firm over time? What agreements and governance mechanisms might be useful to launch and grow the enterprise?

By reading this book, you are already ahead of most entrepreneurs in establishing entrepreneurial family firms. Most business founders fail to think of themselves as being in family enterprises in the start-up stage. We have already encouraged you to prepare a business plan in starting up, and part of that business plan should involve preparing your family for the struggles that the new venture might face. Your immediate family members in particular should not be caught by surprise by the demands this business will impose. If budding entrepreneurs are candid with their loved ones at origin about what the business will consume in time, money, and effort, they will quickly learn from the reactions of spouse, parents, and children whether they will face support or resistance.

Leaders of successful entrepreneurial family firms think of the evolution of their enterprise right at the start-up stages, sowing the seeds for disciplined governance even before the venture is launched. Intuitively or consciously, they use the three circles model we discussed in Chapter 4 (Figures 4.2 and 4.3) to comprehend the roles that will be played by family and nonfamily stakeholders in different stages of the venture's growth. In a later chapter, we discuss the governance tool kit that is useful in different stages of an entrepreneurial family firm. A few tools useful at the start-up stages are mentioned here.

Written agreements are used to explicate the roles and responsibilities of different stakeholders in the venture. For example, when hiring family members to assist with the venture, it is useful to have their terms of employment (roles, responsibilities, and term of appointment) agreed upon through a written document that both parties are comfortable with. Similarly, while borrowing money from family members (or friends), written agreements are extremely valuable. Being clear on the terms and conditions of repayment of the money is important as it helps to build strong and trusting relationships over the long term.

Entrepreneurs often make the mistake of taking on investors as partners at early stages of their ventures, only to find out later that these partners begin to seek and often play a more active role in determining the strategic direction of the firm than the entrepreneur had envisioned. Forward-thinking entrepreneurs distinguish between the costs and benefits of debt versus equity financing, regardless of whether the sources of funding are family members or outsiders. While debt financing brings with it the burden of paying interest at a time when the venture needs all resources to help it grow, it removes the burden of sharing the profits at a later stage or losing control of the venture.

Once the current and potential future players become clearer, the appropriate governance mechanisms are put into place. Two foundational structures that are helpful for entrepreneurial family firms at the start-up stage are the *board of advisors* and *family meetings*. While both of these may be relatively informal governance structures, having them in place and using them enable entrepreneurs to have a support network within which ideas can be shared and evaluated. Family meetings help to ensure that stakeholding relatives have a venue to participate in the developments of the venture. Neither of these governance mechanisms needs to be cumbersome or time-consuming, but having them sows the seeds of disciplined governance of the enterprise.

PROBLEMS, OPPORTUNITIES, AND STRATEGIES IN THE START-UP STAGES

In this section, we discuss the problems, opportunities, and strategies that can be used at the inception of a venture. A summary is presented in Table 7.2. As you go through this section, we encourage you to think of other points that may be relevant to a business in the inception stages that you may be examining at this time.

PROBLEMS

We distinguish between problems related to individual, family, business, and environmental levels.

INDIVIDUAL-RELATED PROBLEMS

If you are not passionately committed to creating a venture and making it work, stop now. Ventures driven by pull factors are likely to do better than those driven by push factors. However, for nascent entrepreneurs, it is often difficult to fully distinguish between the pull versus push factors, as there may be some aspects of both driving them toward an entrepreneurial pursuit. A good soul-searching and objective assessment is needed to know clearly why one is attracted to an entrepreneurial career.

FAMILY-RELATED PROBLEMS

Even when propelled by the pull factors, as an entrepreneur, you can count on plenty of family members, friends, and business associates who will stand ready to tell you why your idea will fail. The start-up stage can be a discouraging time for those who feel the need for positive reinforcement. Family members often have their own requests and demands for limited familial resources, for example, household repairs, auto replacement, and new clothes. If they are not convinced about the potential of the venture or in general about the idea of an entrepreneurial career path, they are likely to resist the efforts of the nascent entrepreneur, using various pathways of influence at their disposal.

The case of Roy and Walt Disney demonstrates that complementary strengths tend to have corresponding weaknesses. In their collaborations both

TABLE 7.2	Problems, Opportunities, and Strategies in the Start-Up Stage		
	Problems	*Opportunities*	*Strategies*
Individual related	• Distinguishing between motivations of pull and push factors • Persevering toward launch amid limited resources and setbacks	• To be one's own boss • To establish an entity to express personal values and aspirations • To earn the full benefits of the value generated by ones' hard work	• Previous work experience • Networks and alliances developed
Family related	• Convincing skeptical family members about the potential of the proposed entrepreneurial initiative • Learning to work with family members • Complying with family requests for resources needed	• Global start-ups or multinational ventures created by immigrant families • Venture created by junior-generation family members	• Leveraging relationships of family members who are already in business • Building on the "assets of maturity" of family members • Using physical and financial capital of family
Business related	• Accessing the business opportunity • Conducting the preliminary feasibility analysis under resource constraints • Coping with unanticipated expenses and setbacks such as zoning ordinances and trademark violations • Forming the venture team	• Opportunity to start anew without being burdened by reputation of the past • Ability to form partnerships with other new players in the marketplace	• Disciplined governance by using written agreements with all key stakeholders (family or nonfamily members alike) • Start small, dream big
Environment Related	• Accessing information about markets and competitors • Gaining supplier/customer information and access	• Potential to leapfrog a generation of technology as current players are locked into capital investments and long-term relationships • Reap the benefits of niche opportunities that open up with rapid changes in technology, economic, or regulatory environment	• Outside work experience • Developing and presenting business plan to critical outsiders for objective feedback

before and after forming their company, they were as likely to disagree on major issues, especially when money was at stake and they had to find ways to work effectively together. In the start-up stage, contentious relatives with differing worldviews can sink the venture before it has a chance to sail.

BUSINESS-RELATED PROBLEMS

Some individuals open and succeed in creating entrepreneurial family firms with startlingly little preparation. They are rare. Most of us are better off if we invest time and money in planning the venture and testing the waters. Research and planning always take longer than originally expected. This is especially true if you are employed full-time while trying to assess and then organize your business opportunity. And there will be unanticipated expenses associated with this stage. Examples we have seen include zoning ordinances that prohibited the intended signage for the business, attorneys' letters contending trademark violations, presumed equity partners reneging on providing financial support, and many more.

As indicated in the previous section, gaining commitments from individuals that you want on your venture team can be a major hurdle. This may be compounded by anticipated growth. As you prepare to open your doors, do you want generalists who can do many tasks adequately, or do you hire specialists with the skills you will eventually need, but who may be too expensive for your initial cash flow or who may not be willing to perform many of the mundane tasks a new company needs done? If you are relying on family members, do you anticipate that they will be able to grow with the firm, or will it be necessary to replace them? If so, what are the implications for family relationships?

ENVIRONMENT-RELATED PROBLEMS

For a nascent entrepreneur working outside the rubric of an existing family firm, accessing information about competitors and market conditions with limited resources can be a significant challenge. While much of the information is readily available on the Internet today, it is often the tacit information that is essential to determine the feasibility of the new launch. Another challenge to overcome is to gain cooperation from suppliers and customers who may be contractually or otherwise obligated to competitors or alternate offerings in the marketplace. Convincing family members to launch an independent venture is no easy task either.

OPPORTUNITIES

INDIVIDUAL-RELATED OPPORTUNITIES

The foremost opportunity in the mind of many nascent entrepreneurs is to be free from someone else's routine, even if this someone else might be a parent. Being one's own boss is a draw for many to embark on an entrepreneurial career path. Even if they are fully cognizant of the fact that the business may take control of their lives, many people welcome that as opposed to having a supervisor, especially a family member, controlling them. Personal values and objectives can determine how opportunities are perceived. Factors that draw an individual toward an entrepreneurial career vary. Some, like Professor Muhammad Yunus of Grameen Bank,[29] seek to make a positive impact on their community or the world. Others may believe that they can organize a profitable business from a hobby or personal interest so that they will enjoy rather than dread how they spend their days. There have been cases of inventors who formed businesses to maintain control of their inventions instead of selling or licensing the products. George and Bock discuss strategies for such entrepreneurs at length in another book in this Series, *Inventing Entrepreneurs*.[30]

Individuals growing up in business families gain the confidence of starting independent ventures as they are exposed to the highs and lows of an entrepreneurial career path by observing their family members. They understand that entrepreneurs hire employees to make money for the venture and its founders. They also realize that employees get paid less than the value they generate for the venture or else it becomes difficult to justify their continued employment.[31] Such experiences and ways of thinking often propel junior-generation family members toward entrepreneurial career paths.

FAMILY-RELATED OPPORTUNITIES

Entrepreneurship scholars have studied phenomena they refer to as **global start-ups or multinational ventures**. These are companies that have been created specifically to exploit international business opportunities. Immigrant families with relatives in other countries who can engage in trade through family members are prime examples of global start-ups. As an example, in the early 1990s, Nina Gupta established Lamptronics, the North American marketing arm for her family's compact and fluorescent lightening (CFL) manufacturing plant in India. In 1996, with the cooperation of her family, she renamed the company Greenlite Lighting Corporation, focusing on importing CFLs into Canada and the United States. Government initiatives to reduce energy usage fostered exceedingly fast growth of this immigrant's venture from sales of $500,000 in 1996 to $30 million in 2007. Estimated sales for 2008 were over $50 million.

BUSINESS-RELATED OPPORTUNITIES

Nascent entrepreneurs may enjoy unblemished reputations when competitors have been accused of legal or ethical lapses. Junior-generation family members such as the Brown cousins we discussed earlier in this chapter reaped the benefit of the strong reputation of their family's wineries as they harnessed their collective entrepreneurial spirit by launching the Kid You Not wines. While such next-generation members can make their own entrepreneurial mark on a multi-generational family firm, the good family name can be particularly valuable.

---

[29]http://www.grameen-info.org/index.php?option=com_content&task=view&id=19&Itemid=114

[30]George, G., and Bock, A.J. (2008). *Inventing Entrepreneurs: Technology Innovators and Their Entrepreneurial Journey*. Prentice Hall Entrepreneurship Series, edited by R.D. Ireland and M.M. Morris. Upper Saddle River, NJ: Prentice Hall.

[31]Case: Prairie Mill Bread Company: Personal qualities in entrepreneurship. In Longnecker, J.G., Moore, C.W., Petty, J.W., and Donlevy, L.B. (1998). *Small Business Management: An Entrepreneurial Emphasis*. ITP Nelson.

Environment-Related Opportunities

For new start-ups, opportunities often exist to leapfrog a generation of technology. Competing firms may be locked into capital investments that make it prohibitively expensive to introduce a new product or adapt a new technology. A new venture may be able to enter the market more cost efficiently. Rapid adjustment to changes in economic conditions, technology changes, and regulatory requirements often provide opportunities for nascent entrepreneurs to build upon.

Strategies

Individual-Related Strategies

Research shows that most entrepreneurs start businesses based on experience they obtained with a previous employer or within their family firms. They acquired product or service knowledge that they put to use in a different way. They developed job-related skills that formed the basis for the new enterprise. They used contacts from the former employer, perhaps with the thought of the employer becoming a customer. These examples suggest alliance strategies. Nascent entrepreneurs may be able to negotiate contracts with erstwhile employers that help them obtain financing to launch the venture. Alternatively, they may be able to link with other corporations in the supply chain, assuming they do not violate any noncompete clause that was in their employment agreement. Branching out from an existing family firm by expanding into related products or markets can prove valuable for novice or first-time entrepreneurs.

Family-Related Strategies

If the nascent entrepreneur has family members who are already in business, those relationships may lead to alliances that would not be available to competitors. These connections may take the new venture into entirely unexpected directions.

Although we recognized how the liability of newness is a problem in attracting talented members to the venture team, the entrepreneur with capable, well-networked relatives may be able to involve those relatives in a new venture in ways that nonrelated new business owners could never do. Because the entrepreneur is family, the relatives may be more willing to gamble on the survivability of the enterprise. Minimally, they may be willing to give time and resources to help start the business. In other words, the nascent entrepreneur strategically uses the **assets of maturity** available through his or her family members and relatives.

The resource issue speaks directly to the financial capital strategy. For most nascent entrepreneurs, traditional financial institutions are not viable lending options. In Chapter 6, we encouraged you to treat family members professionally when borrowing money, specifically charging you to enter into written agreements. There is no reason, however, for you not to negotiate terms that are advantageous to your fledgling situation. Your strategy may be to defer payments until cash flows begin or until you decide to terminate your plan to start a venture. Another approach could be to pay interest only until certain conditions are met for the revenues to the proposed firm. Regardless of what terms you are able to negotiate, you should have written agreements that clarify the roles and responsibilities of all key stakeholders in a venture. Such agreements become the basis of disciplined governance of the family enterprise.

Nascent entrepreneurs can draw on the social networks of relatives to identify business opportunities, gain access to financial capital, or attract key employees. Furthermore, family members often use the physical capital of relatives, as did Walt Disney when he started his first company in the family garage.

BUSINESS-RELATED STRATEGIES

Later-generational family members often deal with the difficult issue of how large their new enterprise should be. As they have grown under the shadow of successful ventures of their family, they often feel hesitant to start small, fearing how such initiatives may be perceived by their successful family members or friends. This self-consciousness might lead to two opposite reactions of junior-generation members—"freeze and do nothing" or "invest family's wealth in risky untested ventures that are too large in scope for the individuals' abilities." Neither of these strategies is fruitful, however. Instead, successful entrepreneurs "start small but dream big." That is, they understand the need to begin developing and testing their entrepreneurial skills through smaller projects and ventures. As their comfort level develops, they either grow these ventures to achieve the big dreams they have or launch larger ventures. Such a strategy enables them to test business ideas to the maximum feasible and cost-effective extent to determine if there is truly a customer for their product or service and whether they actually have a sustainable competitive advantage before fully investing themselves or their families into the venture.

ENVIRONMENT-RELATED STRATEGIES

Gaining outside work experience and using business plans to attempt to gain funding from banks or other critical outsiders are two pragmatic strategies that entrepreneurs can make use of in the pre-start-up stage.

We end this chapter with a warning. Life-cycle analyses have proved to be valuable in understanding and predicting behavior and in grasping actions that need to be taken, given the conditions an entrepreneur finds himself or herself in. However, you must not look at a single life-cycle stage and assume that it describes everything you need to know. One of the most critical mistakes you can make is to ignore the juxtaposition of life cycles. While you may be in the growth stage of your individual life cycle, your parents are likely to be in the mature or declining stage of theirs. The result is very different perceptions of risk and goals for the use of resources. Similarly, the venture you are launching may be in a mature or declining industry, presenting opportunities and threats that may not mesh with the vision and enthusiasm that you bring when starting up. A key objective of this book is for you to be prepared for the clashes that will certainly occur among the stages of the various life cycles that impact the success of your venture.

Summary

- Start-up stages are typically characterized by strained resources.
- Family members may prove to be sources of support or of discouragement to the venture founder.
- Even though a firm is in the start-up stage, its owners, investors, employees, and customers may be in different, conflicting stages.
- A start-up firm may be entering an industry in another life-cycle stage or may be introducing products, services, or technologies that are in different stages.
- Life-cycle analysis can be used to identify conflicts and seek resolutions for family businesses.
- The start-up stage requires an entrepreneur to find his answers to the following questions:
  - o Why is she or he being drawn to an entrepreneurial career?
  - o What should be the target market scope for the products or services to be provided by the venture?
  - o Who should form the venture team?
  - o How can the venture be organized to lay a strong foundation for disciplined governance?

Discussion Questions

1. According to the Small Business Administration, restaurants have the highest rate of failures of any industry in the United States. What do you think are some of the risks associated with starting a restaurant?
2. How might family participation increase the likelihood that a new restaurant might succeed? How might family involvement lead to a failure?
3. What conflicts do you think are most likely to come up when parents start businesses with their grown children? How would you resolve those conflicts?
4. Research suggests that each generation of a family firm uses different pathways to embark on innovation and opportunity exploitation. In going through the opening vignettes in each chapter of this book, can you identify examples of the following pathways?
   - Regeneration of the existing firm and its offerings
   - Creating spin-offs from the family firm
   - Creating entirely new ventures.

Can you think of other examples where such regeneration strategies have been used by next-generation family members? Under what conditions is each of these strategies likely to be effective?

5. Table 7.2 provides a list of problems, opportunities, and strategies in the start-up stages. On the basis of your experiences, can you think of additional points in each of these categories?

Learning Exercises

1. Identify a start-up business in your community. What problems are they experiencing? What opportunities do you think they have? What strategies would you recommend to them?

2. Families often develop idiosyncratic ways to share their regrets or love with other family members. That is, to say "I am sorry" and "I care for you." Can you think of some such ways in your family or others that you know of?

3. Ask your classmates if they want to own their own businesses. Of those who do, how many are actively engaged in trying to start one, and what are they doing? Are they involving members of their family in this process? If so, in what ways?

4. Interview a student who has already started a company. How much preparation did she or he put into it? If she or he could do it over again, what would that person do differently before starting?

Other Resources

• McCann, G. (2007). *When Your Parents Sign the Paycheck*. Indianapolis: JIST Works.
• Thomas, B. (1994). *Walt Disney: An American Original*. New York: Hyperion.
• Thomas, B. (1998). *Building a Company: Roy O. Disney and the Creation of an Entertainment Empire*. New York: Hyperion.

8

GROWING, FOR BETTER OR WORSE

ORGANIC GROWTH

Frank Gerten's vision of quality garden goods in the early 1900s began with a simple motto: "Buy from the Grower." This vision was reflected in the produce he grew on his beloved 22-acre farm and sold to the local residents of South Saint Paul, Minnesota, through his small garden center and truck farm.

Because of his passion and dedication to providing people with quality, locally grown plants, and produce, Gertens continued to fulfill the desires and needs of the patrons. When Frank retired, he handed over his firm to his sons, Robert & Jerry. During their time as primary owners, the brothers gradually and devotedly grew the business into a 12,000 square feet retail store and greenhouse.

In 1989, two sons of Robert—Lewis and Glen, along with their brother-in-law Gino Pitera, bought their uncle Jerry's half of the business. A few years later, when Robert retired, he gifted his shares equally to the third generation. When the trio bought their initial shares, sales were about $700,000. [Within fifteen years] it blossomed to almost $30 million.

Gertens grew "organically"—without a formal plan—said Glen. It evolved into a nursery, run by Glen; a greenhouse overseen by Lewis; and a 50,000-square-foot indoor retail and 500,000-square-foot outdoor store selling gifts, plants and garden supplies year-round, with Gino at the helm. Although he's retired, Robert still stops in to help now and then. The company's extensive Web site (www.gertens.com) also sells shrubs, trees, perennials, landscape supplies, gifts and barbeque grills. A newsletter is e-mailed to about 10,000 customers throughout the Greater Twin Cities area.

"As the city grew up around us, we started broadening our product lines," explained Glen. Soon after the trio took over, they phased out the labor-intensive truck farming and branched into more profitable bedding plants for home gardeners. Soon they began growing and selling pumpkins, poinsettias, and Christmas trees. This venture extended their seasonal business from eight weeks to eight or nine months; today, they stay open year-round. The most recent addition was a 15-acre contractor yard, which separates the wholesale and retail business so trucks don't clog up the parking lot.

These expansions required more land. While the original land, with frontage on the main road into St. Paul, is still owned by Robert Gertens, the "boys" almost quintupled that to about 100 acres in the surrounding area. But lack of space is still the company's biggest challenge. Glen remarks, "If we had more room, we could have grown the company a little quicker, possibly," but he adds there is very little available land left in their area.

The family flew by the seat of their pants for many years, Glen acknowledged. He reported that the challenge of maintaining double-digit growth motivated the partners to write their first formal business plan. "I still see us as a mom-and-pop operation," he explained, "but as it does get bigger, it runs more like a corporation. We have to have some things in place, like employee handbooks and an HR person. But we're trying to keep the family business flavor to some degree."

While their success has made the business more exciting, "I still enjoy going out and working in the nursery," Glen said. "I feel better after a hard day's work [in the nursery] than in the office, but as you grow you can't do that as much."

Since they've been in charge, the partners haven't suffered much from economic downturns. "The Minnesota economy has been kicking pretty good," he said. Low interest rates made it less expensive to purchase land. Rising fuel prices, terrorism fears, and unemployment dampened travel, so "instead of traveling, people stay home and work in their yards," he noted. But he worries that a slowdown in construction could hurt contractors—an important market for the business.

Uncertainty and the company's expanded size make planning more essential than ever. Glen acknowledged, "I'm not sure what dividends formal planning will pay, but with three partners, everyone can't have their own plan."

Sources: Pearl, J.A. (2004). What a difference 15 years makes. *Family Business*, 15(4): 36–38 and www.gertens.com.

Questions

1. How large does a business have to be before the owners need formal planning and written policies to guide actions?
2. Can Gertens continue to grow and still maintain the feel of a family business? Why or why not?

Entrepreneurial family firm leaders whose firms survive the start-up stages have established their products/services and markets to sustain their enterprise through this tender but potentially precarious life-cycle stage. If all ventures were to follow the standard life-cycle model we introduced in Part A (Figure A1), they should be going through an "S shape" growth, showing a smooth, gradual start-up, leading into a steep growth phase, leveling off in maturity, eventually trailing off toward termination, or renewing as an upward trend. However, the real life of an entrepreneurial venture rarely, if ever, follows abstract models precisely.

In a later chapter, we will examine the governance structures that can help entrepreneurial family firms continually grow across generations of leaders and economic life cycles. You will see how to make good use of formalized governance structures, legal instruments, and policies to enjoy family harmony and business growth. Well-designed and administered structures can help entrepreneurial family firms avoid much heartache in later years. In this chapter, we examine questions related to the growth stage that leaders of entrepreneurial family firms must understand and address. What factors drive an enterprise into a growth stage? What steps do you take to position your firm for rapid growth? Why do some entrepreneurial firms experience high growth while others languish in low- or no-growth modes for generations? What are the consequences of varied levels of growth? How might family firm leaders prepare themselves and other involved family and nonfamily members for high growth?

GROWTH: BLESSING OR CURSE?

The growth stage is not similar for all entrepreneurial family firms as the timing and extent of growth can vary significantly. Some family firms experience abrupt growth spurts, while others grow slowly over generations of leaders and economic life cycles. Some plateau, experiencing slow or no growth or decline and die without a growth stage. The Gerten family business entered its growth spurt as a third-generation company. This enterprise was a successful low-growth business for two generations, supporting the life styles of the founder, his two sons, and their families. Over 60 years after Frank Gerten started selling his produce, his grandsons and grandson-in-law launched the business on a high-growth trajectory. The experience of the Gertens conforms to the conditions associated with a business in the growth stage. The vision and foundations laid down by the founder and the second-generation leaders provided the base for the third-generation leaders to engage in high growth.

The challenges and issues faced by a growing firm differ significantly from those experienced during the start-up phases. When the business is starting, family members may pull together without asking difficult questions as to how their investments will be returned. Once the business begins to generate profits, this issue and others begin to surface. The conflicting life-cycle stages of individuals, families, business, and environment may lead to disagreements as some family members may want high growth, while others prefer to reap returns on their investments in the form of more leisure time or harvesting some of the profits. You may recall from Chapter 2 how Richard Lumpkin's ideas for expanding the business distressed his parents, who were accustomed to the stability of Consolidated Telephone Company.

It is natural for us to see the world through the lens of our own experiences, desires, and ambitions. Leaders of entrepreneurial family firms who sustain their ventures through generations have the capacity to empathize, grasping the ideas and beliefs of others. Beyond comprehending how others view the world, they are able to accept that there can be varying viewpoints. Such understanding becomes the foundation for disciplined governance and for producing win-win solutions. One means of preempting conflict among family members in the growth stage is to design organizational structures and policies before they are needed. As observed by Ward:

> Wise business-owning families recognize that predictable issues are going to come up that will create some conflict or friction. They ask, "When this issue or that one arises, how are we going to deal with it?" They answer that question by establishing policies *before* the policies are actually needed.[1]

For most entrepreneurs entering the growth stage, this is something new as they are consumed in the start-up stages to "make and sell."[2] In most business textbooks, choices of structure tend to be functions of growth strategies, tax consequences, cost efficiencies, and managerial effectiveness. But leaders of entrepreneurial family firms know the critical importance of ensuring that family values regarding the role of family in business must be respected when making related decisions. For example, Family First enterprises[3] (which we labeled "Fb's" in Table 3.1, Chapter 3) may be more inclined to pursue low-growth strategies if growth begins to compete with their desire to retain family control of the business or their ability to engage family members actively in the business. Others, like the Rumpke Consolidated from Chapter 6, continue to find ways to balance the family and business systems (labeled "FBs" in Table 3.1) to ensure high involvement of family in business while continuing the enterprise on a high growth trajectory.

THE IMPETUS FOR GROWTH

We have all heard the clichés—"The harder I work, the luckier I get"[4] and "Chance favors the prepared mind."[5] Although it is possible for an entrepreneurial family firm to grow through lucky happenstance by being in the right place with the right product at the right time, what appears to be a lucky occurrence usually results from an entrepreneur having the qualities, qualifications, and

---

[1]Ward, J.L. (2004). *Perpetuating the Family Business: 50 Lessons Learned from Long-Lasting, Successful Families in Business*. New York: Palgrave Macmillan, p. 23.

[2]Greiner, L.E. (1972). Evolution and revolution as organizations grow: A company's past has clues for management that are critical to future success. *Harvard Business Review*, July–August.

[3]Ward, J.L. (1987). *Keeping the Family Business Healthy: How to Plan for Continuing Growth, Profitability, and Family Leadership*. San Francisco, CA: Jossey-Bass Publishers.

[4]Attributed to Thomas Jefferson

[5]Attributed to Louis Pasteur

insight to take advantage of opportunities. As we examine family firms, we find examples of companies that seem to have achieved their status despite how they have been managed; only the smile of good fortune saved them from disaster. Without a doubt, such *permanently failing*[6] family firms exist. But we would be doing you a serious disservice to encourage you to rely on luck for your success.

Keep in mind the preparation factor. When we look at Gertens, we learn that Glen and Lewis grew up in the business. Love of the land and what it produces was instilled in them at early ages. Their brother-in-law Gino started working in greenhouses at 13 and added a degree in marketing to his practical experience. When the opportunity to own Gertens came along, the three partners were prepared not only to manage it, but also to grow it. Also noteworthy are the courage and business savvy of the senior-generation family members to pass the baton of the firm's leadership to the next generation in a timely manner.[7]

Why do some family enterprises stay permanently in the "mom and pop" category, while others grow into major corporations? There is no single answer to that question. We do find patterns and recurring conditions, however; and we can learn important lessons by studying those conditions. From a more proactive perspective than simply relying on luck to knock on the door, entrepreneurial family firm leaders are opportunity seekers who allow their aspirations to grow while continuously working to expand the resource stocks available to support growth.

Identifying an opportunity is not restricted to the start-up stage of a venture. Successful entrepreneurs are open to new experiences, keeping in touch with the environment, scanning continuously for opportunities. They know these may come in the form of environmental changes in legislation or regulation, or in the sociological, technological, or economic trends we discussed in an earlier chapter. Some business operators look at environmental disruptions as threats, but not the leaders of entrepreneurial family firms. For them, underlying threats and environmental disruptions are invariably opportunities. For the Gertens, the environmental disruptions of rising fuel prices and terrorism fears proved to be triggers for high growth. Similarly, you may recall from Chapter 5 how the Roberts brothers of St. Louis grew an empire worth over $820 million by pursuing opportunities presented by environmental changes.

So, what prompts the move from start-up or slow growth into a rapid growth phase? Similar to the start-up stage, growth may occur both due to positive (pull) or negative (push) factors that are driven either from within the firm (internally driven) or through the environment (externally driven). In the case of push propellers, family firm leaders may be forced into a growth mode. If they do not move forward, their firm may cease to exist. In the case of pull propellers, entrepreneurial family firm leaders may proactively seek to grow their firms.

---

[6]Meyer, M.W., and Zucker, L.G. (1990). *Permanently Failing Organizations.* San Francisco, CA: Sage Publications.

[7]Dyck, B., Mauws, M., Starke, F.A., and Mischke, G.A. (2002). Passing the baton: The importance of sequence, timing, technique, and communication in executive succession. *Journal of Business Venturing,* 17: 143–162.

TABLE 8.1	Growth Drivers of Entrepreneurial Family Firms	
	Pull Factors	*Push Factors*
	Positive triggers	*Negative triggers*
Internally driven factors	• Joining of new family members with skills, ideas, and perspectives that may be absent earlier • Passion and desire by the next-generation family members to make their mark on the family firm • Increased competence and confidence of the enterprising family through the family incubator and readiness to undertake larger initiatives • Family culture of innovation, creativity, continuous development, and growth • Inspired by entrepreneurial role models in family, close relatives, or friends	• A significant milestone in the individual, family, or organizational life-cycle stage (as an anniversary), reminding the leader of the need to grow • Increase in family size or in the number of family members dependent on the income from the firm, suggesting a need to grow to help sustain the standard of living of the family member • Recognition that the firm has entered a gradual decline that must be reversed for the business to survive
Externally driven factors	• Formation of alliances with family members in other geographic regions, enabling the firm to enter into new markets and/or introduce new products • Inheriting wealth, enabling financial resources now available to invest in growth • Young firm finding an unexploited market niche, leading to increased demand that launches the growth stage • Overcoming the liabilities of newness, leading customers, suppliers, and creditors to encourage firm to grow • Increased competence and confidence of the entrepreneur, leading to new product or market development • An opportunity to acquire a competing enterprise	• Closure of a key supplier, leading to growth via backward integration • Natural disasters necessitating regeneration of the business • Change in competitive landscape, leading to a desperate need to redefine the business if it is to survive • Product/services moving to a decline phase, leading to a reduced demand and a dire need to renew the business • Loss of a key player in a social network that may have been instrumental in previous sales of the firm • Facing of a crisis such as litigation or drop in demand of products/services, suggesting the need to reinvent the business

In the Gertens case, the following statements indicate that both push and pull factors, from within and outside the family firm, impacted growth.

> During their time as primary owners, the brothers gradually and devotedly grew the business into a 12,000 square feet retail store and greenhouse. [Internal Pull]

The most recent addition was a 15-acre contractor yard, which separates the wholesale and retail business so trucks don't clog up the parking lot. [Internal Push]

"As the city grew up around us, we started broadening our product lines." [External Pull]

"If we had more room, we could have grown the company a little quicker, possibly", but Glen adds there is very little available land left in their area. [External Push]

As we discussed in Chapter 6, established and then growing entrepreneurial family firms require inflows of resources of all types—financial, social, physical, and human. The timely availability of appropriate quality and quantity of each of these resources is critical for growth. Entrepreneurial family firm leaders are adept at the preparation of their enterprises to ensure that they have adequate resource bundles to take advantage of growth opportunities. A small number of possible stimulants to growth are listed on page 174 (Table 8.1) Can you think of other drivers of growth?

SPEED AND DIRECTION OF GROWTH

How fast and in which direction should my family firm grow? Are my family, our firm, and I ready for growth? Can we sustain rapid growth, or must we tread slowly? What will happen if growth outpaces the resources? When such questions begin to cross an entrepreneur's mind, it is evident that the family firm has moved beyond the start-up stage.

For the family business owner, the growth stage of the life cycle presents different types of dilemmas than the strategic management of limited resources in the start-up stages. There are the added burdens of whether family members who performed effectively in the start-up possess the right talents for a larger, more complex company. Will the familiness that tied everyone together as resources flowed from the family to the business be a source of distinctive competence when the business generates profits and the resource flow may be reversed? Can the demands of the family be met while reinvesting in new opportunities? Are the patriarchs and matriarchs ready to accept the responsibilities that accompany growth? When thinking of the mode and pace of growth, entrepreneurial family firm leaders must consider a few critical points.

FIRST, WHY GROW?

Not all family firms desire growth, and some consciously avoid it. Reasons for growth avoidance can vary from one firm to another but may include a high desire to retain family control of the business in terms of both ownership and management, coupled with a perception that family control will be lost when the growth of the business exceeds some threshold level.

Family values regarding the respective roles of family and business, degree of firm control that a family wishes to retain, and exit strategy for the firm and its leader, influence the growth strategy. Earlier in this book, we discussed how reasons for establishing a family firm can vary significantly. Some entrepreneurs may launch or acquire a venture with an eye to establish an entity that is attractive to transfer across the future generations of their family. They view their business as part of their family's legacy and are likely to embrace slow and steady organic growth, as pursued by the Gertens. You can imagine such a vision being the motivator for firms like Houshi Onsen of Japan, which was founded in 718 AD and is now run by the 46th generation, or Barone Ricasoli of Italy, founded in 1141 and run by the 30th generation.[8]

Other entrepreneurs may launch or acquire a firm to use it as a vehicle to grow their family's investment in the shortest possible time frame. While these family firms have significant family involvement in business through ownership, the intent in these firms, which are sometimes called **gazelles**, is to find a venture that has high growth potential, ride the wave, and then reap the rewards for themselves and their families. Their exit strategy may include merging or being taken over by a larger corporation. Thus, before deciding on the extent and mode of the growth strategy for the family firm, each leader needs to reflect on the desired role of the business in the family and the family in the business.

HOW TO GROW?

Looking back at Figure 4.1 in Chapter 4, which growth strategy should the venture choose? The three variables in this diagram are the products or services offered by the firm, by markets in which it operates, and by the leading team. A combination of industry, product, and macroenvironmental life-cycle stages can help decide whether a firm should grow in the same product/services and markets categories or must change on one or both of these dimensions. The greater the degrees of change, the greater are the liabilities of newness.

It is in the growth stage that some family business owners discover that while they enjoyed and were effective entrepreneurs in the start-up stage of the enterprise, their skill sets or interests do not match the new demands for keeping the company successful. When this happens, they may either choose to recruit new leadership or struggle to maintain control. The likely outcome of the latter is either business failure or a weakened company at the end of the growth spurt.

Contrary to the popular belief that business founders do not have the personality or skills to manage a larger enterprise, there are multiple success stories. At the time this chapter is being written, the Gerten company is one such example. We do not want to discount the odds against success, nor underestimate the changes that must take place for the transitions instigated by growth to be successful.

The extent and mode of family involvement in business needs to be reevaluated at this stage if a firm wishes to continue or embark on a high growth trajectory. Family involvement both in terms of ownership and management of the firm

---

[8]For a list of world's oldest family firms, see http://www.familybusinessmagazine.com/worldsoldest.html

needs to be determined. To do this, it is often useful to identify the current stake-holders in the family firm using the three circles model that we introduced you to in Chapter 4 (Figures 4.2 and 4.3). The entrepreneur determines who would or should be the occupants of the overlapping parts of the model, projecting 10 to 15 years into the future. Think why you want the different family or nonfamily members in each of the regions of the three-circle model.

Given the emotionally driven relationships within a family, it is often chal-lenging for a family firm leader to avoid becoming bogged down in sentiments when thinking about the role of family members in business. Growth-oriented, successful entrepreneurs know when it comes to business they face stiff competi-tion where there is no room for distractions by resentful family investors who would rather have cashed out their shares. Nor can the family firm afford to carry the additional load of noncontributing family managers. Instead, creative ways must be found to use family members interested in ownership or management of the business. As the firm grows, cutting back the family's involvement in the busi-ness has been found to improve both the financial performance of the business and family relationships.[9]

Let us begin with the ownership aspect of the firm. Family investors often help the entrepreneur by providing financial support during start-up periods. As we noted in the last chapter, savvy entrepreneurial family firm leaders know the importance of drafting clearly understood repayment plans for all investors in the business. Before launching into a growth mode, it is best to ensure that all equity investors are comfortable with such growth. If not, some investors may have to be bought out, an outflow of cash that may alter growth plans in the short term but may prove crucial over the long term. As noted by Glen in the opening vignette, "with three partners, everyone can't have their own plan," suggesting the critical importance of a clear understanding among family members.

In addition to involvement in ownership of a growing family firm, policies and procedures need to be established to help determine the role of family mem-bers in the firm's management. It is critical to put in place the "Rules of Entry" (Appendix 6A, Chapter 6) so that family members recognize the qualifications needed for managerial jobs in the business. Regardless of their levels of expertise, family members are well positioned to provide different types of support at the start-up stage. As the business becomes more complex, not all members are suited for or may be willing to accept careers in the family firm. Successful family firm leaders understand that it is only by attracting and retaining the very best talent that they can hope to grow their enterprise.

In addition to the importance of abilities and their fit with the firm's needs, entrepreneurs also keep in mind that there can be varying motivations of family members for wanting to pursue a career in the business. Some family members may be drawn by their desire to contribute toward the growth of the firm while others may be attracted to it because of the potential to reap benefits or their

---

[9]Lambrecht, J., and Lievens, J. (2008). Pruning the family tree: Family business continuity and family harmony. *Family Business Review*, 21(4): 295–313.

inability to secure as lucrative a job outside the family firm. The "Commitment Index" provided in Chapter 6 (Appendix 6B) can be used to gain a preliminary understanding of the reasons driving a family member's desire to work on the family firm.

Enterprising families engage in proactive entrepreneurial career planning for capable family members with potential to contribute toward the growth of their family firm. A growth stage provides excellent opportunities to develop the entrepreneurial skills of family members. Moreover, there may be opportunities outside of the firm as well that could be used to speed up the learning processes and to bring insights from outside. As the firm grows, leaders need to move from doing everything themselves—the norm at the start-up stages, to working with others, then to working through others, while keeping an eye for growth opportunities.

In the Woody Allen movie, *Annie Hall*, Allen's character at one point comments to Annie, portrayed by Diane Keaton, that an intimate relationship is like a shark . . . it has to keep moving or it dies (to which he adds, "And I think what we got on our hands is a dead shark."). Entrepreneurial family firm leaders often face a similar situation as they must engage in continuous learning to avoid having their firm slip into stagnation and decline, or seeing the firm's needs outgrow the capabilities of the entrepreneur. In the highly competitive arena of our times, these leaders need to continue on developmental paths to avoid falling prey to the "Peter Principle,"[10] that is, each advances to his or her level of incompetence. Toward this end, forward-thinking and talented entrepreneurs know that it helps to gain experience at different levels of operating and analysis. As one becomes comfortable with one level of operating and what had been the "liabilities of newness" become "assets of maturity," it is time to think of the next stage of growth and learning. Such continuous moves help to broaden one's horizons and grow the firm.

A word of caution—it is important to ensure that all who invested their time and efforts to help establish the family firm are treated with dignity and respect. Especially important is the careful management of farewells for those family or nonfamily members whose services will not be needed in future phases of the business.

NAVIGATING ENTREPRENEURIAL GROWTH

Entering the growth stage changes the business, for both better and worse. We talked about transitions between life-cycle stages—how difficult it is to recognize when your venture is moving from one stage to another, the problem of matching resources from the old stage to the new one, and the precariousness of trying to be two types of businesses at once. In much the same way, you can think about

---

[10]Peter, L.J., and Hull, R. (1993). *The Peter Principle: Why Things Always Go Wrong*. New York: Buccaneer Books.

the entire growth stage as one of transition. This was made excruciatingly clear in the comments from Glen Gerten:

> I still see us as a mom-and-pop operation, but as it does get bigger, it runs more like a corporation. We have to have some things in place, like employee handbooks and an HR person. But we're trying to keep the family business flavor to some degree.

You can sense both excitement and agony in Glen's words. There is pride in what they have accomplished and a view toward even greater opportunity. But there is also a feeling of loss or the potential loss of the core family values for the business. As the third-generation owners, Glen, Lewis, and Gino carry the heritage of Frank, Robert, and Jerry as they work hard to preserve the core values of "quality garden goods from the grower," while embracing progress.[11] They want the pioneers to be proud of what they have accomplished. They want to take the firm to a new level. But this company carries the Gerten name. With continued growth, will the Gerten family values remain the foundation of the enterprise? Will new employees, new managers, even new family members entering the firm still perceive this as a family business? Will formalization and professionalization cause the special nature of this business to disappear?

DEALING WITH RESISTANCE TO CHANGE

There is a large body of literature addressing resistance to change in family firms. Topics such as intergenerational transition,[12] exit from the founder's business, and professionalization of the firm all have resistance to change at the core of the issues involved. We will not devote excessive space to that subject here, but at the end of this chapter we provide some references that could facilitate your efforts to further examine this issue if you desire to do so. You will encounter resistance both inside and outside the firm when you embark on the growth curve. Recall the Consolidated Communications case. Richard A. Lumpkin's own parents were skeptical of his intent to grow the company. On the inside, employees, including family members, may feel threatened by the changes taking place, wondering if their jobs or the company itself are secure. Outsiders—suppliers, customers, and others—may resist change as that may necessitate changes at their ends too. On the other hand, innovative family-controlled firms such as W.L. Gore & Associates (creators of miracle fabrics such as Gore-Tex), SC Johnson, and Tetra Pak make change their way of life.[13]

---

[11]Collins, J.C., and Porras, J.I. (1997). *Built to Last: Successful Habits of Visionary Companies.* New York: HarperCollins Publishers.

[12]Lansberg, I. (1988). The succession conspiracy. *Family Business Review,* 1: 119–143; Miller, D., Steier, L., and Le Breton-Miller, I. (2003). Lost in time: Intergenerational succession, change and failure in family business. *Journal of Business Venturing,* 18(4): 513–531.

[13]Miller, D., and Le-Breton Miller, I. (2005). *Managing for the Long Run: Lessons in Competitive Advantage from Great Family Businesses.* Boston, MA: Harvard Business School Press.

At this point, we ask you to keep one thing in mind. Resistance to change is not necessarily bad. Rather, when you find resistance to your plans, it should tell you to take a step back. Are people resisting my idea because it disrupts their comfort level, or are they resisting because what I propose to do will not work? Not every change is for the better. Therefore, treasure those objections. Make sure that you have assessed how your strategy will actually lead to long-term improvements. If they do not, abandon your proposal and develop another one. As an example, in reporting about another family firm in the growth stage — "Affairs to be Remembered"[14] — a Broomall-based event design company in Pennsylvania cofounded by four sisters and eventually employing ten family members in the business, author Jayne Pearl noted:

> In the seven years the company has existed, the family has had to handle typical family disagreements, Marie [one of the four sisters who founded the company] says. "For instance, I'm more eager to take risks, but we have checks and balances," she explains. "Every major decision goes through all four partners."
>
> The company, which oversees about 100 events a year, is currently considering purchasing new trucks. Marie would like a 15- and 24-footer and a van, but Eileen [cofounder], who tends to be more cautious, is not convinced.
>
> "Sometimes [a decision] goes by majority," says Marie. "I know Eileen is not just saying no for the sake of it, that it's because she has our company's interests at heart. Most of the time, we learn to trust unconditionally that we have each other's back, and you can't put a price tag on that."[15]
>
> Marie says the siblings take care not to pick fights. But she adds that they know they can take advantage of each other. For instance, Marie says, when tempers occasionally flare, "We don't have to apologize. Our form of an apology is getting iced tea for each other."

As you can see, disagreements among family members occur frequently during a business's growth stage. But successful families ensure that different opinions are voiced. In Chapter 11, we discuss various governance mechanisms that are used by family firms for this purpose. In addition, many families tend to develop their own idiosyncratic ways to communicate apologies to others when necessary without disrupting family harmony or the work of the enterprise.

PROFESSIONALIZING THE FAMILY FIRM

In the Gerten case, we find the classic tension between running a casual, family-oriented enterprise and instituting the policies associated with a formal business. After years of success in collaborative working relationships, the owners are acknowledging that policies and procedures must be put in writing. A plan for

---

[14]http://www.affairstoberemembered.com/
[15]Pearl, J.A. (2007). Dealing with dissent: Planning for family time. *Family Business,* 18(1): 63–66.

keeping the business healthy in a changing environment must be formalized and put into place. Parallel planning of the business and the family's involvement in the business needs to be undertaken.[16] The respective responsibilities of the family owners must be delineated. As you can see from Glen's comments, he did not relish the prospect. He did not want to sit in the office preparing plans; he wanted to put in a day's work in the nursery. But he knew what had to be done.

Glen Gerten made another cogent comment. He felt they had needed formal policies for years, but that they did not have time to work on them while devoting themselves to growing the business. This is an almost universal excuse that business owners and managers use for not doing something that needs to be done. Running a business fills your day ... and your night ... and your weekend. There is always some demand that a business of your own places on you. Ultimately, the only way to move your business forward is to step back from day-to-day activities and invest your time in planning. Otherwise, be assured that no matter how hard you try, you will lose control. It is those policies you formulate that enable your managers and employees to know what actions to take or not to take without seeking you out to make every decision.

USING EXPERT ADVISORS

Today, there is an abundance of expertise available to business owners who take time away from everyday operations. The Family Firm Institute, an international association of family business consultants and advisors, has more than 1,500 members around the world. There are more than 150 university-based family business centers that are currently operating. Associations like the Family Business Network, Family Business Australia, and Canadian Association of Family Enterprises all provide resources for family business owners who are eager to professionalize their firm. We list these resources at the end of the chapter.

In addition, workshops conducted by trade associations, chambers of commerce, the United States Small Business Administration and its equivalent in other countries, community colleges, and so on all offer value in managing a company more effectively. Bankers, accountants, attorneys, and other professionals can provide invaluable advice in excess of any expense they charge for their services. It is quite evident that those business owners who seek advice from qualified external parties are more successful than those who do not.

PROBLEMS, OPPORTUNITIES, AND STRATEGIES IN THE GROWTH STAGE

We now turn to our model of problems, opportunities, and strategies associated with life-cycle stages, in this case, the growth stage. Table 8.2 presents examples of individual-, family-, business-, and environment-related conditions that might be

---

[16]Carlock, R.S., and Ward, J.L. (2001). *Strategic Planning for the Family Business: Parallel Planning to Unify the Family and Business.* New York: Palgrave Macmillan.

TABLE 8.2 Problems, Opportunities, and Strategies in the Growth Stage

	Problems	Opportunities	Strategies
Individual-related factors	• Failure to recognize that growth is occurring • Lack of expertise for growth stage • Inability or unwillingness to move to the next level of analysis or operations of the firm • Lack of time and resources • Loss of control • Threat of personal failure and loss of job	• Potential to create wealth and legacy for next generation • Develop entrepreneurial and leadership skills • Expanded responsibilities and opportunities to build networks with the community	• Grow own competence • Train and develop others—learning the critical yet difficult skill of delegation and working through others
Family-related factors	• Business resources reinvested rather than spent on family • Less quality time among family members • Some family members may want to cash out their investments • Life-cycle needs of family may compete with resource needs of the growing firm	• Grow the firm to leave a legacy for next generation • More positions in the company available to engage more family and nonfamily members • Potential to create wealth for the family	• Opportunity to reevaluate family involvement in business • Increase or decrease active family involvement in business • Develop more external interests and careers • Form a family council or other governing mechanisms • Establish family participation rules and entrepreneurial career plan for the most talented family and non-family members in the firm
Business-related factors	• Threat of company failure • Need to develop capabilities in new markets or with products/services • Liabilities of newness as growth occurs • Lack of resources	• Increase span of operations and influence of the firm • Enhanced responsibilities and opportunities to build competence levels in the firm • Financial benefits, short and long term	• Entrepreneurial career planning • Education and training opportunities • Exiting under-performing employees or highly demanding investors

(continued)

	Problems	Opportunities	Strategies
TABLE 8.2 *(continued)*			
Environment-related factors	• Threat of retaliation from competitors who might have ignored a start-up but become vigilant of a growing firm • Threat of new entrants and replicators • Economic, political, or financial low turns, leading to drop in demands and low consumer confidence • Inability to obtain credit, supplies, or distribution difficulties	• Potential to develop new markets, services, and products • Enter into new alliances, acquire or merge with other firms • Contribute to community's growth by providing employment and products in need • Build networks in the community	• Build social capital and networks • Enter into cooperative alliances or acquire competitors • Diversify into growth segments of the industry • Take advantage of economies of scale as the operations become larger

faced in the growth stage, and what actions might be available to each set during a period of rapid growth. As you go through this list, think of other points that could be added to the table.

PROBLEMS

As with every stage, there are both positives and negatives of growth. From our prior discussion, we can expect that the primary threats are associated with capacity issues and with potential resistance to change. For the **entrepreneur**, the capacity problems may creep up in terms of his or her willingness to adapt to the demands for a new management style, as well as insufficient resources to meet the demands resulting from growth opportunities. Delegation does not come naturally to many entrepreneurs, but a growth stage necessitates learning this essential skill. Time and resource constraints are high, causing stress for the entrepreneur as she must attend to the growth needs while patiently training others.

For the **family**, the concerns are time demands, especially by those participating in the business, and the sacrifice of resources (especially income) that can occur when company revenues must be reinvested to support growth. Some family members who might have invested in the business during start-up stages may not want to continue with the business and ask to cash out their shares. Life-cycle stages of family may conflict with the resource needs as well. Examples include a new birth in the family, educational expenses for children, and health needs of aging family members. These all consume family resources, which an entrepreneur might otherwise need to invest in the growth of the firm.

For the **business**, capacity issues can be related to personnel as employees may not possess adequate skills needed for growth, or there may be inappropriate policies in place to handle the system needs that arise with the growth stage. The need to hire more employees to handle growth may not be aligned with the inflow of cash.

Environment-related problems may emerge with financial turbulence that the entrepreneur cannot control. Political instability might influence consumer confidence, leading to reduced demand. Technological or sociological changes and competitive landscapes all influence the environmental impact for growing a firm.

OPPORTUNITIES

Growth stages bring forth individual, family, business, and environment-related opportunities. The obvious ones for the **individual** entrepreneur are the potential to create a legacy and wealth, to generate employment, and to build entrepreneurial competence and skills for herself and prospective successors. As the business expands in size, it provides the potential to employ more **family** members and outsiders in the firm. Family members have more opportunity to participate in the company or to find fulfillment elsewhere. For some families, the business becomes a vehicle to build family identity and relationships.

Growth provides opportunities for the **business** to serve more customers and markets, to expand its scope, and to make a mark on the community. The increased span of operations allows some employees to learn new skills that make them more valuable and provide career satisfaction and advancement. The potential to enter into alliances or to buy out competitors might exist as the entrepreneur overcomes the liabilities of newness and gains the confidence of investors and customers. **Environment**-related opportunities include the potential to increase the span and scope of business operations through expanding the mix of products and markets. As the firm becomes more noticeable in a community, it begins to encounter opportunities to contribute to the community, which in turn helps build valuable networks.

STRATEGIES

Several strategies are available to the entrepreneurial family firm leader to overcome the challenges of problems listed above and take advantage of opportunities. Most relate to adding to the resource mix in order to accomplish the growth. For **individuals** involved in the business, one of the learning and growth opportunities must be harnessed and taken advantage of. Growth is a great time to reevaluate the role of family involvement in business and make amends for past sacrifices. For **family** members, a key aspect in this stage involves determining their current and future roles in firm governance. These might include increasing family investments or buying back some of the family members' shares so as to consolidate ownership and control. One way or another, policies regarding governance will be established in this stage. All too often, those policies evolve unplanned, and a price will be paid later.

Critical strategies for **business** at this stage relate to making prudent decisions regarding how to grow—the direction and pace of growth. Career planning for employees must take place. This is the time to make sometimes difficult decisions about which employees should stay (and grow with the firm) and which ones may have to leave. Those who remain must acquire the expertise necessary to contribute to the business in its new form. **Environment**-related strategies include building networks in the community and social capital that can help with further growth. As the firm becomes more attractive, it may receive invitations to form alliances with other growing firms or find opportunities to acquire other firms; these strategies can lead to economies of scale.

Growth is both exciting and dangerous. The mode and extent of growth varies from one family firm to another. It is not unusual for the family firm to experience multiple growth spurts over the course of its life cycle. It is important for entrepreneurial family firm leaders to recognize that familiness can be both distinctive and constrictive. That is, the tensions raised and resources needed to keep the firm healthy are likely to trigger stresses in the family. Similarly, family conditions are likely to influence success in the business domain. Family firm leaders who fail to consider these interactions are likely to lose the business or the family or both.

Summary

- Although we portray firms as entering growth stages following start-up, rapid growth can occur at any point in a company's life cycle.
- Companies can experience growth because they are pushed by conditions beyond their direct control or because they pull themselves into a new stage.
- Push conditions may include actions by competitors, customer demand, technological advances, legislative or regulatory changes, and more.
- Pull tactics include entering new markets, introducing new products, changes in leadership, and more.
- Growing a business means changing the business. Change can be disruptive, uncomfortable, and threatening. Resistance to change can be both positive and negative.
- Similar to other life-cycle stages, there are problems, opportunities, and strategies that are characteristic of the growth stage.

Discussion Questions

1. Identify some family businesses that have sustained rapid growth over a period of years. What life-cycle stage were they in before entering the growth stage?
2. Were those companies pushed into growth, or did they strategically pull themselves into the stage? Were the stimulants of growth internally or externally driven?

3. Suppose you were running a stable small business. Think about your own family members. How would they react if you told them that after years of operating your firm you were going to do something radically different to turn it into a big enterprise?
4. Pick a type of business with which you are familiar. If you wanted to grow that business by raising money from outsiders, what strategy would you use to give them a return on their investment in five years?

Learning Exercises

1. Review the cases appearing at the beginning of the chapters in this book. Given what you have learned to this point, what factors, conditions, or influences do you believe contributed to the growth of the family firms that are examined in the cases?
2. Identify a faculty member at your school who studies change, perhaps someone in biology or computer science or psychology. What has that person observed about how people, especially family members interacting, respond to rapid changes in their environments?

Readings

- Birch, D. (1987). *Job Creation in America*. New York: The Free Press.
- Gerber, M.E. (1995). *The E-Myth Revisited*. New York: Harper Business.
- Johnson, S. (1998). *Who Moved My Cheese?* New York: Putnam Adult Publishers.
- Kuratko, D.F., and Welsch, H.P. (2001). *Strategic Entrepreneurial Growth*. Fort Worth, TX: Harcourt College Publishers.
- Ward, J.L. (1987). *Keeping the Family Business Healthy: How to Plan for Continuing Growth, Profitability, and Family Leadership*. San Francisco, CA: Jossey-Bass.

Resources for Family Business Owners

- Canadian Association of Family Enterprise — *http://www.cafecanada.ca/*
- Family Business Australia — *http://www.fambiz.com.au/*
- Family Business Network — *http://www.fbn-i.org/*
- Family Firm Institute — *http://www.ffi.org/*

THE MATURING FAMILY VENTURE

BREAKING OUT OF THE "24/7" TRAP

Overwork and family business tend to go hand in hand. "Most family business owners and members put in backbreaking hours," said family business consultant Wayne Rivers of Raleigh, N.C. "They sacrifice their personal health, their family togetherness, their social lives, their spiritual lives—everything—for their business."

But does it have to be that way? In 2002, more than five decades after its founding, one family of real estate investors decided that grueling hours might not be such a necessary ingredient after all. They agreed to begin an unusual experiment to see if they could run their fast-growing real estate investment and lending empire on a four-day-a-week schedule, along with three months off in the summer, and one or two extended winter vacations.

It was in 1949, that the late Alvin Wolff Sr. founded a real estate brokerage and development company. When he retired in 1970, he passed the company to his son Alvin "Fritz" Wolff Jr. For its first 50 years, the Wolff Company's schedule followed conventional lines. The days were long as the Wolff's tried to follow the founder's philosophy of accommodating with the homebuyers' schedules. Alvin Sr. believed that "If somebody's willing to talk, now's the time to do it."

But in the late 1990s, as the third generation joined the business and the firm began to focus mostly on investments in apartment buildings, the four sons and their father—Chairman Alvin "Fritz" Wolff Jr.—decided they wanted to do things differently.

[A]s much as they liked their work, the Wolffs liked spending time with their young families more. "We made a conscious decision that this company would work for us, not us for it," said Fritz. Alvin Sr. said spending time with the family had always been extremely important to his son. Alvin Sr. said he recalled Fritz once telling him "[W]hen I get to be your age, I'm going to have plenty of time for family."

And Fritz actually followed through on that promise, according to his wife, Jeanie. . . . He always made sure he was home in the evenings, and the Wolffs impressed upon their children the importance of being home for dinner. Television was kept to a minimum, and after dinner, they often played board games. (Monopoly, of course, was a favorite with the budding real estate investors.)

The idea of the four-day week resulted from watching their employees work four long days in order to give themselves extended weekends. The adjustment for the Wolffs was difficult and resulted in a number of mistakes along the way. The summer experiment was even harder. The setting up of home offices, regular conference calls, and staggered time off among the principals helped make the schedule work.

A strong second tier of nonfamily managers helped, as well. About ten years earlier, Fritz said, he began hiring strong managers who could be trusted to mind the shop when the family went away. Before that, he admitted, "We had had a history of paying peanuts and getting monkeys." Paying more for someone more talented yielded spectacular results, he found.

The family also reorganized at the top. Before, Fritz acted as the CEO, according to his son Jesse. Afterward, they began running the firm as five equal co-presidents, with all decisions made by the principals on the basis of "five yeses or one no." While this arguably could be seen as less efficient, it may have made it easier for them to take time out of the office, by preventing the kind of political problems that can arise when someone feels out of the loop.

Amazingly, in the years since the Wolffs changed their work schedule, they've been more successful than ever, they say. The value of the firms' real estate investments stood at about $175 million in 2001 and had grown to about $1 billion [by 2006], with another $1.5 billion under development. Jesse reported that production has doubled every year since 2001.

Sources: Voyles, B. (2006). Family leave. *Family Business,* 17(3): 52–55 and www.awolff.com.

Questions

1. Can five copresidents run a company together successfully? Why or why not?
2. What message are the family members of the Wolff Company conveying to nonfamily employees?

Why did we choose the Wolff Company to introduce this chapter? Because this company was founded in 1949, we are not talking about the recognition of the original concept, the role played by the entrepreneur in creating a new venture, or its growth and stability over the years as the next-generation members took leadership roles in the company. Instead, here is a firm, now three generations old, fundamentally in the same line of business as it was when founded about six decades earlier. The real estate industry has certainly evolved over this time, and the Wolff Company evolved and grew along with it. The Wolff family is finding ways to keep a mature company, in a mature industry, fresh.

In the case of the Wolff family, we find a novel approach to firm governance implemented with the advent of the third generation into leadership roles. The foundation for the governance changes, however, was laid by Fritz, the second-generation leader of the company. He grew up observing his father's dedication to building an enterprise. He saw the successes, but he also saw the sacrifices. He vowed that his life would not be exclusively devoted to the business. Fritz's children learned not only from their father, but also from their employees. Recognizing that the company did not collapse when employees worked four-day weeks or took vacations, they concluded that they did not have to commit to the company on a 24/7 basis. As explained in the case, the road to this change in style has not been completely smooth, but increases in revenues and profits speak for themselves.

What do mature family firms look like? How is a family firm leader to know that his or her firm is in a mature stage of a life cycle? And if that leader recognizes it, what is he or she to do—harvest the business or regenerate it? When is it appropriate to seek each of these outcomes? Do individual and family life-cycle stages influence the options available at the maturity stage? Does the mode and nature of family involvement in business change when a firm matures? These questions and more are addressed in the sections that follow.

SYMPTOMS OF MATURING FIRMS

The term "mature" implies stability. In Chapter 1 (Figure 1.1), we introduced you to two types of family firms, *plateaued* and *entrepreneurial*. The former are run by *cruising kin* who have an established firm with the same products/services and markets, using the same processes for a long time. Entrepreneurial family firms are run by *enterprising families* who seek transgenerational value creation through continuous innovation and regeneration of products, processes, markets, and so forth. As you can imagine, maturity looks different in these two types of family firms.

It was not so long ago that our stereotype of the mature company was a business started and grown by an entrepreneurial founder with a relatively low level of education who sent the children to college to acquire a business education. Those children would then return to be the professionals who could administer what the parent had built. Plateaued family firms are likely to be serving a niche business that provides an acceptable life style for the family. Their leaders are most likely comfortable with their employees, markets, and products or services, and resist change on any significant dimension.[1] However, the enterprise may not

[1]Salvato, C., Chirico, F., and Sharma, P. (in press). A farewell to the business: Championing exit and continuity in entrepreneurial family firms. *Entrepreneurship and Regional Development.*

provide an exciting career for family or nonfamily members involved in the business. Research[2] suggests that individuals in plateaued family firms

- accept business performance below the potential of the firm,
- expend lesser efforts to achieve business objectives,
- spend increased time or effort on nonbusiness pursuits, and
- show little desire to improve their managerial skills.

The following comments by a satisfied yet bored family firm leader are indicative of a mature plateaued firm:

> My business is successful but really isn't growing that much. My products are relatively mundane industrial supplies. And the least of my problems is raising capital. My company is relatively debt free, and we have amassed a pretty good amount of cash. . . . I miss the excitement that I felt when I started my company. Now I don't want to go back to the days when I didn't know if I was able to meet the weekly payroll, but, to be honest about it, I really find my business to be a little boring.[3]

Maturing entrepreneurial family firms are harder to spot. Leaders of these firms understand that the economic environment is too dynamic for a company to shift into idle gear. As noted by one German family firm leader, entrepreneurial effort helps ensure a "strong competitive position of their companies, enables organic growth and thus promotes the family's capital assets that are tied to the company."[4] A survey[5] of 788 family firms in the United States indicated that 93 percent of family firms have little or no income diversification. That is, the family's income is highly dependent on the performance of the family firm. Enterprising families realize that continuous innovation and regeneration must become the norm for sustained high performance and longevity of their family firm.

Innovation in family firms can take varied forms. In this book, we have shared examples of two types of family firm innovators. Firms that move from one industry to another after recognizing viable opportunities to satisfy their customers' needs represent the first type of family firm innovator. Arbill Safety (Chapter 4) and Roberts Brothers (Chapter 5) are examples of this type of innovator. You may recall that Arbill Safety started as an industrial laundry supplier, moved or changed to become a glove company, again transformed itself to become a comprehensive supplier of personal protective equipment, and then changed again to become a national supplier of safety products and services. As fourth-generation leader Julie Copeland noted, this enterprising family shared

---

[2] Malone, S.C., and Jenster, P.V. (1992). The problem of the plateaued owner-manager. *Family Business Review,* 5(1): 25–41.

[3] Malone, S.C., and Jenster, P.V. (1992). Ibid.

[4] Bergfeld, M.M.H., and Weber, F.M. (in press). Dynasties of innovation: Highly performing German family firms and the owners' role for innovation. *International Journal of Entrepreneurship and Innovation Management.*

[5] http://familybusinesssurvey.com/pdfs/LNT_FamilyBusinessSurvey_2007.pdf

one common goal across generations—"to keep Arbill one step ahead of its customers' needs."

Firms such as the Wolff Company and Consolidated Telephones (Chapter 2) demonstrate the second type of family firm innovators. These firms remain in the same industry but transform themselves as the industry evolves over time. In the case of Consolidated Telephones, the telephone industry changed over the years to include wireless services, high-speed Internet, pagers, conferencing, and so on. Consolidated grew by taking advantage of changing industrial trends. The Wolff Company started as real estate brokers and developers, evolving into real estate investors over time. With the Wolff family, we find that 2002 marked an innovative turning point in the management of the company. The firm introduced a four-day work week, signaling the importance of quality-of-life issues for this enterprise. Learning from their employees, they chose to work smart rather than work more so as to leave themselves time to attend to their individual, family, and strategic business needs.

Entrepreneurial family firms engage in three levels of innovation, incremental, progressive, and radical innovation.[6] **Incremental innovations** are efficiency-focused improvements on the existing business without significant changes in the products/services, markets, or processes used by the firm (Figure 4.2). Such innovations ensure a secure base of core business that generates revenues for the firm to meet its expenses and support its growth-oriented innovative initiatives. **Progressive innovations** are movements into adjacent markets, products or services, and related processes. These are extensions or continuations of the current business, involving limited liabilities of newness. Such innovations help maximize the benefits that can be reaped from the current levels of product/service, market, technical expertise, and experiences. **Radical innovations** are moves into significantly new industries, technologies, markets, or products/services. While the uncertainties and liabilities of newness are high in radical innovations, long-lasting family firms understand the critical importance of engaging in such corporate renewal initiatives "behind the scenes" to ensure sustained high performance.[7]

An entrepreneurial family firm can be recognized by its involvement in several initiatives. These initiatives are strategically staggered to ensure continuous renewal and growth of the firm. Some incremental modifications are made to be most efficient in serving the current customers with existing products or services. Such innovations ensure short-term profits for the firm. Other innovations are directed to adjacent or related markets and products using familiar technologies so as to reap the maximum benefits from the assets of maturity possessed by a company. These initiatives ensure medium-term growth and revenues for the firm. Still other renewal "projects" are either being seeded or in various early stages of development. These may involve new technologies, products/services, or

---

[6]Bergfeld, M.M.H. (2008). Global innovation leadership: Towards a practical framework for the strategic development of worldwide innovation competence. PhD diss., Manchester Business School.
[7]Bergfeld, M.M.H., and Weber, F.M. (in press). Op. cit.

markets and are directed to ensure longer-term renewal and growth of the firm. There is likely to be a high level of energy and excitement in entrepreneurial family firms as improvements are being made on the core business, while leaders are always on a lookout for new opportunities.

DRIVERS OF MATURITY

What factors drive some family firms in the maturity stage into a plateau mode while others continue to regenerate and sustain high performance across generations of individual, family, industry, and economic life cycles? To answer this question, we need to become familiar with some of the common features of mature family firms. Then, we can see how leaders of plateaued and entrepreneurial family firms vary in their orientation and behaviors related to these factors. Research[8] suggests that established family firms are often characterized by the following:

- Long owner-manager tenures often spanning three to four decades
- Practical and psychological difficulties of older family members to exit the business
- A large number of family members, possibly from multiple generations, involved in the business as owners and/or managers and/or directors
- Family identity associated with the firm
- Dependence of family on income from the business
- Family control and autonomy
- Feelings of responsibility or stewardship toward the business
- Committed long-tenured employees with tacit knowledge
- An established based of loyal customers
- Economies of scale as compared to firms in birth or growth stages
- Strong community orientation.

While plateaued family firm leaders are complacent, perhaps even giving the impression of being sedate and slow,[9] entrepreneurial family firm leaders are

---

[8] 2008 LNTyee Family Business Survey, http://www.familybusinesssurvey.com/; Malone, S.C., and Jenster, P.V. (1992). The problem of the plateaued owner-manager. *Family Business Review,* 5(1): 25–41; Miller, D., and Le-Breton Miller, I. (2005). *Managing for the Long Run: Lessons in Competitive Advantage from Great Family Businesses.* Boston, MA: Harvard Business School Press; Milton, L.P. (2008). Unleashing the relationship power of family firms: Identity confirmation as a catalyst for performance. *Entrepreneurship Theory and Practice,* 32(6): 1063–1081; Salvato, C., Chirico, F., and Sharma, P. (in press). A farewell to the business: Championing exit and continuity in entrepreneurial family firms. *Entrepreneurship and Regional Development.*

[9] Bergfeld, M.M.H., and Weber, F.M. (in press). Dynasties of innovation: Highly performing German family firms and the owners' role for innovation. *International Journal of Entrepreneurship and Innovation Management.*

aggressive opportunity seekers. Committed to transgenerational wealth and value creation, they are future oriented. They also understand that their firm enjoys assets of maturity such as customer loyalty, tacit knowledge, and economies of scale. A mature firm has an established base of customers who are prepared to continue purchasing from the business and who may be amenable to new products and services from a company and brand they have come to know and trust. Having passed through the growth phase, the firm should have reached a point where they can be more cost-efficient than new entrants to the industry. If the business has been successful at retaining skilled labor and competent management, the employees of the firm should possess tacit knowledge of their products, industry, and market that new entrants might need years to acquire, providing for rapidly implemented innovations or reactions to moves by competitors. The importance of the assets of maturity is nicely captured by the following dialogue between a British Lord and his American visitor:[10]

> "How come you got such a gorgeous lawn?"
> "Well, the quality of the soil is, I dare say, of the utmost importance."
> "No problem."
> "Furthermore, one does need the finest quality seed and fertilizers."
> "Big deal."
> "Of course, daily watering and weekly mowing are jolly important."
> "No sweat, jest leave it to me."
> "That's it."
> "No kidding?"
> "Oh, absolutely. There is nothing to it, old boy; just keep it up for five centuries."

Although it is an advantage to possess assets of maturity, leaders of entrepreneurial family firms understand that there is an "expiry date" for these assets they enjoy. Unless renewed, these same assets are likely to become liabilities of maturity for the firm. Family business successors, being groomed for leadership in this stage, face a dilemma. They may have been educated to seek a sustainable competitive advantage and may find that advantage embedded in the core competence of the firm. But no advantage is permanently sustainable. While they persevere to protect the core family values, the leaders must embrace change to ensure continuous renewal of their business. Future performance aspiration is the force that is driving these firms and their leaders. What about those who plateau? What drives them? In Table 9.1, we compare the mature plateaued and entrepreneurial family firms on key factors noted above.

---

[10]Dierickx, I., and Cool, K. (1989). Asset stock accumulation and sustainability of competitive advantage. *Management Science,* 35(12): 1504–1513.

TABLE 9.1 Plateaued versus Entrepreneurial Family Firms

Features of a Mature Family Firm	Plateaued Family Firm	Entrepreneurial Family Firm
Long owner-managers' tenures	Complacency sets in	Tenure is used to institutionalize the entrepreneurial spirit in the firm
Practical and psychological difficulties to exit	Fear of newness and unfamiliar holds leaders to defend status quo	Continuous change and learning is a norm, thereby reducing exit barriers
Large number of family members involved in the business	Business is viewed to serve family needs without value being created	Family involvement in management is based on abilities and separated from family's involvement in ownership or governance of the firm
High family identity with the firm	Identity with the firm leads to high resistance to change	Identity with the firm leads to continuous improvement so as not to let the firm go stale
High dependence of family on income from the family firm	High dependence results in inertia, resisting changes	High dependence is translated to urgent need to continue being progressive so as not to lose competitive position
High levels of family control and autonomy	Family control and autonomy are used to resist change	Family control and autonomy are used to undertake incremental, progressive, and radical innovations
Feeling of responsibility or stewardship toward the business	Feeling is guided by past orientation and a desire to retain the founders' business as is	Feeling of responsibility propels toward future orientation and continuous innovation
Committed long-tenured employees with tacit knowledge	High trust in employees leads to hesitation to hire new or different thinkers	Lifelong learning, growth, and career planning of trusted employees
Established the base of loyal customers	Customers are taken for granted	Close to long-term customers and strong efforts to understand and satisfy their evolving needs
Economies of scale as compared to firms in birth or growth stages	Economies of scale allow for comfortable life style	Economies of scale are used to undertake renewal and regeneration of the firm
Community orientation	High involvement in community activities with little or no regard to opportunity identification	High involvement in community activities along with continued efforts to identity entrepreneurial opportunities

NAVIGATING THE MATURITY STAGE

Mature family firms must remain vigilant if they are to prosper over generations of leaders and over product and market life cycles. There are many well-managed firms that remain in mature stages for years, even through multiple leadership transitions. With difficult financial times, shortening life cycles of products and technologies, intense international competition, and changing sociological trends, however, the cruising mode of plateaued firms is likely to result in a negative spiral of shrinking markets and revenues. If some family or nonfamily members in these complacent firms fall into high-consumption modes, the pace of decline will be even faster.

The entrepreneurial family firm leader is open to ideas that may cause disruptions in the marketplace. Before introducing a strategy that has never been tried and that could jeopardize the firm, managers of mature businesses should evaluate the strategies that have been found to fit this stage of development. Below, we consider some of the problems, opportunities, and strategies that are commonly faced by individuals, families, businesses, and industries in maturity. These are grouped in Table 9.2.

PROBLEMS

Individual family members in mature firms, especially founders, feel a sense of accomplishment for the success achieved by their firm. The later-generation family members involved in the business also feel a sense of pride in the family firm. This positive identification can make them wary to undertake significant changes that may lead to risking the current levels of success.

The family firm founders, who usually have long tenures, may be in the later adulthood stages. At these life stages, individuals begin to acknowledge their mortality and may want to slow down a bit to enjoy life. Health concerns can consume the attention of maturing individuals. Comfortable with their employees, suppliers, and customers, they may not be eager to undertake significant changes. As the business generates more revenues, lifestyles adjust, with the maturing family members engaging in more leisure or community-related activities. These forces require extracting cash from the firm and leading to resistance to changing the winning formula on which the business was built.

Problems related to **family** in the maturity stage revolve around conflicting life-cycle stages of multiple generations of family members involved in the business. Company founders may be in later adulthood stages, concerned with retirement security, health issues, and estate planning. The next generation might be in early or middle adulthood stages, which could include being empty nesters, either carrying on family traditions or experimenting with new ideas. As the third generation enters the firm, they may be in provisional adulthood stages, forming households, wanting to introduce new ideas and directions. Family members working together in the firm have serious adjustments ahead as they discover that they come at problems and opportunities from very different perspectives. The addition of in-laws and blended families increases the number of

TABLE 9.2 Problems, Opportunities, and Strategies in the Maturity Stage

	Problems	Opportunities	Strategies
Individual	• High dependence on business income for maintaining personal life style • Practical and psychological difficulties to change • Development of other interests outside of business, requiring time and resources	• Building personal and professional skills • Enlarging social networks • Learning through mentoring of the next generation of leaders • Engaging in community leadership opportunities	• Developing and learning new skills • Build entrepreneurial skills through voluntary activities • Begin leadership transition planning • Provide entrepreneurial experiences to the next-generation family members
Family	• Demands on firm resources • Sense of entitlement • Failure to understand boundaries between family and business • Conflicting roles among extended family members, including in-laws	• Wealth creation • More positions in company available to family members	• Succession planning • Formation of family council, family office, and family foundation • Developing rules of entry, exit, and promotions for family members in business
Business	• Failure to recognize that markets are saturated • Potential loss of market share to competitors and substitutes • Questionable competence of successors • Difficulty in retaining nonfamily managerial talent • Consumer activism and government intervention • Increasing expenses	• New markets • New products • Improve existing products/services • International expansion • Customer loyalty • Tacit knowledge of management and employees • Economies of scale	• Diversification • Formalization of policies and procedures • Increasing investment in marketing • Product differentiation • Market concentration • Engaging in incremental, progressive, and rapid innovation

(continued)

TABLE 9.2 *(continued)*			
	Problems	*Opportunities*	*Strategies*
Environment	• Product/service obsolescence • Threats from international competitors • Access to affordable and qualified labor • Legislation and regulation • Commoditization of products/ services • Price competition • Lower margins	• New technologies • New markets within or beyond national boundaries • Building networks and learning from social, technical, and thought leaders	• Alliances • Research and development • Political lobbying

stakeholders who claim rights to the business and want to provide input to the direction it is pursuing.

As larger numbers of family members from different generations become dependent for their needs on the business, the desire to undertake radical innovations may be reduced. Familiness compels or obliges the family firm leaders to attend to these demands and needs, leaving fewer resources for renewal and regeneration of the business. Many family members may have contributed to the business in birth and growth stages. As the firm begins to enjoy stability in the maturity stage, these family members expect to be repaid for their hard work with more time and resources from the business flowing toward them.

A corresponding phenomenon often occurs with family **businesses**. Families themselves, even multigenerational ones, take on characteristics of the life cycles of their organizations and industries. Thus, the various family members managing a mature company may recognize through analysis or experience that the options of the mature firm are constrained by its very maturity. As a result of previous success, there are strong perceptual biases against recognizing competitive threats, inhibiting thoughts of renewing the firm.

Family enterprises have an additional internal threat, management talent. Is the entrepreneur who created the venture and led it through growth still the right person to ensure long-term prosperity in the mature firm? Are prospective family member successors competent and qualified to move into leadership roles? Is the firm attracting and retaining competent nonfamily managers? Talented individuals are attracted to growth, both personal and of the organization in which they work.

Related to the **environment**, the most obvious problems for the maturing family firms are associated with competition. New competitors in growth or start-up stages see opportunities for innovations where the mature company concentrates on being more and more efficient at something that the market no longer wants or gets excited about. Problems encountered by firms in a maturing industry are reduced profit margins caused by slackening or stabilizing demand and the commoditization of products as competitors learn from each other, adopting and adapting one another's features in accordance with customer preferences.

Another phenomenon that may occur at this stage is government intervention in the marketplace. The financial crises at the end of the first decade of the twenty-first century sparked greater involvement of governments worldwide in the private sector than had been seen since the Great Depression of the 1930s. The wider the acceptance of the products and services provided by an industry, the more experience is acquired, and the more awareness of defects or of business practices that may negatively affect a society. As a result, elected or appointed officials impose regulatory requirements, almost invariably adding to the cost of doing business. Government action is frequently instigated by consumer activism. This necessitates a further need to direct energy and resources toward monitoring public policy, including participation in associations seeking to influence the formulation and implementation of laws and regulations.

OPPORTUNITIES

While the plateaued family firms often find themselves overwhelmed by the problems discussed above, entrepreneurial family firm leaders are able to locate opportunities in all situations. For example, at the **individual level**, maturity may be viewed as an opportunity to delegate the day-to-day running of the business to nonfamily managers, as was done by the Wolff family, and to use the time and resources toward the strategic development of the firm. Many family firm leaders take great pride in mentoring the junior-generation family and nonfamily members. The maturity stage of a business can be a satisfying time to train the next generation of leadership.

At this stage of business, more time can be devoted to meet individual and family needs and desires. While the family firm leaders may be fully consumed by the demands of the firm during the early life stages, the stability characterizing maturity allows for personal and professional development. More time can be carved out to take on leadership responsibilities in the community. Such activities lead to personal growth and building social networks, enabling further opportunity recognition and exploitation.

A mature family business provides several opportunities for **family** members. A family business may serve as the glue that binds a family together. Siblings or cousins who might otherwise go their separate ways and lose touch may remain connected through joint ownership, mutual benefit, or shared legacy of the enterprise. Several opportunities for employment and family involvement in the firm become available in the maturity stage of the firm. Junior members can be trained in different types of jobs in the firm, helping build a company that can become their legacy for future generations.

Harry Luby, founder of Luby's Cafeterias, a major cafeteria chain in the southwestern and midwestern United States, opened his first restaurant with his wife. Her sister and brother-in-law later became partners in the business. Harry was an only child who spent much of his youth with his 11 cousins, 8 of whom eventually became Luby's Restaurant owners. Although Luby family members eventually gave up control of the chain following a public stock offering, they built wealth and valued the trust they had in one another while it remained a family enterprise. Many family members not only served as managers, but also held ownership positions in which they honed their entrepreneurial skills, retaining core values while experimenting with changes in operations. Some effectively transferred those skills to other ventures.[11]

As discussed in earlier sections, a mature family **business** is well positioned to undertake different forms of innovation. Not only are there opportunities to enhance the efficiency of current operations, but also new markets and products can be launched. As the core business of the firm is secured at this stage, more efforts can be devoted toward renewal, reflected in the empowerment of the next-generation or nonfamily managers to run the firm.

Environment-related opportunities range from exploring and expanding into new industries to meeting changing customer needs within the current market and product domains. Mature firms have opportunities to engage younger family and nonfamily members. For example, by hiring university and college graduates equipped with new learning, such firms can provide a stable environment for them to hone their business-specific skills while helping renew the firm. As more time is available to the leaders, they have opportunities to stay close to public policy makers and other thought leaders. Such social networks often spur ideas and enhance resources for exploitation of opportunities.

STRATEGIES

As the company matures, what level of risk are the executives prepared to accept? The firm now has more assets to lose than in the start-up or growth stages. Does that result in more conservative management styles? Many family business founders and successors believe that conservation of assets and wealth is the appropriate strategy for the mature firm. But will the competitive environment permit conservation? To reap the benefits of tacit knowledge and build relationships and assets of maturity, entrepreneurial family firms adopt several strategies.

At the **individual** level, entrepreneurial family firm leaders are always eager to learn and develop their skills. As the mature firm provides basic stable income through loyal customers, career development plans for family and nonfamily members can be initiated. These might include further education, traveling, or building entrepreneurial skills and networks through voluntary activities. This is

---

[11]Dawson, C., and Johnston, C. (2006). *House of Plenty: The Rise, Fall, and Renewal of Luby's Cafeterias*. Austin, TX: University of Texas Press.

also a good stage to begin planning for leadership transition, training the next generation of leaders, and providing them with opportunities to hone entrepreneurial skills.

As different generation **family** and nonfamily members may be involved in the maturing business, they may benefit from listening to and appreciating the viewpoint of the other generations. As the business matures, the family in turn creates structures that define the relationships of the members as individuals and groups to one another and to the firm. Furthermore, these structures help individual family members understand and appreciate how they relate to the governance of the firm.

Although family structures can be developed during any stage, it tends to be in the mature stage of the life cycle when family members recognize the wealth that has been created by the venture and that the failure to formulate guidelines may have disastrous consequences for family cohesion and for individual members. Please take note, however, that the earlier family practices are formalized, the fewer problems will likely result at some later point when family members begin contending over the assets that the business has succeeded in building. Some of the structures that have become common include family councils, family foundations, and family offices. In Chapter 11, we will discuss structures that enable disciplined governance of an entrepreneurial family firm. While we would prefer that the process starts earlier, maturity is a good time to develop rules of entry for family involvement in business. As we saw in the Wolff Company, bringing in a cadre of nonfamily managers was a critical factor, enabling the family executives to take time away from the enterprise.

The structures designed and implemented by the maturing family **business** may go a long way in helping to overcome many of the problems we have raised. Similar to the mature family, a mature business should be introducing more formalized structures, policies, and procedures. By this stage, the firm should have an external board of directors. Minimally, there should be a board of advisors to help screen opportunities, make recommendations on hiring and promotion, review financial plans, and help in other ways. Mature firms also concentrate on new and more effective ways of serving existing markets, diversifying risk through the introduction of new products and services and into new market segments. Disciplined governance should provide the means to avoid conflicts in this stage without stifling the innovative behavior that might prove necessary for eventual renewal.

Are the leaders of the firm still engaging in **environmental** scanning? Are they looking for opportunities? We see certain strategies consistently applied in mature industries. Efforts to influence the regulatory environment occur. These are often led by industry associations, seeking to minimize the costs or constraints of complying with government edicts. Firms within the industry may form alliances, not only as part of the lobbying efforts of trade associations, but also to improve distribution systems, add product lines, or take advantage of new technologies. Industries seek to avail themselves of government-sponsored research and development and invest in university-based research projects. For many companies within an industry, these investments are strategies for facilitating the return to a growth stage.

In the dynamic global economy, industries are constantly coming and going. They may be new creations, resulting from an invention or discovery, such as the harnessing of electricity or nuclear power. They may be spin-offs from existing industries, such as the evolution of recorded sound. And they may be globally mobile, chasing new labor markets, consumer markets, and technological advances, such as in garment manufacturing. As with the products or services that characterize them, industries tend to follow a life-cycle pattern of birth and gradual introduction and acceptance, followed by rapid growth, eventually leveling into maturity.

Maturity is accompanied by opportunities for firms currently competing in the industry and for prospective new entrants. Entrepreneurial family firms in a mature domestic environment may find new opportunities beyond the country's borders. New technologies may be developed within the industry or may transfer across industrial boundaries, transforming the nature of competition. Entrepreneurial leaders should be on the lookout for opportunities that can differentiate products or raise profit margins in all stages of a firm's life cycle.

Summary

- Rapid growth is not permanently sustainable. Eventually, families, businesses, and industries mature, although a more moderate level of growth may continue in maturity.
- Maturity implies stability and carries both positive and negative consequences.
- The indicators of maturity are different in plateaued versus entrepreneurial family firms.
- Entrepreneurial family firms engage in incremental, progressive, and rapid innovation simultaneously to ensure short-, medium-, and long-term growth of the firm.
- The maturing family needs to consider and implement formal practices to manage the wealth the business is creating and to ensure future success for the firm.
- The maturing business similarly needs to engage in professionalizing behaviors while not neglecting to seek opportunities.
- Maturing industries possess characteristics that need to be understood by family business owners if they desire long-term, multigenerational survival for their firms.

Discussion Questions

1. Do you believe that a family matures as a unit, or will generational differences always keep members in separate life-cycle stages?
2. What other problems, opportunities, and strategies for maturing family firms can you think of in addition to the ones listed in Table 9.2?

3. How would you go about persuading your family to form a council or write a constitution?
4. What steps would you recommend to business founders who want their children to be entrepreneurial when the family firm reaches maturity?
5. What would be some signals that your family firm has left a growth stage and become mature?
6. How will a family firm leader know whether his firm is plateaued or entrepreneurial in the maturity stage?
7. How would you retain competent family and nonfamily managers in the maturity stage of the business?
8. If your family has a business or if you have work experience, describe the life-cycle stage of the industry in which the company competes.

Learning Exercises

1. Identify a mature industry. How did you determine that the industry is in the maturity stage?
2. In a mature industry, compare six different organizations. Can you identify those that are plateaued and others that are entrepreneurial family firms? If so, what key differences do you observe in terms of the factors discussed in Table 9.1?

Other Resources

- Gerber, M.E. (1995). *The E-Myth Revisited.* New York: Harper Business. www .census.gov for more information on NAICS and business statistics.

10

DECLINE— DEGENERATION OR REGENERATION?

SELLING YOUR COMPANY

For family business owners contemplating a possible sale or merger of their company, family issues are every bit as important as business issues in the decision-making process. In October 2001, we sold our second-generation family business—Hayes Manufacturing Group of Neenah, Wisconsin—a paper converting company. I was 55 years old. My father had started the business in 1968. My two brothers and I took over management of the company in the mid-'80s and grew the business to $70 million in sales with three manufacturing plants and 350 employees.

Our decision to sell our company was driven primarily by business rather than family concerns. The rapid consolidation among customers and suppliers in the latter half of the '90s put us in a position of needing wider distribution to continue growing and affiliation with a paperboard producer to remain competitive. In short, we needed to align ourselves with a national or international company with recycled paperboard mills. We received offers from three strategic buyers and ultimately sold the company to Sonoco Products of Hartsville, South Carolina—an international packaging company. The sale process itself took about five months. Selling a family business is a very emotional decision. No matter how compelling the business reasons for selling, the psychological dimension of family business ownership makes letting go very difficult. Here are some things we learned during the process.

1. *The decision must be unanimous*—It's critical that family business owners, particularly those working in the business, agree on the sale. . . . Once the decision is made and the process starts, any signs of family conflict can discourage current potential buyers as well as future buyers. . . . Selling is tough enough. Don't risk tearing the family apart in the process.

2. *Seek outside help*—Don't try putting a value on the business or negotiating with a buyer yourself. . . . Look to your professional advisers, board members, or outside consultants to help set a value, market your company and negotiate with potential buyers. Hayes Manufacturing Group hired an investment banking firm to help us value and market our company and negotiate the sale. That was money well spent.

3. *Be comfortable with change*—Understand from the start that once you sell your business, it's no longer yours, and it will change. . . . If you continue to manage the business for a new owner, expect changes. . . . If you aren't interested in staying with the business after a change in ownership, be sure to pursue potential buyers who have the resources to take over management. This is often the difference between a strategic buyer and a financial buyer.

4. *Have a game plan for life after the business*—If you decide to leave the business after a change in ownership, be sure you've given serious thought to what comes next. Selling the business may put money in your pocket, but it also strips you of the psychological benefits of business ownership. . . . If you plan to stay, your tenure will probably be shorter than you think. It's tough working for someone else. Currently, I am a principal in a business and real estate investment company, along with my brothers Don, 56, and Bob, 52. In addition, I am an adviser to family businesses and serve as an adjunct faculty member at a local university.

Source: Hayes, J.R. (2005). Points to consider before selling your company. *Family Business*, 16(2): 40–41.

Questions

1. Suppose you were related to the Hayes brothers, but not active in the management of the business. What questions do you think you might have asked when they were considering this sale? Would your questions vary if you had an ownership stake in this business? (Hint: You may find using the stakeholder map introduced in Chapter 4 useful for this exercise.)
2. Now put yourself in the shoes of the business buyer. What would be the advantages and disadvantages to you of acquiring a family-owned company?

If **growth** indicates an increase in size and **maturity** refers to stability, **decline** implies a reduction or decrease in size. However, as we noted in earlier chapters, decline takes a slightly different meaning in the context of individual, family, business, products, industries, or economic life cycles. For example, in individual life-cycle stages, decline refers to late-late adulthood stages (70+) when the health and energy levels tend to deplete for most individuals. For families, it refers to reduction of the family size as junior generations leave home to establish independent households and seniors may begin to pass away. Reductions in performance metrics such as revenues, market size, profits, or the number of employees suggest that a business is in decline. And when the demand for specific products or an industry as a whole reduces, it is symptomatic of the decline stage.

In our standard life-cycle model (Figure A1), we show decline as a negative slope, but the potential of renewal or regeneration at this stage is also displayed. Enterprising families are not caught unaware by the decline stage. Instead, they plan for this stage and potential exit or regeneration of their business in earlier stages of their ventures. Their decisions for continuity or business exit are guided by the desire to ensure long-term value and wealth creation potential of the firm and protecting the investments of family members. When leaders of entrepreneurial family firms find their enterprise in the decline stage, they use various strategies to deal with it. Another point in regard to the transition from maturity to decline or renewal is that many family businesses may have nonfamily investors. Those investors are more likely to be concerned about recouping their investments along with some gains, rather than whether the company can continue to another generation. Thus, the family owners should have contemplated exit strategies for those investors at an earlier stage.

Depending on the underlying source of decline and life-cycle stages of involved individuals and their families, some entrepreneurial family firms engage in regeneration activities through internal development or acquisitions, for example, as we saw in the cases of Illinois Consolidated Telephone Company (Chapter 2) or Arbill Safety (Chapter 4). Others, like the Hayes Group, choose to sell the enterprise and exit as gracefully as possible, when the family venture has run its course.[1] For this group, industry consolidation was the triggering event. The brothers, entering late middle adulthood stage, were running a mature company that was on the verge of decline. They could forecast the future of the industry and determined that the choice was to grow through acquisition or find a buyer. At their personal life-cycle stages, attempting to reenter a growth stage was not appealing.

In this chapter, we investigate the various causes that may lead a family firm to the decline stage. Problems, opportunities, and strategies that entrepreneurial family firms may find useful for negotiating this stage are discussed.

CAUSES OF DECLINE

Decline is a natural part of the life cycles of individuals, families, family firms, products, or industries. We do not wish to depress you, but for living organisms, such as the individual family members, the decline stage will eventually end in death. Regeneration at individual or family levels more likely means finding

---

[1]DeTienne, D.R. (in press). Entrepreneurial exit as a critical component of the entrepreneurial process: Theoretical development. *Journal of Business Venturing*.

and developing others to extend a legacy. For family firms and products, innovative strategies may trigger revitalization. But closure, liquidation, or sale of an enterprise are possible alternatives too. In general, failure to stay attuned to the changes in the internal and external environments and to anticipate the need for adjusting strategies has a much higher probability of leading to degenerative pathways such as closure through liquidation, rather than regeneration through the sale or renewal of the firm.

When a firm goes into a decline stage experiencing negative growth of sales and revenues, entrepreneurial leaders concern themselves with the reasons for decline, not just the symptoms. Is the decline temporary or permanent? Are the triggers of decline individual, family, business, or environmental factors? Can these factors be altered? At times, owners may engage outsiders who are not emotionally involved in the family firm to conduct an objective review of the firm and report on factors causing decline. This understanding enables them to adopt appropriate strategies for their family firm. Table 10.1 lists various factors that can lead a family firm to the decline stage. Can you think of other factors that should have been included in this table?

TABLE 10.1 Causes of Decline	
Driving Factors	*Causes*
Individual driven	• Deteriorating health of current leaders • Desire to retire • Resistance to change • New career or life interests of firm leaders outside the family firm
Family driven	• No capable relatives interested in rejuvenating or growing the firm • Conflicts among family members over affection or resources • Disagreements on vision and course of action for the family firm • Joining of new family members or attachments taking up more time and attention of firm leaders
Business driven	• Ineffective or plateaued leadership • Philosophical orientation of the family deters hiring of capable nonfamily employees needed to turn around the family firm • Obsolete facilities and equipment • Technological obsolescence • Family firm has moved into other high-growth areas, leaving the original firm in a state of neglect
Environment driven	• Emergence of new competitors who are more effective in meeting the demand • Substitute products have emerged to satisfy customer needs • Consolidation in industry necessitated by low demand • Changes in customer preferences • Government regulations • Technological changes • Depressed economic environment • Natural disasters impacting key stakeholders of the firm

NAVIGATING THE DECLINE STAGE

While in itself the decline stage indicates a negative trajectory, individuals and their firms can accelerate the speed of decline, eventually degenerating toward death or closure, or take strategic actions to stop or reverse the decline, leading to rejuvenation. In this section, we discuss the problems, opportunities, and strategies in the decline stage at the individual, family, business, and environmental levels — summarized in Table 10.2.

TABLE 10.2	Problems, Opportunities, and Strategies in the Decline Stage		
	Problems	*Opportunities*	*Strategies*
Individual	• Deteriorating health • Infirmities associated with age • Burnout • Loss of interest in the business • Resistance to change • Procrastination of succession planning • Sudden loss of entrepreneurial leader • Intensifying competition	• Harvest wealth created by the firm • Senior generation: Time available to pursue outside business interests post semi or full retirement • Leave a legacy through mentoring of others • Successor: Engage in innovative and creative changes • Exercise leadership and entrepreneurial skills	• Key decision: Extent and mode of involvement in the business for family and key nonfamily members • Formulation and implementation of succession and leadership plans • Postsuccession developmental plans for all family members
Family	• No next-generation members available or interested in the firm • Dispersion of relatives • Conflict over affection and resources • Disparate life styles	• Developing talented nonfamily members • Harvesting the wealth tied up in the firm • Employment within the firm as elders depart • Support for education and venturing	• Creation of family governance mechanisms such as family constitution, protocols, family councils, family offices • Most appropriate forms of family involvement in business for the growth of family firm • Mentoring programs for the next-generation family members
Business	• Declining market share • Obsolete facilities/equipment • Increasing competition	• New product/ service introductions • New market penetrations • Strategic alliances	• Merger or acquisition • Liquidation • Diversification • Bankruptcy

(continued)

TABLE 10.2 *(continued)*			
	Problems	*Opportunities*	*Strategies*
Environment	• Technological obsolescence • Evolving customer preferences • Increasing costs • Substitute products • Government regulation	• Product/service innovation • New market expansion • Complementary products or alternate uses of current products • Technological advances to increase efficiency of operations	• Vertical integration • Product discontinuance • Use of existing products as cash cows to fund new initiatives • Research and development • International expansion • Government support

DECLINE STAGE IN INDIVIDUALS

When individuals enter into later adulthood stages of decline, our stereotypical image is that of the degeneration of mental and physical prowess. Yet, with advances in medical care, nutrition, and general quality of life, examples of productive octogenarians are not too hard to find today. Consider, for example, David Oreck, founder of Oreck Corporation, designer of the lightweight Oreck Vacuum Cleaner and other products, and famed Infomercial personality. At the time of this writing, the Oreck Corporation Web site states, "At 85, David Oreck isn't about to slow down."[2] Can you think of other octogenarians who are actively running their family firms? While these are clearly remarkable individuals, given the limitations of human life, they too will eventually die. For family firm owners, departure through death is not unusual. We are never truly prepared for the death of a beloved family member, even when the decline has occurred over a period of time. Multigeneration family businesses are often characterized by family members congregating on two occasions: weddings and funerals.

While many family firm leaders tend to procrastinate on succession and retirement planning, leaving their firms inadequately prepared for their departure,[3] entrepreneurial family firms should not take this unnecessary risk. Instead, the leaders proactively plan for their inevitable departure from the world and prepare the next-generation family and nonfamily leaders to set the stage for continued growth of their family enterprise. Thinking in terms of the various forms of capital we discussed in Chapter 6—financial, social, physical, and human (moral, physical, intellectual, and psychological)—tends to help. Astute entrepreneurs know that while some forms of capital may indeed deplete in the later stages of life, the stocks

---

[2]http://www.oreck.com, accessed February 13, 2009.
[3]Ward, J.L. (2004). *Perpetuating the Family Business: 50 Lessons Learned from Long-Lasting, Successful Families in Business.* New York: Palgrave Macmillan.

of other forms of capital may be the highest they have been over the entire life span. So, instead of assuming that all family entrepreneurs in the late adulthood stages go into degenerative phases or all younger ones are in their prime on all dimensions of capital, they adopt strategies that enable making the best use of assets of individuals in different stages of life.

Some, like the Hayes brothers, sell their firms when they can reap the harvest. Others pass on the leadership to the next-generation family or nonfamily leaders to allow themselves time to pursue other interests. As long tenures are a norm in successful family firms, some entrepreneurs who may have become plateaued or worn out by their business commitments may blossom when those obligations are lifted. At last, they are able to travel, golf, fish, paint, or engage in other fulfilling activities. What appeared to be decline may turn into rejuvenation.

There is evidence that family firm leaders with no interests outside the company either struggle to maintain control or deteriorate rapidly both mentally and physically after retirement.[4] The senior-generation members should be developing hobbies and interests in which to invest themselves postretirement. Some enterprising families establish a foundation or office in which the former executives could devote some time and effort. Experienced senior-generation entrepreneurs can be invaluable on advisory boards of family firms, as well as mentoring junior generations of family and nonfamily members. Even if the leaders' departure ends up being sudden and the successors are ill prepared to step into leadership roles in their family firm, enterprising families act energetically at such times to prohibit the business from slipping into decline. They know well that competitors will use these occasions to encourage customers to switch their loyalties.

The Hayes brothers are examples of individuals who carried their entrepreneurial spirits into other ventures. As we notice in the opening vignette of this chapter, not only did the brothers launch another venture together in the real estate industry, James Hayes has also become a consultant to family businesses and teaches at a local university. We have introduced you to the notion of the habitual or serial entrepreneur. Creativity does not have to cease because an individual enters the late adulthood stages of life, or decides to retire, or closes down a family firm.

DECLINE STAGE IN FAMILIES

The decline stage in family refers to the reduced number of family members in a household due to death, divorce or separation, or establishment of new households by family members. Although the household size may decline, the number of family members involved in the family firm may increase or decrease over time. Synchronized growth of both systems is rarely achieved, necessitating entrepreneurs to think of strategies for continued growth of their firm.

---

[4]Kenyon-Rouvinez, D. (2001). Patterns in serial business families: Theory building through global case study research. *Family Business Review,* 14(3): 175–191.

Family enterprises that survive for more than two generations tend to pass through the following sequence: (1) controlling owner, (2) sibling partnership, and (3) cousin consortium.[5] At any point along the way, the business may enter into a decline stage, although such stages are disproportionately observed at transitions. Similarly, families themselves may decline, and such declines may occur at transition points when the senior generation dies or steps aside or is forced aside by the succeeding generation. A popular phrase in the family business literature is "shirt sleeves to shirt sleeves in three generations," implying that the wealth created by the business founders is squandered by the inheritors.

Businesses, as we have reported, are often launched by lone entrepreneurs, by entrepreneurial teams, or by enterprising family members (Figure 1.1). These start-ups are typically supported by families through financing, labor, and in other ways. Family businesses that transition to subsequent generations are affected by how many or few family members there are and by how many or how few participate actively in the firm. Larger families tend to become dispersed; there may not be sufficient wealth to go around to all branches, and the relatives may eventually feel less part of a family than of an extended clan. The familiness feature may diminish or even cease to exist. Pierre S. du Pont IV, who began his career with the du Pont Company before entering politics, was quoted as saying, "there's still a bond of heritage holding us together, but I don't feel it as strongly as my father did, and my children don't feel it as strongly as I do."[6]

As senior family members approach retirement age, hierarchical relationships often shift. The generation that had been in charge may become dependent, physically, financially, emotionally, on younger family members. In North America, those younger members have sometimes been referred to as the *Sandwich Generation*. They find themselves caring for their parents while still being responsible for supporting and rearing their own children. These conditions create innumerable stresses that can in turn lead to the breakdown of relationships and the desire to be free from family obligations. It is not unusual for founding entrepreneurs to have virtually all of their personal wealth tied up in the assets of the business. When they retire, their financial security may be dependent on the company revenues generated under the leadership of their children. While they may have given up ownership, they remain stakeholders and may be forceful in expressing their opinions and may attempt to continue to exercise control. Their actions may not only create schisms with their children, but they also become visual lessons to their grandchildren, who could decide the last thing they want to do is enter the family firm.

Alternatively, there are many successful regeneration examples. The Hayes family is one in which the three brothers could easily have parted ways upon the sale of the company, yet the relationships they had developed over the years made it possible for them to continue venturing together. In other cases, new

---

[5]Gersick, K.E., Davis, J.A., Hampton, M.M., and Lansberg, I. (1999). *Generation to Generation: Life Cycles of the Family Business.* Boston, MA: Harvard Business School Press.

[6]Allen, M.P. (1987). *The Founding Fortunes.* New York: E.P. Dutton, p.107.

roles have been defined for family members upon their departure from the business. When retiring family members take on affiliated roles, it almost always results from serious and lengthy prior planning. We suggested previously that retirees may follow employment by making second careers from their hobbies. Now we discuss how they may engage in activities that make further contributions to the business and the family, without interfering with normal business operations.

More and more multigenerational family businesses are finding ways to extract value from the outgoing senior generation. This can happen through formalizing an advisory or consulting position in which a retiree may be called upon in some periodic or ad hoc manner. At Management & Engineering Technologies International, Inc., CEO Renard Johnson designed the administrative offices such that his father Alvin would have an office adjacent to his. The title on the door reads "Dad." In other cases, family cohesion and involvement is maintained by having members of the senior generation sit on the governance bodies such as boards of directors, family foundations, family councils, or family offices. Each of the structures has the potential of providing opportunities for senior family members to continue their involvement beyond retirement from the business. More importantly, they institutionalize the family relationships beyond the lifetimes of the business founders. The governance mechanisms used by entrepreneurial family firms are discussed in the next chapter.

DECLINE STAGE IN FAMILY BUSINESSES

Organizational life cycles are real, regardless of whether or not the organizations are family-owned and -operated. This book has taken you through numerous examples of life cycles and their stages. We have examined the excitement and struggles of starting a venture, the opportunities and challenges of growth, the rewards and frustrations of maturity, and now the dangers and prospects of decline. It is not hard to identify a business in decline. The wear and tear typically shows in the physical facility. Equipment is becoming obsolete or wearing out. Market share is decreasing, margins tightening, reducing discretionary income for replacing assets and supporting personnel.

The foremost concern at this stage is entropy, the tendency toward degradation to a state of inert uniformity.[7] In the corporate, nonfamily business world, a key tool for reversing entropy is to change the top management team. Empirical evidence tells us that family businesses are characterized by longer tenures in the CEO position than are nonfamily firms. The liability is inherent but can be overcome.

If family firms do not find a means to revitalize, their energy will eventually run out, resulting in, euphemistically, its nonexistence. We have seen with individual life cycles that the leaders of a family enterprise can deteriorate physically and mentally as they age. In their decline stage, they may become risk averse. The

---

[7]Malone, S.C., and Jenster, P.V. (1992). The problem of the plateaued owner-manager. *Family Business Review,* 5(1): 25–42.

traditions established through past successes become entrenched with managers, applying yesterday's solutions to tomorrow's problems.

The dilemma facing those inside the firm is whether they recognize the decline, the underlying reasons of the decline, and what they intend to do about it. In the family firm, the situation is complicated by the demands of those family members who derive benefits from the business, but who are not directly employed in the company.

Entrepreneurial family firm leaders look under the surface toward causes of decline in their business before taking actions. If the decline is caused by industry conditions as it was in the case of the Hayes Group, strategic sale is an option. But the window of opportunity for such a sale is usually limited, necessitating quick action. If competitors learn that the company is for sale, they will use that information to try to undermine the firm's reputation with suppliers and customers. The solution chosen by the Hayes brothers was to sell their business. This is particularly viable when the business possesses assets of value, such as intellectual property, or when it has market access that would be expensive for a competitor to duplicate. On the family side, the issue is whether there are family members in the wings with the desire and competence to take charge of the firm. For other businesses, the regeneration approach might be to identify and introduce new products and/or services. Some will choose to seek new market outlets at this stage, often across international borders. The most innovative solutions are likely to be triggered by management and ownership transitions.

On the other hand, if the source of decline lies within the family firm, such as the need for technology upgrades, new product development, opening of new markets, or even change of leadership, entrepreneurial family firms engage in such revitalization strategies. Some may opt for growth through acquisition, by becoming one of the industry consolidators or by using the acquired firm to change directions. Family firms that fail to find solutions at this stage will typically find themselves in bankruptcy. Others might choose exit by liquidation or by merger into another firm. For the family business, survival as a family-controlled entity may be a function of prior planning, especially through investing in management and ownership development of successors. What we find critical at this point is for the successor to be prepared not just to govern, but also to be entrepreneurial. The firm in decline will not prosper simply by being efficiently managed. The new top management team must be capable of identifying and exploiting opportunities and of implementing innovative practices for the venture.

DECLINE STAGE IN THE MACROENVIRONMENT

Many family businesses find themselves competing in declining industries if those businesses survive long enough. You may recall from Chapter 5 (Figure 5.3) some examples of such industries we shared with you—wringer washers, manual typewriters, black-and-white televisions, and so on. What causes such declines? Typically, we see external factors at work. Technological advances result in substitutions that make the dominant products, services, or processes of an industry obsolete. Customer preferences change. Witness the effects of nutrition concerns on the quick service restaurant industry (what we used to call "fast food"). Economic conditions change. For example, spikes in fuel prices have ripple effects on transportation and tourist industries. A significant variable for many industries is government regulation. New laws or rules issued by regulatory bodies can dramatically influence costs or may require the removal of products from the market, such as for the pharmaceutical industry.

Although oligopolies[8] do exist, in most situations family businesses will not be able to alter general industry conditions. The question facing the family business owners is how to adjust to industry declines. Interestingly, such declines may present new opportunities to smaller family enterprises. Large corporate competitors, sensing declining industry conditions, adopt redirection strategies, disengaging from one industry and seeking more fertile grounds in which to compete. The departure of dominant players can open market growth opportunities for the remaining firms that are frequently smaller family firms. The cigar industry represents a classic case where such behaviors were documented. Thus the new, innovative approaches might be to look for opportunities where other contenders are leaving the field.

Family business owners must keep a close watch not only on their direct competitors, but also on substitutes that customers may begin to select over their primary product mix. Although there is much talk about high failure rates of ventures, scholars have observed that the failure rate of new product introductions is even higher. Most new product concepts never make it to the marketplace, even those that are awarded patents. And for those that are actually introduced, 9 out of 10 quickly disappear. In a previous chapter we referred you to one of the seminal contributors to the entrepreneurship literature, Joseph Schumpeter, who is best known for describing the entrepreneurial event as **creative destruction**, that is, the entrepreneur disrupts existing patterns by introducing something that destroys the old order. Few products achieve that objective of destroying what is currently accepted by customers. And when it does happen, eventually that product is creatively destroyed by something new.

What conclusions can we draw for the family enterprise regarding product life cycles? First, avoid the trap of complacency. One of the major assets of a family enterprise can also be one of its major liabilities. When the entrepreneurs have laid a solid foundation of the business, it is only natural for the company to adhere to policies and strategies that led to the success. But the environment changes, tried and true products are approaching the end of their life cycles, yet top management stays wedded to them. It is essential that the original entrepreneurial attitude be maintained and infused within successors. How can we build on prior achievements? What are we seeing in the environment that our competitors may be missing? What have they observed that we may have overlooked?

---

[8]As you may recall, an oligopoly is an industry dominated by a small number of sellers, making it easy for collusion and knowing the actions of each other. The decisions of one firm influence and are influenced by those of other firms in the industry.

What new products represent opportunities for the next generation? Should we be the leaders in research and development for our industry to keep our products fresh, satisfying customer needs?

Product development and introduction can serve as a great training program for the next generation of family business leaders. The impetus for innovation by the next generation does not always have to come from the senior generation, however. An inspirational example is provided by the fourth-generation cousins of Australia's Brown Brothers,[9] the renowned family-owned wine company from Victoria, Australia, which was founded in 1889 by John Francis Brown. In early 2000s, six 18- to 35-year-old Brown cousins banded together in secret from their parents to develop a new line of wines called Kid You Not.[10] Unlike the traditional classic wines that Brown Brothers have been well known for over 100 years, these cousins launched a new business under the umbrella of the parent company to produce wines for their own generation. While they had a lot of fun building a business together and getting to know each other, this junior generation used the family incubator effectively to develop their entrepreneurial skills by launching new products. Such activities not only help strengthen the bonds among the next-generation family members, but also help juniors gain respect of their senior family members, nonfamily employees, and other key stakeholders. Learning to work with their cousins and siblings and moving up the learning curve together can become valuable for the family and their firm.

The caveat, however, is to be accepting of failures. Unfortunately, most businesses, both family and nonfamily, choose to punish failure rather than to view it as an investment in acquiring entrepreneurial capacity. Conscious attempts to build skill sets can pay off for companies with subsequent new product introduction and long-term firm survival.

CONCLUSIONS

The decline stage of life cycles is unavoidable but should not be looked upon with terror. Nor, however, should it be ignored. Decline simultaneously represents threats of degeneration and opportunities to renew and regenerate. The biggest threat results from a failure to diagnose decline. Complacency and the continuation of past strategies are the certain routes to death. For some families, the most appropriate response to decline is to exit. Hopefully, exit can take place gracefully with the capture of the wealth the business has generated. In other cases, entrepreneurial initiatives are the best course of action. Success here is often a function of how well the family and nonfamily managers have prepared successors to bring entrepreneurial attitudes and styles to the venture.

It is prudent to keep in mind that for a particular family firm, each of the four categories could be in a different life-cycle stage at any point in time. And within

---

[9]http://en.wikipedia.org/wiki/Brown_Brothers_Milawa_Vineyard, accessed February 16, 2009

[10]http://www.thecoolhunter.com.au/food/The-Brown-Brothers-Kids-Launch-New-Wine, accessed February 16, 2009

the family unit, different members who are active in the business may be in different and conflicting stages. In a multigeneration business, it would not be surprising to find the senior generation in decline, with potential successors in the growth stage. They may have very different attitudes toward risk as they formulate strategies for the business.

The entrepreneurial family firm recognizes that risks exist on both sides of the equation. There are risks associated with innovative behaviors. But the risks of continuing previous practices may be far higher. In the two chapters (11 and 12) of Part C of the book, we present our final recommendations for preparing the family inside and outside of the business for infusing a tradition of thoughtful entrepreneurship into the enterprise.

Summary

- It is inescapable that life-cycle models have a decline stage. Human organisms will eventually die, but that can happen to families and businesses as well.
- Although for individuals death is inevitable, the legacy can be continued through the family and the firm.
- For businesses and for families, regeneration is possible though rarely occurs accidentally.
- Strategically engaging in entrepreneurial approaches can extend the lives of both families and businesses.
- There are identifiable patterns of problems, opportunities, and strategies that are recurrent in individual, family, business, product, and industry life-cycle decline stages.

Discussion Questions

1. What products have you used that are no longer on the market? Why do you think they were discontinued? What happened to the companies that sold those products?
2. There is a good chance that you may one day work in an industry that does not exist today. On a global scale, what industries do you think will prosper in the twenty-first century? Which ones do you believe are in decline? Do the ones in decline present any opportunities?

Learning Exercises

1. Look again in the list of the America's largest family businesses that we cited in Chapter 1 (www.familybusinessmagazine.com). Pick one, go to the company Web site, and identify a founding family member. What can you learn about how that person left the firm? Was it through death, retirement, sale, or something else? How did the firm perform at the time that person left?
2. Entrepreneurial family firms vary in the strategies they adopt when in decline stages. Using the chapter opening case vignettes in this book, develop a list of varied strategies used by these firms.

3. Pick out a foundation that carries the name of some well-known business family (e.g., Ford, Rockefeller, Mellon, and Kellogg). How and why was it created? Are any of members of the family still involved?

Other Resources

- Cohn, M. (1992). *Passing the Torch: Succession, Retirement, & Estate Planning in Family-Owned Businesses*. 2nd ed. New York: McGraw-Hill.
- Friedman, S.E. (1998). *The Successful Family Business*. Chicago: Upstart Publishing Co.
- Lansberg, I. (1988). The succession conspiracy. *Family Business Review*, 1(2): 119–143.
- Leach, P. (2007). *Family Business: The Essentials*. London: Profile Books.
- Sonnenfeld, J.A. (1988). *The Hero's Farewell: What Happens When CEOs Retire*. New York: Oxford University Press.

PART C

ENTREPRENEURIAL FAMILY FIRMS: SUCCESS THROUGH LIFE STAGES

Part A of this book introduced you to life-cycle stages of an individual, family, organization, and the environment in which a venture operates. In Part B, we take a closer look at each stage in the life cycle of a firm. It should be evident to you by now that family businesses are heterogeneous, as they vary in terms of size, industry or market served, age, and extent and mode of family involvement in business, among others. Environmental conditions such as technology, society, legislation, and the economy impact these firms in different ways.

As a result, there is no magic button to push to ensure effective functioning of either the business or the family. Yet research shows us that there are certain problems that come up in family ventures over and over again, opportunities that family members encounter when running their businesses, and strategies that have higher probabilities of leading to success. In Part B, we discussed strategies that help family firm leaders coordinate the life-cycle stages of a family and business so as to anticipate the obstacles that can be expected, opportunities that come along, and strategies that can be useful for high performance on family and business dimensions.

In the concluding Part C of this book, we cull the lessons learned from this reflective journey focused on entrepreneurial family firms. What are some of the most successful and enduring family firms doing? How do they get to the coveted lists of the largest or oldest family firms in the world that we shared in the first chapter? Like all other firms, they make mistakes too, but these long-lived firms do not make the same mistake twice. Instead, they use the opportunities that come about as a consequence of changes in life cycles to amend past mistakes and prepare ground that will nurture the entrepreneurial spirit in the family and nonfamily members of the firm. Chapter 11 is focused on the governance of family firms, while the last chapter presents 25 winning strategies that are more frequently used by enterprising families for the success of their entrepreneurial family firms.

GOVERNANCE TOOL KIT FOR ENTREPRENEURIAL FAMILY FIRMS

AN EVOLUTIONARY PERSPECTIVE ON BUSINESS GOVERNANCE

Where in the life cycles of business development, family leadership, ownership, and continuity across generations is *your* family business? Knowing the answer can greatly improve both the role and the value of governance for your family and its enterprise.

Achieving continuity across generations is a . . . challenge that involves a balance between legacy and renewal of a family's culture, values, and business practices. The dual governance structures of a board and a family council can help foster the right balance as the family and the business grow. While the board manages risk and ensures that the business follows the right strategic direction, the family council's ultimate responsibility is achieving continuity of family ownership through the generations.

Virtually all businesses come from modest beginnings. A family business's first advisory group often consists of (family and) longtime friends whose loyalty and deference can be counted on. At this stage, governance of the business—and the family, for that matter—is accomplished at the kitchen table.

With each new level of formalized business governance, a founder's willingness to share information, to be held accountable and to be evaluated on the basis of financial performance and leadership is challenged. In a family business, this is a significant test.

At some point in the evolution of a family company, the value of establishing a board of independent directors overrides the advantages of less formal governance. The timing of this shift depends on the growth in size and complexity of the business, the ownership configuration, and progression from founder to second generation and beyond. An independent board's responsibility is to ensure that the business will follow the strategic direction set by the owners and articulated in the management's strategic plan.

When a family company has reached the mature stage of development, its board should have a majority of independent directors, selected based on the skills and experience needed to help the business achieve its strategic direction. To ensure strong links among the board, family, and management, the CEO and another family member should also serve on the board.

Just as the board oversees the business, the family members who share ownership oversee the board. This begins with the family communicating to the board a strategic direction for the company, determining an acceptable level of risk and setting financial goals for revenue, profits, and dividends. Best results are obtained when there is effective dialogue between the family and the board.

Just as the business and the board progress from informal to formal practices, family governance undergoes a similar progression. What begins as informal discussions over meals progresses to more formal communication at family meetings and shareholder assemblies. Some families form a family council. The most important responsibility of a family council is to achieve family consensus and to serve as the channel for family communication to the board.

Source: Moore, J., and Juenemann, T. (2008). Good governance is essential for a family and its business. *Family Business Magazine*, Summer: 63–66.

Questions

1. Moore and Juenemann advocate dual governance structures for family firms. Do you think entrepreneurial family firms run by 2 siblings, or by 6 second-generation cousins, or by 35 third-generation owners need different governance structures for success in family and business? Why?
2. What types of activities can a family council leader organize to achieve its objectives of building family consensus, maintaining family ownership, and serving as family's communication channel to the board?

Entrepreneurial family firms create value across generations of leaders, products, and economic life cycles. Family involvement in management and ownership of the firm varies over such extended time frames. As noted by Moore and Juenemann, most entrepreneurial ventures are established by one or a few family or nonfamily members with discussions taking place around the kitchen table. In the first generation, ownership and management are usually wrapped up in the founders. If the venture succeeds as a family business beyond the founding generation, you can expect the number of family owners to increase. This happens when there is an equal distribution of ownership among family members and the number of the next-generation members is larger than the number of founders. For example, the Laird Norton Company, founded in 1855 by two brothers and a cousin, now in its seventh generation, has more than 400 family member owners. Even though the company installed its first nonfamily CEO in 2001, about 140 family member owners actively participate in the family enterprise.[1]

THE CHALLENGES OF GOVERNANCE

The Laird Norton family has successfully managed to remain a cohesive unit through effective family and business governance, simultaneously managing family harmony and development of their business. Continuing the entrepreneurial spirit of a family firm against the backdrop of dispersed and differentiated ownership, with many owners distant from the functioning of the firm, is a challenging task.[2] Krister Ahlström, a fifth-generation family member CEO of the $3 billion holding company Ahlström Corporation of Finland, observed that "in the second and third generations, a gap forms and gradually widens. Owners become more removed; they are less able to see what's happening to the business. But still they retain control. . . . We needed some ways to bring the family together so that its 200 members could function in an organized way as *owners*"[3] In response to this challenge of managing entrepreneurial family firms against dispersed family ownership, both Ahlstorm Corporation and Laird Norton Company developed separate mechanisms for the governance of the family and business, as suggested by Moore and Juenemann. As you may recall from Chapter 1, governance mechanisms help establish the overall strategy of the family firm, including the nature of family involvement in business, performance standards, and codes of conduct. It is through these mechanisms that the family owners guide management, who provide operational leadership to ensure that the work of the company gets accomplished.[4]

Other firms such as the German superstore chain Aldi, the Dutch shoe producer van Bommel, the Italian luxury jeweler Bulgari, Australia's self-storage and equipment hire company Kennards', and America's S.C. Johnson and Co. and Marriott International followed a different path. Over the life cycle of their family firms, they pruned their family trees by reducing the number of family shareholders and/or managers or by splitting up the family business into parts, each of which is led by different family member.[5] Such pruning introduces

---

[1]Steen, M. (2008). Continuity through change. *Family Business,* 19(3): 48–52.

[2]Lambrecht, J., and Lievens, J. (2008). Pruning the family tree: An unexplored path to family business continuity and family harmony. *Family Business Review,* 21(4): 295–313.

[3]Magretta, J. (1998). Governing the family-owned enterprise: An interview with Finland's Krister Ahlstrom. *Harvard Business Review,* January–February: 113–123.

[4]Gersick, K. (2006). *Generations of Giving: Leadership and Continuity in Family Foundations.* Lanham, MD: Lexington Books, p.176.

[5]Lambrecht, J., and Lievens, J. (2008). Op. cit.

simplicity in the ownership and/or management, enabling continued growth of the family firms while promoting strong family relationships.[6] It may occur for any number of reasons. Most frequently, it involves decisions by individual family members to refrain from working in the business and to pursue other interests. On occasion, the decision may be imposed on a relative who has been determined by the managing owners not to be a fit with the firm. And, in the extreme, conflicts over ownership and the exercise of control may result in one family member or branch being ousted by another.

Amid varying levels of family involvement in the ownership and management of the business, how can family firm leaders grow their firm, while maintaining family legacy? What governance mechanisms are needed to simultaneously develop individual family members, promote family harmony amid changing family structures, and maintain the entrepreneurial spirit in the firm? Long-term survival and success of family firms are dependent on the ability of firm leaders to strategically choose from an array of governance choices to fit with the core values of the family and the environment in which the firm operates.[7] In this chapter, we discuss the features of the various governance mechanisms that can be strategically used by entrepreneurial family firms to ensure value creation across life-cycle stages of individual leaders, their families, businesses, and changes in macroenvironment.

THE GOVERNANCE TOOL KIT

Two mechanisms available to govern family firms are the (1) governance structures or bodies that meet at regular intervals and (2) legal or social contractual instruments that are written and binding on all parties involved. The three-circle model proves helpful in terms of thinking about the governance structures that may be useful for a family firm (Figure 11.1). The preferences and views of owners can be expressed through a family office, family foundation, and/or shareholders assembly. An executive or management council is often used to ensure that the viewpoints of the top management team are shared. Family meetings and councils are governance structures that ensure that the family's vision for the firm and the family's involvement in the firm across generations are clearly articulated, communicated, and developed over time. Boards of advisors or directors are the governance structures that ensure that the perspectives of the three subsystems of family, owners, and management are brought together for value creation and longevity of the entrepreneurial family firm.

These governance structures are complemented by legal instruments such as shareholder agreements, buy-sell and call options, wills, employment contracts, and prenuptial agreements. Added to this is the family constitution that is a written

---

[6]Montemerlo, D. (2005). Family Ownership: Boost or Obstacle to Growth? Paper presented at the FBN Ifera World Academic Research Forum, EHSAL, Brussels.

[7]Coles, J.W., McWilliams, V.B., and Sen, N. (2001). An examination of the relationship of governance mechanisms to performance. *Journal of Management*, 27: 23–50.

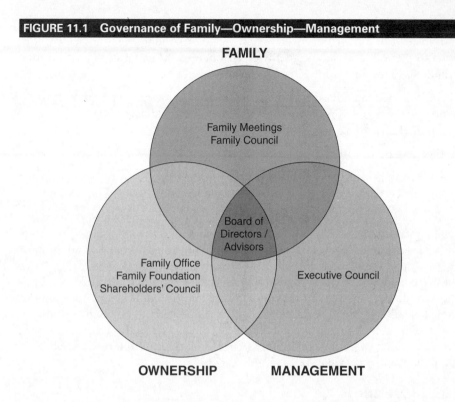

FIGURE 11.1   Governance of Family—Ownership—Management

socially binding instrument guiding the role of family in business and vice versa. Together, these structures and instruments form the governance tool kit available to family firms. While the legal instruments can be used by the smallest of family firms, experts prescribe the adoption of governance structures for growing firms to voice different perspectives of key stakeholders in a firm.[8] Next, we discuss the governance structures from boards of directors to family subsystem structures of family meetings and councils. This is followed by the ownership subsystem governance structures of family councils, family foundations, and shareholders' assemblies. Last, executive councils are discussed as the governance structure aimed to provide a voice and ensure synergistic efforts in the management subsystem.

BOARD OF DIRECTORS OR ADVISORS

It is generally agreed that an active board of directors or advisors positively influences the quality of decision making in family firms, as objective counsel is helpful for the leader. The major difference between a board of directors and that of advisors is the legal status. Advisory boards have no legal power or status,

---

[8]Spector, B., ed. (2006). *The Family Business Policies & Procedures Handbook*. Philadelphia, PA: Family Business Publishing Co.

while the boards of directors do. Many family firms prefer to have an advisory board instead of a board of directors as this allows them to get advice without having to share decision-making power. As one second-generation member of a medium-sized family business owner has observed:

> I started with an advisory board in order to accumulate experience. If it doesn't work out, it is always easier to dissolve an advisory board than a board of directors.

Another stated:

> I want to receive advice, but I don't want to be directed. After gathering the advice from experts, I want to be able to decide by myself. I don't want to let the power out of my hands.[9]

Many family firms use an advisory board as a step toward a board of directors with outsiders. Regardless of whether it is set up as a board of advisors or directors, the effectiveness of this advisory body is dependent on its being active in both frequency of meetings and influence over the strategic direction of a business. A rubber stamp board filled with family and friends who are unwilling or unable to challenge the directions of a leader is not likely to be of any significant benefit to the firm. You may recall the critical role played by this advisory body in the regeneration of both Arbill Safety (Chapter 4) and the Illinois Consolidated Telephone Company (Chapter 2).

FAMILY MEETINGS

The least formal structure available to families in business is the periodic scheduling of family meetings. For an entrepreneurial family firm, few steps are more critical than initiating such meetings at early stages of a firm's life cycle and continuing them throughout the later stages. In the early stages of a firm, family meetings can be held around the kitchen table. As the families go through stages of life and may become dispersed, it becomes important to plan for family meetings so as to maintain open channels of communication. In larger firms and families, such meetings usually precede the more formal structures described below. In their monograph on family meetings, Aronoff and Ward made the case for engaging in those activities:

> Family meetings can help build a stronger family *and* a stronger business. They help the family plan for the future of the business in an orderly and constructive way. They can smooth such difficult transitions as the succession of new leadership or the professionalization of the business. They can avert painful and costly conflict by helping the family address early and openly the issues that inevitably arise in family business ownership.
>
> In fact, we believe family meetings are one of the two most important steps a business owner can take to ensure the continuity of the family

[9]Lambrecht, J., and Lievens, J. (2008). Pruning the family tree: Family business continuity and family harmony. *Family Business Review,* 21(4): 295–313.

business. (The other is to establish an active outside board of directors.) Once begun, family meetings often take on a momentum of their own, sparking family mission statements, family-education projects, shared vacations, philanthropic efforts, family histories, venture or scholarship funds and other creative efforts.[10]

Regardless of the size of a family, it is often useful to hold the family meetings away from the family home or business premises, as this helps to avoid distractions. The meetings provide family members an opportunity to bond, inevitably helping to understand each other better and build family harmony. Bastianich recommended that family meetings

- be held on a regular basis
- adhere to an agenda and document any agreements reached
- be run by a facilitator
- include younger family members as well as seniors
- encourage sharing and free-flow of ideas
- be nonconfrontational
- appoint an arbiter to ensure smooth progress of meetings.

She adds that family should invite an expert on some relevant topic and should even consider inviting a customer.[11]

FAMILY COUNCILS

Families in business create family councils for a variety of purposes, but typically to facilitate communication among family members and to formalize decision-making processes as they relate to the company. The council is a means of family governance. It is an organizational and planning arm for the family, allowing members to participate in shaping values, policies, and directions for the family regarding their relationships with the enterprise that led to the formation of the council.[12] Councils may formulate standards for family behavior, support educational programs, organize events, provide venues for conflict resolution, or perform other services for or on behalf of the family members.

Councils are sometimes structured in accordance with charters or constitutions or may evolve out of family meetings. Council members are typically elected to represent other relatives, but the formalized documents may provide for other means to select council members. In turn, the councils themselves may draft charters or by-laws for their functioning. The by-laws establish the rules of membership, which can range from all members of an extended family to a rotating, elected group of representatives. Councils are established to ensure that

---

[10]Aronoff, C.E., and Ward, J.L. (1992). *Family Meetings: How to Build a Stronger Family and a Stronger Business*. Marietta, GA: Business Owner Resources, p. 3.

[11]Bastianich, L. (2004). Savoring the family meeting. *Family Business*, 15(4): 16–18.

[12]Martin, H.F. (2001). Is family governance an oxymoron? *Family Business Review,* 14(2): 91–96.

members of the family, especially those not employed by the firm, feel informed about the company's health and direction, and to prepare policies that will resolve conflicts before they occur.

Family constitutions may be drafted before the formation of a council or may be instituted by a council. Constitutions are also known as protocols, and the term is sometimes used interchangeably with charters. Montemerlo proposed multiple benefits from adopting protocols such as providing opportunities for

- defining a common vision of the future
- providing a change catalyst to strengthen the company
- preparing for succession
- grooming responsible owners
- improving interpersonal relations, especially through better communication
- preventing and resolving conflicts.[13]

According to family business consultant Lansberg, there are typical components of a family constitution:[14]

- A mission statement that defines the family's fundamental desire to be in business together
- A statement of the family's fundamental values and beliefs
- A family code of behavior that specifies the family's norms and expectations with regard to how the members treat one another and conduct themselves
- Policies for regulating the relationship between the family and the business
- A performance policy
- A retirement policy
- A dismissal policy
- Stock redemption policies
- A noncompete agreement that all family shareholders are willing to abide by
- Job descriptions for the key positions in the governance structure
- Funding mechanisms for governance.

The Rules of Entry introduced to you in Chapter 6 (Appendix 6A) are likely to be part of the family constitution. Montemerlo cautioned that constitutions and protocols are not guaranteed to succeed. Causes of failure include different values among individuals, unhealthy attitudes of powerful family members, and the lack of trust among family members.

---

[13]Montemerlo, D. (2000). Regulating relations between family, ownership and company: The role and variety of formal agreements—some Italian experiences. In Panikkos, P. (Ed.). Tradition or Entrepreneurship in the New Economy? Proceedings of the Family Business Network Academic Research Forum, London, p. 215.

[14]Lansberg, I. (1999). *Succeeding Generations: Realizing the Dream of Families in Business.* Boston, MA: Harvard Business School Press. pp. 323–325.

FAMILY OFFICE

The financial success of many family businesses has led to the formalization of family investments. Family offices have been established to enable family members to invest as a group similar to private portfolio management firms, but without imposing those external costs. The primary purpose of a family office is to provide centralized planning for the investment of family wealth. Offices are created when families determine that they have a surplus beyond the immediate needs of the venture and the maintenance of family members, and when there are a substantial number of family members who are not directly involved in the business. An office provides economies of scale in buying and in reducing investment management costs. The theory behind such offices is that they will be efficient and effective in asset management. In addition, they often provide advisory services for family shareholders. According to de Visscher, the family office exists to perform the following:

- Provide stewardship of capital
- Tighten family bonds
- Determine rules of entry
- Help with family philanthropy
- Educate relatives
- Perpetuate heritage
- Maintain communication
- Resolve conflicts
- Review business plans
- Sponsor educational programs.[15]

The family office operates separate from the business and helps preserve and build wealth for shareholders who may not possess investment expertise.[16] Smaller family businesses sometimes make use of multifamily offices to reduce the operating expenses one firm would have to incur.

Family foundations are philanthropic entities designed to accumulate excess revenues from the firm and family members, to invest the contributions and receive tax-exempt returns, and to make charitable donations in accordance with the shared values of the family. For families whose enterprises have created wealth, the elders may decide that the time has come to "give back." They may work with the team running the business to form a philanthropic foundation carrying the name of the enterprise or the family. In their early stages, foundations are generally run by family members.

---

[15]De Visscher, F. (2008). A structure to aid large, dispersed families. In Spector, B. (Ed.). The *Family Business Shareholder's Handbook*. Philadelphia, PA: Family Business Publishing. pp. 73–74.

[16]Leach, P. (2007). *Family Businesses: The Essentials*. London: Profile Books.

In a study of 30 family foundations in the United States and Canada that have survived through at least two generations, Gersick suggested three commonly observed motivations for founding of foundations:

- Minimizing taxes
- Enacting a set of philanthropic values
- Promoting and strengthening family relationships and interactions.[17]

Although the purposes and administration of such foundations vary enormously, each must conform to tax regulations and relevant legislation in the countries in which it is located. Among the best known are the Ford Foundation and the Rockefeller Foundation. One that specializes in supporting entrepreneurship is the Kauffman Foundation, launched by and named for Ewing Marion Kauffman, founder of Marion Laboratories pharmaceutical company. Foundations are established as tax-exempt organizations through which families make charitable contributions that benefit their communities or particular social issues while enhancing the reputation of the family.[18]

SHAREHOLDER COUNCIL OR ASSEMBLY

In firms with a mix of family and nonfamily shareholders and majority and minority shareholders, the shareholder council is often found useful to provide a venue for different types of shareholders to express their perspectives and understand those of others. Where shareholders are geographically distanced, the board of directors or advisors should ensure that their perspectives are sought and taken into consideration in the strategic decision making of the firm.

Family firms that survive over generations face the challenge of complacent owners. Krister Ahlström captures this challenge as follows:

Family-owned companies that manage to survive into the third generation are vulnerable to the complacency of their owners. By then, the family takes for granted that the company will always be there to support them. They've been pampered and sent to the best schools. It's natural for them to think the business was handed to them by the gods and they are just along for the ride.[19]

Entrepreneurial family firms negotiate this challenge by distinguishing the family's role in management from ownership of the business. As they moved into the fifth generation, the Ahlström's decided the role of the family was to own but

---

[17]Gersick, K.C. (2006). *Generations of Giving: Leadership and Continuity in Family Foundations.* Lanham, MD: Lexington Books.

[18]Lansberg, I. (1999). *Succeeding Generations.* Boston, MA: Harvard Business School Press.

[19]Magretta, J. (1998). Governing the family-owned enterprise: An interview with Finland's Krister Ahlstrom. *Harvard Business Review,* January–February: 113–123, p. 119.

not to manage the firm. However, the family members were expected to be enlightened, not simply passive, owners of the firm. This was accomplished by holding formal training for all family members in their early 20s and 30s through three workshops run by experts from a university. Each workshop lasted two very full days focused on teaching the students what does it mean to be an owner? How is strategy formulated? What is personnel management? How are the company's values put into practice? How does the company budget its resources? What accounting principles does an owner need to master? What questions should an owner ask?[20]

An **executive or management council** is a top management team that meets regularly to discuss the developments and strategies to achieve the objectives of the firm. In the context of family firms, with a mix of family and nonfamily managers, this body gains particular significance as family members are more likely to meet in social gatherings. Entrepreneurial firm leaders try to ensure that the talented nonfamily employees are kept informed of the key issues and their input effectively used in decisions. Capable and talented nonfamily employees are likely to lose interest in making contributions to a firm where the strategic decisions are made around a family table.

GOVERNANCE OVER LIFE-CYCLE STAGES

One shoe does not fit all,[21] nor does the same shoe fit one over the life-cycle stages. Clearly, not all these structures and instruments are likely to be equally effective in all firms and at all life-cycle stages of a firm. Moreover, the selection of a governance kit that suits a firm at one stage of its life cycle may not be suitable in another stage. Timely adoption of appropriate governance mechanisms for the firm is the challenge entrepreneurial family firm leaders must face. Depending on the current and potential extent and mode of family involvement in the business, stage of the family and firm's life cycle, and size of the business, appropriate governance structures must be adopted. In general, the more the complexity and diversity of stakeholders, the higher the need for varied governance mechanisms.

As discussed earlier, in firms like Laird Norton Company or Ahlström, which are richly complex due to the numerous and differentiated shareholders, and multigenerational family members, all governance structures discussed in this chapter are likely to be useful. Many family firms are choosing the route of simplicity in ownership and management of their firms. A few studies in Europe suggest that the number of shareholders in the first-generation family firms (five to nine) does not differ significantly from those in multigenerational family firms

---

[20]Magretta, J. (1998). Ibid.

[21]Corbetta, G., and Salvato, C. (2004). The board of directors in family firms: One size fits all? *Family Business Review,* 17(2): 119–134.

(five to six).[22] This strategy of pruning the family tree from time to time seems to work well as family owners' commitment to the business has been found to correlate negatively to the number of shareholders in the business and positively to the relative amount of equity owned by the family member.[23]

On the basis of a study of 17 family firms that had pruned their family tree, Lambrecht and Lievens[24] concluded:

- Signals such as divergent owners' vision, uninterested or incompetent family members, highly capable and well-motivated nonfamily employees, competing family members or family branches—all indicate it is time to prune the family tree.

- Pruning the family tree entails that the remaining family owners and managers are the same persons or that the shareholders are concentrated in a single family branch, thereby simplifying the governance of a family firm.

- Timely pruning of the family tree is a worthwhile path to family harmony and business performance.

- Not pruning in time can generate a high opportunity cost and impose a burden on business performance.

- The aim of pruning is to keep the majority of shares in the hands of managing family owners. This does not mean that there cannot be passive shareholders but it does mean that such shareholders must act as responsible owners.

- When there are multiple shareholders in a pruned family firm, the CEO generally possesses more shares than other family members.

- While some family firms prune their family tree in one phase, others employ multiple phases of pruning. The latter eases the financial stress on the firm as the family sellers must be bought out by the family buyers.

- The value of the business is often determined by external advisors to ensure that fair value of the firm is determined.

- Financing of the buyout is often made feasible by using a payment plan, bank loans, or in cooperation of a venture capitalist.

- Family businesses that prune themselves before the generational transition save themselves a great deal of time, money, and effort.

[22]Labaki, R. (2007). *Contribution à la connaissance des liens familiaux dans les enterprises familiales francaises cotées: Renforcement versus atténuation.* Bordeaux: Université Montesquieu-Bordeaux IV; Westhead, P., Howorth, C., and Cowling, M. (2002). Ownership and management issues in first generation and multi-generation family firms. *Entrepreneurship and Regional Development,* 14: 247–269.

[23]Vilaseca, A. (2002). The shareholder role in the family business: Conflict of interests and objectives between non-employed shareholders and top management team. *Family Business Review,* 15(4): 299–320.

[24]Lambrecht, J., and Lievens, J. (2008). Pruning the family tree: Family business continuity and family harmony. *Family Business Review,* 21(4): 295–313.

- Pruning is a complex and delicate process. Family firm leaders are well advised to use expert help when simplifying their ownership, management, or governance.

In conclusion, the tool kit available to entrepreneurial family firms offers many choices in terms of family and business governance.

Enterprising family firm leaders adopt governance mechanisms, that is, systems of structures and instruments to efficiently direct, control, and promote accountability of their firms.[25] While they are aware of the importance of developing structures that enable them to routinely monitor and understand the needs and concerns of key stakeholders, they are wary of adding unnecessary complexity that might hinder the creativity and flexibility of their enterprise.

Either too much or too little support from governance mechanisms is likely to hinder the achievement of organizational objectives. When a family firm has a diversity of stakeholders involved in its ownership and management, it must be adequately supported by structures such as the shareholders' assembly or executive council to ensure that there is a forum for these legitimate and powerful stakeholders to express their perspectives. In the absence of such forums, these stakeholders are likely to use their pathways of influence to express themselves, thereby obstructing or slowing down progress toward firm objectives. On the other hand, when a firm has a simple ownership and management structure, too many governance mechanisms are likely to consume unnecessary resources, leading to inefficiencies and perhaps causing frustrations for those responsible to achieve organizational objectives. Timely adoption of appropriate governance mechanisms is necessary for the success of an entrepreneurial family firm.

Summary

- Various governance mechanisms—structures and/or instruments—are available for an entrepreneur to choose from. Savvy leaders adopt governance mechanisms that enable their entrepreneurial initiatives rather than unduly consume precious time and resources.
- Governance instruments such as partnership agreements, buy-sell agreements, wills, employment contracts, prenuptial agreements, and family constitutions can be used by the smallest of firms.
- An active board of advisors or directors has proven helpful for entrepreneurial family firms.
- Structures such as family meetings and family councils are useful to ensure that family members remain well informed about the business and have an accepted venue to share their perspectives.
- Governance structures related to family and nonfamily shareholders may include family office, family foundation, and shareholders' assembly.

---

[25]Neubauer, F., and Lank, A.G. (1998) *The Family Business—Its Governance for Sustainability.* London: Macmillan Business.

- Executive or management councils prove helpful in firms with a mix of family and nonfamily managers.
- Simplicity in terms of governance, management, and ownership can be achieved through timely pruning of the family tree.

Discussion Questions

1. What governance mechanisms are available to family firms? Can you distinguish mechanisms that focus on governance of family versus those that help govern the business?
2. Family business consultants contend that pruning the family tree to simplify the management, ownership, and governance of the family firm has many advantages. Do you agree with this strategy? What complications do you think can be caused by adopting this strategy?
3. If you were running your family's business and you were to propose that they form a family council, how do you think your relatives would react? What objections or concerns do you think they would raise?
4. If you ran a family business and formed a family council, how would you expect nonfamily employees to react? Do you think they would feel relieved or threatened? Why?

Learning Exercises

1. Locate an entrepreneurial family firm in your community. Develop a stakeholder map for this firm today and explain how the positions held by key stakeholders is likely to change over the next decade. What governance mechanisms are being used in this firm, and how effective has each proven to be?

Other Resources

- Gersick, K.E. (2006). *Generations of Giving: Leadership and Continuity in Family Foundations.* Lanham, MD: Lexington Books.
- Greiner, L.E. (1972). Evolution and revolution as organizations grow: A company's past has clues for management that are critical to future success. *Harvard Business Review,* 50(4): 37–46.
- Huse, M. (2007). *Boards, Governance and Value Creation.* Cambridge: Cambridge University Press.
- Lambrecht, J., and Lievens, J. (2008). Pruning the family tree: An unexplored path to family business continuity and family harmony. *Family Business Review,* 21(4): 295–313.
- Magretta, J. (1998). Governing the family-owned enterprise: An interview with Finland's Krister Ahlstrom. *Harvard Business Review,* 76(1): 113–123.
- Neubauer, F., and Lank, A.G. (1998). *The Family Business—Its Governance for Sustainability.* London: MacMillan Business.

- Spector, B., ed. (2006). *The Family Business Policies & Procedures Handbook.* Philadelphia, PA: Family Business Publishing Co.
- Ward, J.L. (2001). *Creating Effective Boards for Private Enterprises: Meeting the Challenges of Continuity and Competition.* 3rd ed. Marietta, GA: Family Enterprise Publishers.
- Zall, R. (2004). *The Board of Directors in a Family-Owned Business.* National Association of Corporate Directors.

CHAPTER

12

CONCLUSIONS: SECRET RECIPES OF ENTREPRENEURIAL FAMILY FIRMS

PRESERVING THE ENTREPRENEURIAL SPIRIT

The Grupo Ferré Rangel is predominantly a media group operating in Puerto Rico and the U.S. mainland. Now in its fourth generation, the company has 1,600 employees and generates annual revenues of $300 million. *El Nuevo Día*, the flagship newspaper, enjoys 50% market share and commands 80% of the newsprint advertising in Puerto Rico. The family, controlling shareholders of the NYSE-listed Puerto Rican Cement, approved the sale of that earlier-generation business to Cemex in 2002. That company itself had $250 million in annual revenues.

The family's first business was a foundry. As the company grew, it added paper and cement to the mix. Over the generations, the company expanded to Florida, Panama, and Cuba and then lost some of those businesses—in some cases, for obvious political reasons; in others, because the businesses were mismanaged. In the 1960s, the second-generation leader, Luis A. Ferré, entered politics and became the governor of Puerto Rico. Soon afterward, the company confronted a financial crisis that led to its restructuring and breakup. Some of the businesses, now owned by individual third-generation family branches, survived; others did not.

One of Luis Ferré's sons, Antonio L. Ferré, became the CEO of the cement company and bought a little daily newspaper in Ponce, Puerto Rico's southernmost city, for $400,000 from his father. The purchase of *El Día*, as it was named then, took place at a time when the northern and most populous city, San Juan, was controlled by two other papers, *El Mundo* and *El Imparcial*. In one generation, Ferré's little paper from a secondary city ended up taking 80% market share in the most important market on the island.

In collaboration with fourth-generation family members, Antonio Ferré grew the company by, among other things, launching a new publication—*Primera Hora*, a *USA Today*-style newspaper. The Grupo Ferré Rangel now consists of these two major papers plus a couple of smaller city newspapers, a Hispanic newspaper in Orlando, Fla., a printing company, an Internet company, a direct-marketing company, and a recycling company.

"Our success with continuity in this generation comes from learning from the failure of the second- and third-generation transitions," says María Luisa Ferré, fourth-generation president of the Grupo Ferré Rangel. "My father [Antonio L. Ferré] really set out to do it differently, and he approached it very conscientiously, with a lot of discipline, having learned in his generation that a group of entrepreneurially prone individuals without a coherent structure can get into a lot of trouble."

Perhaps because of the journalistic culture that runs in the family, the opinions of each of the children, however different, were constantly sought and appreciated as they grew up. "Our success in continuing the entrepreneurial spirit is a result of five professionals who knew they complement—they need—each other, to be successful," says María Luisa Ferré. "We respect each other and our differences. The siblings have selected me to lead them. We are entrepreneurs with a coherent structure among us. So the major distinction between us and the previous generation is the sense of confidence that comes from knowing that we now have a coherent structure to govern the relation between people who are naturally entrepreneurial."

She says that after the fourth generation joined Antonio in the top management team, its first value-added function was "the identification of problems and opportunities in the paper that Antonio did not see because his parallel responsibilities as CEO of Puerto Rican Cement made him over-committed. As a fourth generation, we also fundamentally bought into the idea that we have to grow, experiment, create new business plans, or we would end up becoming our own enemies."

Source: Poza, E. (2006). Building a family company that lasts. *Family Business*, 17(2): 39–43.

Questions

1. Why do you think Grupo Ferré Rangel was able to survive, given what María Luisa Ferré described as "the failure of second- and third-generation transitions"?

2. María Luisa describes herself as having been "selected" to lead the company. What are some procedures by which a president might be selected to head a family enterprise?

Family Business magazine provided the opening vignettes for each of our chapters. We deliberated over many stories in choosing one for this concluding chapter.

Do we bring things to a close with a family firm that survives or one that died? Or, with a large publicly traded family firm or a small independent one? Or, perhaps one, as with the Hayes family in Chapter 10, that sold out? There are lessons to be learned from each example. We settled on Grupo Ferré Rangel for a variety of reasons. A major one is the fact that, at the time of this writing, it still exists, and you can go to the company's Web site (www.grupoferrerangel.com) and see the top management team of five siblings. And you can speculate about the firm's future. Will the brothers and sisters continue to get along? Will the company survive to the next generation? Are the members of the fourth generation making efforts to prepare the fifth to be entrepreneurial leaders? If you read their corporate values, you will see the self-description of being "resourceful, creative, innovative, and agents of change," terms that we have argued characterize entrepreneurial family businesses that prosper.

In this concluding chapter, relying on past research, we compile a list of 25 tenets or principles that entrepreneurial family firms use to create value across the life-cycle stages of their leaders, families, products/services, markets, and the environment. The strategies and tactics that emerge from these tenets help instill or maintain the entrepreneurial spirit in the family and help family members to take entrepreneurial actions in the firm. Disciplined governance of the family and the firm becomes a core value. The mechanisms—structures and instruments—developed as a consequence of this discipline help to ignite and nurture the entrepreneurial spirit across generations and into ventures that family members launch/acquire and build. Our discussion starts with the family of origin, focusing on how **enterprising families**[1] infuse and nurture the spirit of entrepreneurship in family members. Then we highlight the tenets used by entrepreneurial family firms as they go through the four life-cycle stages of start-up, growth, maturity, and decline to ensure regeneration and value creation.

SEEDING ENTREPRENEURIAL SPIRIT IN A FAMILY

Before the business can be launched, someone must conceive of its eventual existence and recognize the opportunity. As discussed in Chapter 3,[2] **family of origin** and **family of attachment** significantly influence an individual's perspective on entrepreneurship. They may encourage or discourage the pursuit of entrepreneurial activities by family members. Relatives may support the launching of new enterprises or making innovative changes in existing family firms in several ways. For example, they may highlight the success of other entrepreneurial families or point toward the long-term, valued-added benefits of such actions. Alternatively,

---

[1]As you may recall from Chapter 1 (Figure 1.1), *enterprising families* are those that create value across generations, achieving longevity while sustaining their firm's competitive advantages over time.

[2]In Chapter 3, we described *family of origin* as the family in which we are born or adopted into, while we used the term *family of attachment* for the new family or families that we launch during the course of life by partnering with another individual and in most cases extending to include members of junior and/or senior generations.

they may diminish the entrepreneurial desires of family members by drawing attention to the potential of failure and the consequences of putting the savings of the individual or family in jeopardy. We offer five tenets that help enterprising families seed and grow the entrepreneurial spirit in family members.

1. ***Respecting Within-Family Differences:***   Enterprising families understand that not all members of a family are alike. Differences within family members are respected and nurtured. In entrepreneurial firms run by such families, junior-generation members are not expected to be clones of senior-generation leaders or family firm founders. Nor is one sibling expected to be a perfect replica of another. The dreams and talents of each individual family member are respected and nurtured.

   It is recognized that the skills that were critical for earlier life-cycle stages of a family firm are not necessarily the skills needed to grow the firm into future life-cycle stages. As firms move through life-cycle stages, different skills are needed for success as the passage of time brings new competitors, technologies, and a changing social and economic landscape in which the family firm must compete. The primary growth challenge amid evolving life cycles necessitates innovation and updated skills. Efforts are made to understand and build upon the inherent talents, abilities, and interests of each family member so as to develop the full potential and entrepreneurial abilities of each family member.

2. ***Role Modeling:***   Research suggests that more than half of business owners come from families in which a close relative has been self-employed.[3] While being in the vicinity of self-employed family members provides confidence to launch an entrepreneurial venture, only those who actually worked in this business were successful with their new ventures. Enterprising families seem to naturally use the opportunities of role modeling to imbue the spirit of entrepreneurship in family members.

   Close relatives who own businesses serve as entrepreneurial role models for family members as they understand what it means to operate an independent venture. By watching family members in business, lessons about how core values of integrity, conscientiousness, openness to new ideas, sharing and receiving, and fairness toward employees and other key stakeholders are implemented in the context of an entrepreneurial firm are learned. The effort and honesty it takes to maintain long-term relationships with customers, suppliers, creditors, and so on are brought to life through behaviors of self-employed entrepreneurial family members. It is not only the behaviors in the business arena that get noticed and absorbed by family members but also the nature of relationships of the senior generation with their siblings, parents, and distant relatives. Seeds of behavioral norms are sown in the families of origin and carried over into families of attachment.

---

[3]Fairlie, R.W., and Robb, A. (2007). Families, human capital, and small business: Evidence from the characteristics of business owners survey. *Industrial and Labor Relationship Review,* 60(2): 225–245

Families that do not currently own a business but wish to inculcate the entrepreneurial spirit in the next generation encourage family members to gain practical experience and develop business skills by working in other entrepreneurial firms that are well respected in their community. Family members are encouraged to gain new experiences and develop habits of conscientiousness and responsibility that prove useful for the pursuit of entrepreneurial opportunities.

3. *Practicing Entrepreneurial Skills:* Enterprising families provide opportunities to their members to practice and develop entrepreneurial skills in all stages of their lives. Such families strive to develop both the general business and enterprise-specific skills of their family members, as they understand the importance of such skills for success in entrepreneurial ventures. While general business skills refer to administrative and personnel management skills, enterprise-specific skills are focused on job- or industry-specific knowledge.[4]

Enterprising families with existing firms ensure that juniors get age-appropriate work responsibilities in the business and their performance is closely monitored. Once family members have mastered a particular set of business skills, they are moved on to other responsibilities as opportunities emerge. In cases where there is currently no business run by family members, similar opportunities outside the realm of family are sought after to help family members learn various aspects of the business, while understanding their own interests and talents. This strategy is often used by immigrant families as the first-generation immigrants take on jobs that become available to them. However, many of these immigrants work toward professionalization of the next generation or to prepare them to launch their entrepreneurial ventures in the adopted countries. Often the ventures of other immigrants are used to train family members in general and specific business skills so as to provide experiential learning in some of the fundamental entrepreneurial tasks of opportunity recognition, resource leveraging, and risk management.

In other cases where there is no entrepreneurial venture in the family at the moment, enterprising families nurture the entrepreneurial desires of junior family members by encouraging or supporting them to start smaller ventures such as the "car spa" or "lawn care services" run by the Roberts brothers as discussed in Chapter 5, or recycling of comic books by Fred DeLuca as a young boy before he opened his first Subway Restaurant[5] at 17 years of age. In still other instances, family members are encouraged to expand their sphere of knowledge and skills by participating in volunteer activities in their communities and by organizing events to raise funds for worthy causes. Such experiences help to build entrepreneurial confidence of family members, expanding their networks and leadership and business skills.

---

[4]Fairlie, R., and Robb, A. (2007). Ibid.
[5]Young Entrepreneurs Network. (No date). *Introduction to Franchising: Case Study:* SUBWAY® Restaurants, videotape, Marina Del Rey, CA.

4. *Educating for Business and Life:*   In addition to work experience, enterprising families encourage their members to gain educational training to broaden their knowledge. Unlike a few decades ago, when many entrepreneurs considered on-the-job training to be equally or even more important than going to college, enterprising families of the twenty-first century do not force in-class and on-the-job training into an either-or option. However, each family member is respected as an individual, and programs of study chosen are aligned with the talents and interests of each person. Ideally, generational family firms would like these talents to benefit the family firm. But, if such is not the case, individual development is given precedence over the needs of the family firm as it is understood that in today's competitive arena, the firm can only compete effectively by hiring family or nonfamily employees who are committed to and capable of growing the firm.[6] In addition, the watchword is *lifelong learning*. Astute entrepreneurs realize that learning does not end with formal schooling. Our study of life cycles teaches us that failing to learn and adapt leads to decline and death.

   In choosing educational programs, however, enterprising families encourage their members to join schools that provide not only excellent training in the foundations of chosen subjects, but also courses and programs focused on entrepreneurship and family business studies. Several universities now offer courses specific to entrepreneurship and family businesses that complement the business training. Many business schools around the world have majors and specializations in entrepreneurship and family business.[7] These programs are specifically geared to educate students to work in entrepreneurial family firms.

5. *Adhering to Rules, Roles, Responsibilities:*   Enterprising families communicate clearly. In such families, the rules of behavior in family and business, role of family in business, and responsibilities of family members at home and outside are clearly understood, followed, and monitored (Appendix 5A). Although strict adherence to rules could run against the grain of some entrepreneurs, family firms that successfully negotiate the overlap between family and business systems learn how to balance accountability and responsibility, with allowing family members leeway to test new approaches.

   When disagreements emerge, they are dealt with in a candid and respectful manner. This culture of clear communication is imbued in the family–of origin and carried on into the families–of attachment, sowing seeds for strong, respectful, and open relationships among family members, regardless of their mode and extent of involvement in the family firm. When family members do work with each other in the business, they have a strong foundation of basic rules of behavior to build from, trust, and open communications already developed from the family's culture.

---

[6]Sharma, P., and Irving, P.G. (2005). Four bases of family business successor commitment: Antecedents and consequences. *Entrepreneurship Theory and Practice*, 29(1): 13–33.

[7]For a list of universities and colleges with family business centers and programs, please check the Web site of the Family Firm Institute, http://www.ffi.org/default.asp?id=294.

LAUNCHING AN ENTREPRENEURIAL FAMILY FIRM

When most people see or hear the word *entrepreneur*, they think of someone who starts a business. It is the classic definition of business founder as risk taker. Research has now revealed that about 80 percent of new ventures are launched with significant involvement of family members in the business.[8] The extent of support a founder gets from his or her family can make the difference between the success and failure of a new venture. Family values inevitably seep into the firm, setting its foundational culture. Tenets that help develop a strong foundation for family firms are the following:

6. *Agreements in Writing:* One of the key advantages we attribute to family businesses is the trust among members. Family business owners sometimes feel that putting things in writing suggests a lack of trust. However, enterprising families understand the importance of dealing with family members in a professional manner to avoid conflicts resulting from miscommunication.

   For launching a new venture, practically all entrepreneurs depend on family resources. Entrepreneurial family firm leaders who successfully launch and grow ventures and maintain strong family relationships understand the critical importance of being grateful recipients of resources—financial, physical, social, and human (discussed at length in Chapter 6). They honor the commitments made to family givers to help launch their business and look for ways to return the gifts bestowed upon them as opportunities present themselves.[9] Family members who devote themselves to the firm are treated with as much respect and professionalism as are nonfamily members.

   Family firms that enjoy enduring family relationships and business performance tend to engage in clearly understood and respected agreements wherever there is a flow of resources between the family and business. For example, if capital is borrowed from a family member, the terms of repayments are agreed upon and honored. Similarly, family employees are paid at market rates, and terms of their employment are agreed upon and these agreements respected.

7. *Incubating Family Members and Enterprises:* Existing family-owned firms can serve as incubators for start-ups. Not only are business-owning relatives role models for entrepreneurs, they may also be the stimuli for launching the venture. Many entrepreneurial family firms branch out to different markets or product/service lines as the next generation of family members begins their entrepreneurial careers. These new ventures gain the advantage of growing under the umbrella of existing firms, while enabling the next-generation members to build the new entity as well as their entrepreneurial skills.

---

[8]Chua, J.H., Chrisman, J.J., and Chang, E.P.C. (2004). Are family firms born or made? An exploratory investigation. *Family Business Review,* 17(1): 37–54.

[9]Hoy, F., and Sharma, P. (2008). Entrepreneurial governance in the family firm. In Spector, B. (Ed.). *Shareholder's Handbook: Tips and Strategies for Effective Ownership and Stewardship of Your Family Company.* Philadelphia, PA: Family Business Publishing Co. pp. 10–12.

Although opportunities for market and product/service line expansion may be feasible for existing family firms, entrepreneurial families are careful not to force family members into predetermined roles. Instead, they encourage them to discover their own talents and passion, and then determine the appropriate career path for them within or outside the family firm. As an example, the husband and wife, co-owners of a rapidly growing business, came to one of the co-authors to complain about their son's job performance. They had given him a specific job description related to product sales and service but kept finding him spending his time on information technology projects, often for other companies. When asked whether they would have hired him if he had not been related to them, the couple looked at each other with sudden awakening and announced, no, they would not. They immediately returned to their firm and helped their son develop a business plan for his own information technology venture. That company has since surpassed the parents' firm in revenues.

8. *Learning from Failure:* Enterprising families know the power of failure and persistence. They also understand that the first venture that a family member launches is not necessarily going to be successful. Several reasons may cause failure of the first venture attempted by a family member. For example, she or he may have underestimated costs or efforts it would require to exploit an opportunity, miscalculated the appeal of the identified opportunity to the market, or made mistakes in hiring of employees or choosing partners. Enterprising families treat each attempt at new venture creation as an important part in the journey toward successful entrepreneurial creation.

Lessons from failures are idiosyncratic and sticky, and those learned through mistakes made by one generation are not easily transferrable to the next-generation family members. Although sharing of experiences is helpful, each generation needs opportunities to make their own mistakes and learn from them. Thus, each failure is used as a necessary step toward success and given its due respect as an opportunity to learn and grow a family's entrepreneurs. Failure of a venture must not be confused with failure of the individual. Each is encouraged to start small—learn from mistakes—and dream big.[10]

9. *Delegating:* The start-up stage of a venture necessitates hands-on and personal attention of the entrepreneur. While most founders have difficulty delegating tasks to others, successful entrepreneurs have the courage to delegate to family or nonfamily employees. Delegation is often accomplished very early in the life of a venture by using incremental steps, starting with routine tasks and increasing task complexity as confidence is gained. For example, Fred DeLuca and Dr. Peter Buck, the cofounders of Subway Restaurant, delegated the task of operating the stores to employees from the very first day they opened doors to customers. This strategy not only enabled them to stay focused on the strategic growth of their enterprise, but also

---

[10]Deluca, F., and Hayes, J.P. (2000). *Start Small, Finish Big*. New York: Warner Books.

empowered employees to build their business and entrepreneurial skills. In order for the entrepreneurial firm to succeed, however, it is critical that the family and nonfamily members held responsible work hard to prove worthy of such trust. Delegation in family firms provides opportunities to build generational partnership wherein the assets of maturity and youth are combined to mitigate the liabilities of newness and pleateauing.

10. ***Forming Advisory Boards:*** Entrepreneurial family firms sow the seeds of disciplined governance at the very early stages of the venture. This is done through written agreements, clear rules of family members' participation in the firm, and setting up an advisory board with external members. These mechanisms expose the family firm leaders to being held accountable for their performance and questioned by external parties. While not exercising legal authority, if carefully selected, the body of advisors can bring professionalism and accountability in entrepreneurial firms. As mentioned by María Luisa Ferré in the opening vignette, such structures can help entrepreneurial family members build their firm.

GROWING AN ENTREPRENEURIAL FAMILY FIRM

Businesses that survive for long periods of time tend to enter growth spurts. The growth stage may occur once or on multiple occasions. It may represent a short burst or may continue for years. If you look at the various lists of fast-growing companies (see *Inc.* magazine, *Hispanic Business* magazine, and others), you will find companies that have sustained growth rates. And you will see that many of them can be classified as family businesses. We think of growth as something positive for a business, but research suggests unplanned growth can put a family firm in jeopardy, straining both the business performance and family relationships. In the growth stage, the following tenets have been helpful for entrepreneurial family firms that survive over generational life cycles:

11. ***Managing Growth*** Leaders of successful entrepreneurial family firms understand that growth can be a two-edged sword. While it is good to be in a stage where survival is not the most critical concern, growth can highlight limitations in the founder or his or her family members. Founder characteristics that brought about the birth of the venture may work against the firm when growth opportunities arise. The successful entrepreneur may have provided that 24/7 dedication at the start-up stage of the venture but may not have the capacity to carry that workload when expansion begins. While we encourage founders to engage in delegation even in the start-up stage (tenet #9), it becomes a "must do" in the growth stage.[11] The hands-on focus of the founders that is crucial to launch a venture can become a hindrance in the

---

[11]Greiner, L.E. (1972). Evolution and revolution as organizations grow: A company's past has clues for management that are critical to future success. *Harvard Business Review,* 50(4): 37–46.

growth stage if she or he is unable to delegate when the company needs more talent to manage the growth. It is only by delegation that she or he can explore strategic entrepreneurial endeavors for the firm. For example, when a successful retail store expands beyond a single location, the complexity of management increases geometrically.

Family members that were crucial for the launch stage may not have the abilities to handle the complexity of growing a firm. Long-lived family firms strategically manage growth of their firms by paying careful attention to their own life-cycle stage and that of their families. For example, when a family is going through life stages such as caring for ailing family members or providing for university education expenses for children, it may not be the best time to engage in business expansion as well. On the other hand, when family resource needs are less, expansion may be more feasible. The desires and talents of next-generation family members should be taken into consideration when deciding the timing and pathway of growing the firm.

12. *Professionalizing the Team:* Entrepreneurial growth is all about putting the right talent in the right places at the right time. Whether this talent is available within the family or not is a difficult question for family firms to address objectively, as emotions are involved. Family members who were absolutely critical and dependable in the start-up stage may prove to be liabilities when the firm grows. As the market demand increases, specific skills become more important. Those family members who were loyal at start-up may now not be able to satisfy performance demands for the company as it has evolved. How can an entrepreneur fire a relative? As the venture begins to take off, relatives expect the firm to provide employment for any family member in need. How can the entrepreneur refuse relatives' requests to be hired by the growing firm?

To attract and retain the best talent among family as well as nonfamily members, entrepreneurial family firms professionalize. Despite being stretched thin, successful entrepreneurs take time to establish some policies for recruiting, retaining, and promoting employees. They follow the best practices of hiring, recruitment, and performance evaluation. These principles are applied to both family and nonfamily members. For employment in the firm, clear position descriptions and qualifications needed are developed. Applications are invited, candidates screened, and hired. All are welcome to apply, but the best candidates get the job. Advisory boards often prove extremely helpful with recruitment and promotion for key positions in the firm.

13. *Involving the Family in Ownership:* Not only is it critical to put into place rules of entry for new employees, as the firm grows and more resources are needed, but also it becomes important to reevaluate the participation of family members in the firm's ownership as well. For a growing firm, revenues tend to lag expenses. The company may not have funds to pay bills or may not have the skill set to reach the next level of customer demand. Growth requires borrowing of funds from external parties as well as reinvesting some of the firm's profits into the business.

Entrepreneurial family firm leaders understand that it is a mistake both for the firm's growth and family relationships to assume that the relatives who invested or loaned funds to start a business should all continue as owners in the growth stages as well. It is important to reevaluate the ownership structure, discuss the vision of the firm with those early investors, and provide an option to cash out. The rules for exit and entry of owners need to be developed and legal agreements put into place. The growth stage offers a window of opportunity to exit not only underperforming employees but also demanding investors. Strategic pruning of the family tree at this stage can lead to healthy growth of the enterprise and family relationships.[12]

14. *Creating a Family Council:* When the entrepreneurial firm begins to grow and it becomes evident that there is a sustainable venture, it is a good time to form the family council so that the relatives affected by the business can come to terms with how that relationship will grow and develop. A family council can help to formulate policies on the conditions for family members to join the company and for the distribution of profits. It helps to govern the family involvement in business and the role of business in the family so that policies can be developed before they are needed. Enterprising families avoid many serious problems down the road by proactively putting into place this formalized system of family governance.

15. *Growing Through Successors:* As mentioned before, family firms can experience multiple growth stages for various reasons. Environmental conditions that stimulate growth include technological innovations and legislative/regulatory actions. Successful family firm leaders stay attuned to their competitive environments, fostering an entrepreneurial spirit in the company that extends beyond the top management.

Often, growth spurts follow management and ownership transitions as successors almost always bring new approaches and management styles. If the successor has been developed to be entrepreneurial, resurgence of a mature or declining company may well follow. For a business that enters a growth stage once a generation, the impact on the organizational culture can be traumatic. Employees, customers, creditors, and others have been accustomed to steady behavior and may not react to rapid change with enthusiasm. On the other hand, many of these people may have been troubled by the stagnation or decline they have observed and may applaud the new initiatives.

The burden is on the successor to recognize the situation she is inheriting and to engage in effective management practices that would be appropriate for either a family or nonfamily enterprise. The complicating factors of the family business are to value the history and traditions of the preceding family members and, if the predecessors are still living, to continue to give them

---

[12]Lambrecht, J., and Lievens, J. (2008). Pruning the family tree: An unexplored path to family business continuity and family harmony. *Family Business Review,* 21(4): 295–313.

a feeling of involvement and appreciation while simultaneously encouraging them to acquire new, external interests. Enterprising successors are cautioned to approach family members early to assess their entrepreneurial dispositions and to develop them as appropriate.

No growth stage can be sustained forever. The issue is to ensure that growth will be followed by maturity, not by decline or death. Facilitators used by entrepreneurial family firms to accomplish this are discussed next.

MATURING FAMILY FIRMS

Some family firms may never experience the rapid increases in sales associated with the growth stages and may move directly from start-up to the slow- or no-growth stage of maturity. These tend to be companies that serve local markets, employment substitution lifestyle ventures focused on hobbies rather than growth, or part-time enterprises with no expectation of job creation. In this book, we have been focusing on entrepreneurial family firms that are focused on cross-generational wealth and value creation. Such enterprises, if they survive independently, will level off or plateau at some point following growth. Many factors may contribute to a company entering a maturity stage, among them market saturation, economic conditions, substitute products/services, and management intent. The critical idea that entrepreneurial family firm leaders must keep in mind is that even if they choose not to grow their firm beyond a certain level, they cannot assume that everything will remain stable and that they can prosper without changing. If a firm is to survive, an entrepreneurial culture cannot be allowed to die in the maturity stage. The following strategies and tactics have been found useful in maintaining the entrepreneurial spirit in a mature family firm:

16. *Tiered Innovating:*   Entrepreneurial family firms engage in multiple levels of innovation simultaneously.[13] Incremental innovations are efficiency-focused improvements on the existing products/services, markets, or processes used by the firm. Such innovations help secure revenues from the core business to meet the operational expenses of the firm. Progressive innovations are movements into related markets, products, or services. Extensions of current business, such innovations help these firms to reap maximum benefits from expertise already developed. Radical innovations[14] are moves into significantly different industries, technologies, or markets. They are aimed to reduce the dependence of the firm on maturing industries and markets. Such initiatives of renewal ensure sustained high performance over environmental life-cycle stages.

---

[13]Bergfeld, M.M.H. (2008). *Global Innovation Leadership—Towards a Practical Framework for the Strategic Development of Worldwide Innovation Competence.* PhD diss., Manchester Business School.

[14]Bergfeld, M.M.H., and Weber, F.M. (in press). Dynasties of innovation: Highly performing German family firms and the owners' role for innovation. *International Journal of Entrepreneurship and Innovation Management.*

17. ***Entrepreneurial Career Planning:*** One obvious strategy for mature family businesses is to prepare prospective successors for governance roles in the company. We need not reemphasize our call for early family preparation. In the mature business, it is likely that a succeeding generation has had family values instilled, completed formal education, possibly gained work experience, and is joining or advancing in the firm. By this stage, the family councils should have devised protocols or drafted constitutions, often with stipulations regarding educational attainment prior to entering the business. Along the same lines, a requirement may be included that the family member must obtain some minimal level responsible work experience in an organization not owned or controlled by the family.

Some of the actions that successful family enterprises have taken to develop the next generation of leadership are

- assigning a nonfamily manager or director as a mentor
- sharing information about the company with the next generation
- sharing decision-making authority with potential successors
- designing an educational program, one that could involve learning about the company, the industry, and the leadership
- designing a career development plan to acquire experience, both internal and external to the firm.

18. ***Financial Planning:*** Entrepreneurial family firms proactively plan both for estate and ownership transition. While it is not uncommon to hear entrepreneurs discuss eventualities with the phrase "if I die," leaders of entrepreneurial family firms do not ask the question of "if," but of "when." Although emotionally taxing for them and their family members, the termination of the entrepreneur's life is a fact that is prepared for in advance.[15]

Research suggests that in more than 90 percent of cases,[16] the business is the primary source of the owning family's income and financial security. With longer career and life spans, it is not just the death of the firm's leader that is a concern. Instead, financial planning must ensure that the lifestyle needs of senior generations can be adequately met, the firm's need to regenerate can be financed, and ownership transition can take place. Failure to plan may result in a family losing a healthy business with a bright future. Professional advisors are critical at this stage.

19. ***Involving Family in the Community:*** Where do entrepreneurial firm leaders go to find reliable advisors or look for opportunities to regenerate the firm? And where do they look when hiring key personnel for a family firm? Community involvement is the answer to these questions. While social networks are critical at all stages in the life of a family firm, having trusted advisors becomes particularly crucial in the mature stages of the

---

[15]Lansberg, I. (1988). The succession conspiracy. *Family Business Review*, 1(2): 119–143.

[16]http://www.familybusinesssurvey.com/survey/survey.htm

firm. By playing an active role in professional associations and voluntary activities in the community, entrepreneurs build their networks and trusted relationships, while gaining access to developments in their industry and community. Family business owners are welcome in associations such as the Canadian Association of Family Enterprise (CAFE), Family Business Australia (FBA), Family Business Network (FBN), and Family Enterprise U.S.A (FEUSA). In addition, family business centers and forums, typically associated with universities, often host programs that are good venues to meet other family business owners and advisors. The Family Firm Institute (FFI) is an excellent source for meeting qualified family business advisors. Of course, with any of these networks, family business leaders need to spend a few years getting to know the individuals so as to choose the ones that are a good fit for their family firm.

20. *Evolving with Macroenvironmental Cycles:*   Firms mature when industry and market saturation is reached, or demand for the products/services reduces due to changes in economic life cycles or social, demographic, and technological trends. Entrepreneurial family firm leaders maintain awareness of these changes and adopt various strategies to adapt their firm to these changes. Moreover, their firm is tailored to evolve with macroenvironmental life-cycle changes. New ideas are encouraged in the firm. High family identification with the firm is a common occurrence in family firms. However, in entrepreneurial family firms, this identity alignment is not translated into resistance to change. Instead, it is redirected toward continuous improvements and identifying with the entrepreneurial spirit of the firm rather than a particular set of products, services, or markets.

REGENERATING A DECLINING FAMILY FIRM

No whistle is blown, no lights flash, no one announces when the decline stage begins. It tends to be something individuals and organizations drift into. The drift reflects the failure of the top management to stay attuned to changing conditions or to listen to those who are advising them of the changes. For people, the decline cannot be prevented. It can be deferred by any number of actions. Health may be declining because of poor nutrition, lack of exercise, avoidance of medications, and so on. By improving a personal regimen, people can restore their health and, in turn, reinvigorate their businesses, at least in the short term. Sometimes, retirement is the genesis of a new and more exciting lifestyle. As explained in an earlier chapter, though, by not preparing for retirement, some entrepreneurs have accelerated the decline.

For family firms, however, decline is not inevitable. The problem is often inertia, which comes about when the top management adheres to past strategies that once served the company well, but which have lost their relevance. In such situations, the decline may be too slow to be recognized by entrenched leadership until it is too late. As we have made clear throughout this book, our recommendation at this stage is entrepreneurial governance of the family firm. Seeds of such governance are sown in the family and carried over into the business from the early stages of its life cycle. How can the entrepreneurial attitudes and behaviors that formed the venture in the first place be sustained or rekindled at this point in the life of the firm? How can family firm leaders resist the tendency to remain on a course that worked so well for so long? Tenets often used to regenerate a family firm that has slipped into decline or to avoid such slippage include the following:

21. *Accepting Joint Responsibility:* There is no question that overt efforts to build organizational cultures that cultivate creativity and innovation, foster calculated risk taking without punishment, and nurture external linkages will enhance the chances for long-term survival. But what happens when that preparation has not been done? Will all be lost, or is it still possible to recover and regenerate? The first inclination of many family members is to blame the senior generation for the decline of a family firm. But entrepreneurial family firms that succeed over generations of life cycles think twice about such an approach. Instead, in such firms, senior- and junior-generation members work together toward innovative solutions to regenerate the family firm. Often, nonfamily members and advisors prove helpful to accomplish this objective.

22. *Bridging Generations:* Many successful family firms turn to outside, non-family members as interim leaders. This strategy is particularly useful when senior-generation leaders wish to retire or must reduce their involvement in the business due to health or other reasons but the next-generation family members are not yet ready or prepared to take on senior leadership roles in the business. Trusted nonfamily leaders provide a bridge and a buffer between the generations. They help prepare the successors for their coming roles in ways that the relatives had been unable to do. For other companies, the solution may not be as drastic as bringing in outside leadership, but may, instead, make use of outside consultants. These third-party interventions can often diffuse the volatile interactions of the principals. Consultants can become communication channels when the relatives have such embedded histories that they have stopped listening to each other.

23. *Trusting Advisors:* Another important facilitator in family firms that endure over generations of leaders, life cycles of products, markets, and economies is the capable and trusted advisors. Such advisors tend to have an intimate knowledge of the family and confidential information about the firm, in many instances through their professional roles as accountants or lawyers for the family firm.[17] However, they move beyond this professional relationship status as their breadth and depth of competence, understanding of family dynamics, and vision help them earn the "right to be heard" and

---

[17]Strike, V. (2008). *Mindful Governance: The Role of the Most Trusted Advisor in Family-Controlled Firms.* Unpublished doctoral dissertation, University of Western Ontario, London, Canada.

capture the attention of family members of different generations. Most trust-ed advisors have been found to have a "strong 'sense of self' including being comfortable in their own skin, not having an ego, not taking things personal-ly, not always having to win, knowing you are not always right, and having a low profile."[18] Such advisors help in making more issues and answers avail-able for family firm leaders and help them question assumptions and norms, which in turn enables more encompassing decisions. They also play an inte-gral role in family dynamics and relationships by helping members under-stand their roles within the larger collective and thinking about decisions that are in the best interest of the whole.

24. ***Embracing Progress:***   More often, we see intransigence on the part of the top management. This involves a refusal to accept change. It is often reflect-ed in such statements as, "We tried that before," or "Our customers won't like that," or "That would be too expensive." In the extreme, founding entrepre-neurs have become jealous of their children's capabilities. They will not accept that the next generation can measure up to their accomplishments. They hold them back, damaging the self-confidence of prospective succes-sors. In such cases, there is little beyond revolution that will bring about a positive result with the firm. Revolutions, however, are unlikely to result in happy, cohesive families. Entrepreneurial family firms carry the spirit of change and progress in them through disciplined governance of family and firm and continuous innovation.

25. ***Orienting Toward the Future:***   While past accomplishments of individuals, family, and their firms are respected, enterprising families remain future ori-ented. Research[19] has indicated that neither the large-scale rebellious rejec-tion of the past nor a blind conservative attachment helps family firms succeed after generational transitions. Instead, it is those who are able to blend progressive attitudes and core foundational values such as hard work and integrity that sustain entrepreneurship across generations of leaders, products, and industry life cycles.

Declines can be turned into regenerations. Achieving the turnarounds is not automatic. In this book, we have provided you with strategies and tactics that have been found to work in family businesses. We have all heard the cliché, "We'll cross that bridge when we come to it." Well, when you know where the bridge is, the kind of condition it is in, which paths to the bridge are full of obstacles, and which are smooth, why wait until you get there when a little preparation in advance can smooth the crossing?

In the first chapter of this book, we encouraged you to treat reading this as a voyage of discovery. We now offer our wish for smooth sailing for you and your family business. In these pages, you have discovered the knowledge that has

---

[18]Strike, V. (2008). Ibid, p. 106.

[19]Miller, D., Steier, L., and Le-Breton Miller, I. (2003). Lost in time: Intergenerational succession, change, and failure in family business. *Journal of Business Venturing*, 18(4): 513–531.

been accumulated about starting and managing a family enterprise, one capable of surviving across generations. But we also leave you with the reminder: Every family business is unique in its own way. You must ultimately chart your own course. We have given you guidelines, drawing especially from what research is showing us from life-cycle models. As you seek success for yourself and your family, you do not need to learn everything by trial and error. Make use of the knowledge that was accumulated for you. But as an entrepreneur, nothing here should stifle your creativity and innovativeness. Challenges await! Make them opportunities!

Summary

- Enterprising families seed the entrepreneurial spirit in their families by
  - respecting within family differences and developing the full potential of all family members
  - senior generations' role modeling both in terms of acceptable behavior in the business as well as the family
  - providing opportunities for family members to practice entrepreneurial skills
  - pursuit of formal education by all family members in areas of interest
  - clarity of rules, roles, and responsibilities of each family member in family and business.
- In the birth stage, facilitators used by entrepreneurial family firms to lay strong foundations for generational value creation include the following:
  - Clearly understood and respected agreements among family members regarding their role in family and business
  - Enabling development of new ventures under the rubric of existing family firms through family incubators
  - Acceptance of failure as part of learning process
  - Delegation
  - Setting up an advisory board.
- In the growth stage of the enterprise, following facilitators prove helpful:
  - Engaging in managed growth, keeping in mind the life-cycle stages of family and key individuals involved
  - Professionalization—developing policies, systems, and routines
  - Reevaluating family's involvement in the ownership of the growing firm and prune the family tree as appropriate
  - Forming a family council to develop policies regarding family involvement in business
  - Using transitions in leadership to grow the firm.
- Maturing family firms depend on the following facilitators:
  - Planning for entrepreneurial career paths for family and key nonfamily members
  - Proactive financial planning to ensure that needs of the family members and the firm are well attended to

o Increasing involvement in professional and local community
o Evolving the firm along with changes in the environmental life cycles
o Engaging in multiple layers of innovation.
* Family firms in declining stage can regenerate using the following strategies:
o Junior and senior generations avoid laying the blame on the other but engaging in joint efforts to regenerate the business
o Using bridge generation of nonfamily members to lead or turn around the firm when such renewals are beyond the ability or interests of family members
o Developing most trusted advisors and using them well
o Embracing progress while preserving the core values of the firm
o Being guided by future opportunities and possibilities, rather than being directed by past achievements.

Discussion Questions

1. What venture opportunity ideas have you developed from comments or actions of any of your relatives?
2. Of the 25 facilitators that help build entrepreneurial spirit across life-cycle stages of individuals, families, and firms, which ones do you think are the most critical? Why?
3. Using ideas presented in this article, what do you think you can do as an individual to build your entrepreneurial skills?
4. Can you think of five strategies that your family could adopt to help build the entrepreneurial spirit of family members?
5. The next-generation family members can help in the resurgence of a mature or declining family firm. Go through the chapter opening vignettes in this book to develop a list of strategies that the next-generation members have found helpful for regeneration of their family firm.

Learning Exercises

1. Pick a business in your community that carries a family name. Does their its Web site tell the story of the family that founded the company?
2. Check the archives of your local newspaper. Review the obituaries. How long does it take you to find someone who was a business owner? Can you determine if any of the survivors listed in the obituary are still with the firm?
3. Find a company listed in the *Fortune* 500 that has members of the founding family still involved as executives or board members. Is that company in the same line of business it was in when it was original created?
4. Think of a local firm that has done well across few generations of leaders, product/service, and industry life cycles. Interview two members of this family to understand what strategies are used by this family firm to build entrepreneurial skills of family and nonfamily members?

Other Resources

- Deluca, F., and Hayes, J.P. (2000). *Start Small, Finish Big*. New York: Warner Books.
- Hughes Jr., J.E. (2007). *Family — The Compact among Generations: Answers and Insights from a Lifetime of Helping Families Flourish*. New York: Bloomberg Press.
- Ward, J. (2004). *Perpetuating the Family Business: 50 Lessons Learned from Long-Lasting, Successful Families in Business*. New York: Palgrave MacMillan.
- Canadian Association of Family Enterprises, http://www.cafecanada.ca/
- Family Business Australia, http://www.fambiz.org.au/
- Family Firm Institute, http://www.ffi.org/
- *Family Business* magazine, www.familybusinessmagazine.com
- Family Business Network, http://www.fbn-i.org/
- Leadership in Family Enterprise, http://www.patandpaul.com/
- National Federation of Independent Business, www.nfib.com
- Rural Minnesota Life, Department of Family Social Science, University of Minnesota, http://fsos.cehd.umn.edu/projects/mnlife.html
- United States Small Business Administration, http://www.sba.gov/

GLOSSARY

Assets of maturity consist of entrepreneurial experiences of the leaders, higher levels of their self-efficacy, and deeper pockets of networks to draw from.

Attitude is described as a fairly stable evaluative tendency to respond consistently to some specific object, situation, person, or category of people.

Bankruptcy is a legally declared condition of a firm's inability to pay its creditors, leading to a restructuring or even termination of the firm.

Beliefs govern the pathways that we think will lead to the desired outcomes. Research indicates that people settle in occupations that are a good fit with their beliefs and values.

Birth order refers to a person's rank by the sequence of birth among his or her siblings.

Business angels may be friends and other wealthy individuals who invest their money in new and young firms being launched by entrepreneurs whom they know and trust. While the size of such investments may be lower in comparison to other sources of funds such as public offerings or venture capitalists, the advantages lie in the potential of longer time horizons and lower threat of liquidity and patient investment.

Co-preneurs are couples who form companies together.

Complementary assets are capabilities or assets that are needed in conjunction with the new products or services.

Creative destruction explains the destruction of status quo by entrepreneurs who introduce radical new products, services, or business concepts that destroy the old order.

Cruising kin are kin leading a plateaued family firm that has not introduced any new products/services, processes, or markets over last few years.

Decline is the stage when a firm moves from no or slow growth to negative growth as it begins losing its customers.

Degrees of newness refers to the extent of newness in a new venture on three key dimensions—products/services, markets, and personnel involved. **Product expansion ventures** are launched to serve new products or services in an existing market or to customers with whom the founders are well familiar with. **Market expansion** ventures are launched to open new markets for existing products or services. **Absolutely new ventures** are launched to serve new products or services in new markets. Any of these ventures may be launched by an experienced entrepreneurial team that has launched ventures together earlier, or by new entrepreneurial team members—the latter increases another degree of newness to the venture.

Demographic trends are related to the changes in population over time and space. Changes in rate of growth, distribution, household size and structure, education, gender, and so on can all have important implications for the size of the market that is of interest to a firm.

Economic life cycles refer to the fluctuation—expansion, stagnation, or decline—in a national economy.

Effective resource management involves (1) structuring, i.e., acquiring, accumulating, and divesting resources so that they are available to the firm as needs and opportunities emerge; (2) bundling or integrating resources to form capabilities; and (3) leveraging, i.e., mobilizing, coordinating, and deploying resources to exploit capabilities to avail advantage of market opportunities.

Entrepreneur is the one who creates a new venture, whether in a start-up context or in an established organization (private, public, or nonprofit). This person is distinguished not because she or he necessarily came up with the idea, but by the fact that she or he implemented an innovative concept either successfully or unsuccessfully.

Enterprising families are families seeking transgenerational wealth creation and understand the importance of continuous innovation and regeneration through all stages of their existence so as to ensure longevity.

Entrepreneurial family firms are firms that engage in innovative actions across generations of leaders and product and economic life cycles. Large or small in size, such firms are influenced by *enterprising families* that create value across generations and achieve longevity while sustaining their firm's competitive advantages over time.

Entrepreneurial human capital is the set of knowledge and skills that individuals bring to bear to create and exploit market opportunities. It consists of physical, intellectual, psychological, and moral dimensions.

Entrepreneurial process consists of the following steps: opportunity recognition, concept development, resource needs assessment, resource acquisition, implementation and management, and harvesting or exit.

Entrepreneurial skills are the abilities required to create value in the context of a new venture or an established organization. They include creativity, innovation, opportunity identification and assessment, risk management, resource leveraging, bootstrapping, and guerrilla capabilities.

Entrepreneurship is the process of creating value by bringing together a unique combination of resources to exploit an opportunity and the pursuit of this opportunity without regard to resources controlled.

Evolutions continue during a stage as each is marked by specific characteristics and incremental changes in organizational practices.

Executive or management council is a top management team that meets regularly to discuss the developments and strategies to achieve the objectives of the firm.

Explicit knowledge is knowledge that can be codified and transmitted in formal and systematic language.

Familiness describes the stocks of social, human, financial, and physical capital resources in a firm that result from the interactions between family and business. Over time, levels of these stocks can either increase or decrease, in one or both systems. While the reduction of stocks indicates a negative or **constrictive** influence of one system on the other, enhanced stocks reflect positive or **distinctive** influences.

Family is a group of people affiliated through bonds of shared history and a commitment to share a future together while supporting the development and well-being of individual members.

Family businesses are organizational entities in which either the individuals who established or acquired the firm or their descendants significantly influence the strategic decisions and life course of the firm, leading to success or failure of the business. The family influence might be exerted through management and/or ownership of the firm.

Family business innovation is the generation or introduction of novel processes or products as a consequence of interactions between family members of one or more generations.

Family council is a means of family governance that allows members to participate in shaping values, policies, and directions for the family regarding their relationships with the family enterprise.

Family entrepreneurial orientation is the entrepreneurial orientation in a family that is nurtured in each generation and transmitted into succeeding generations.

Family foundations are philanthropic entities designed to accumulate excess revenues from the firm and family members, to invest the contributions and receive tax-exempt returns, and to make charitable donations in accordance with the shared values of the family.

Family genogram is a visual representation that simultaneously captures the family tree and key relationships and events in a family's development over time.

Family incubator is the unit in which an individual acquires foundational skills that can be transferred to other contexts and enable the successful pursuit of entrepreneurship.

Family office provides centralized planning for the investment of family wealth.

Family of origin is the family in which we are born or adopted and spend the preadulthood and part of provisional adulthood years of our life.

Family/ies of attachment refers to the new family or families we launch during the course of life by partnering with another individual and in most cases extending to include members of junior and/or senior generations. It is in this family that a large proportion of a person's life is spent.

Family life-cycle models attempt to capture the simultaneous changes occurring in a family as the system evolves over time. Four stages of family life cycles are (1) formation of new family through marriage or cohabitation (birth), (2) joining of new family members through birth or adoption (growth), (3) parenting of these new family members so as to prepare them for independent lives (maturity), and (4) launching these members to form new families themselves while accepting shifting generational roles (decline).

Gazelles are family businesses with a high growth potential that are launched with an intention to harvest benefits from growth in a short time. Their exit strategy may include merging or being taken over by a larger corporation.

Global start-ups or multinational ventures are companies that have been created specifically to exploit international business opportunities. Immigrant families with relatives in other countries who can engage in trade through family members are prime examples of global start-ups.

Governance mechanisms are aimed at establishing the overall strategy for the firm including the extent and mode of family involvement in it, setting performance standards and codes of conduct so as to represent the owners of the firm and guide management. Two mechanisms available to govern family firms are the (1) governance structures or bodies that meet at regular intervals and (2) legal or social contractual instruments that are written and binding on all parties involved.

Growth is the stage when a venture becomes a workable business entity. It has sufficient number of customers who have accepted its products/services, and it has satisfied their needs enough to retain their business.

Habitual entrepreneurs are distinguished from novice entrepreneurs (first-time venture creators) by having held an equity stake in two or more businesses that they might have established, purchased, or inherited.

Incremental innovations are efficiency-focused improvements on the existing business without significant changes in the products/services, markets, or processes used by the firm. Such innovations ensure a secure base of core business that generates revenues for the firm to meet its expenses and support its growth-oriented innovative initiatives.

Individual life-cycle models suggest that human beings go through stages of life influenced by a combination of biological (age) and sociological (era in history through which they are living) imperatives. The personal and professional aspirations of firm leaders depend on life stage. Six stages of individual life cycles are preadulthood (birth through 15); provisional adulthood (16–20); early adulthood (31–45); middle adulthood (46–60); late adulthood (61–75); and late-late adulthood (over 75).

Industry is the set of suppliers or producers of a particular product or service.

Innovation refers to the conversion of knowledge and ideas into benefits, which may be for commercial use or the public good, and which may include new or improved products, processes, or services.

Insolvency is a firm's inability to pay its bills when they are due. If left unattended, insolvency can lead to bankruptcy.

Liabilities of newness describe the problems that newly formed organizations face which render them prone to failure.

Life cycle is a series of stages through which something (as an individual, culture, or manufactured product) passes during its lifetime.

Life expectancy is a statistical measure of the average length of survival of a living entity and is often calculated separately for differing genders and geographic locations. It means the expected age at death for a given human population

Macroenvironment cycles include the economic, industry, and product/service market life cycles that impact the external environment of a firm, determining the opportunities presented and challenges posed.

Management provides leadership of operations and is responsible for the actual work of the company.

Market is the set of buyers or consumers of the product or service.

Maturity is the stage when an organization has established its niche with loyal customers, kinks in production processes or service offerings have been straightened, employees have well-established roles, and cash flow is not a problem anymore. The company provides stable income and a lifestyle that the founding team feels comfortable with. The business is successful, but not growing much.

Nascent entrepreneurs are individuals who are actively involved in thinking about creating a new venture either independently or as part of an existing family or nonfamily firm.

Necessity entrepreneurs start businesses because they are pushed into such careers by need.

Opportunistic entrepreneurs are those who intentionally want to be in business for themselves. They may be pulled by an opportunity that they or others have recognized.

Organizational life-cycle models maintain that growing organizations go through distinguishable phases of development, each with relatively calm periods of growth interspersed by revolutionary stages of substantial change and turmoil. Although a varied number of organizational life-cycle stages have been proposed in the literature, most of these follow a pattern of birth, growth, maturity, and death or decline.

Paralysis by analysis is the term used for nascent entrepreneurs who scan so many opportunities that they exhaust themselves and never start, or become confused by the comparisons, or bypass good ideas in search of the perfect one.

Personality is the relatively stable set of psychological characteristics that influences the way individuals interact with their environment. It summarizes an individual's distinctive style of dealing with the world and reacting to people, situations, and events.

Primogeniture accords the common law right to the firstborn son to inherit the entire estate, to the exclusion of other siblings. In his special position as the future heir, he receives particular attention from parents as they attempt to prepare him for the leadership of the family and its business.

Product life cycles refer to the succession of stages a product goes through from its inception to when it becomes obsolete in a market. Four stages of product life cycle are introduction, growth, maturity, and decline following an S-shaped curve.

Progressive innovations are movements into adjacent markets, products or services, and related processes. These are extensions or continuations of the current business, involving limited liabilities of newness. Such innovations help maximize the benefits that can be reaped from the current levels of product/service, market, technical expertise, and experiences.

Push-pull theory of motivation for an entrepreneurial career path suggests that broadly speaking, individuals are either drawn or pulled toward entrepreneurship by the positive forces, or thrust into an entrepreneurial pathway by the push of negative forces in their environment.

Radical innovations are moves into significantly new industries, technologies, markets, or products/services.

Related or unrelated entrepreneurship refers to the degree of differentiation in terms of product/service and market scope of the new venture from existing family firms.

Revolutions are the transitional stages that involve substantial turmoil and quantum changes in organizational life.

Seed money or capital is the investment of funds to help start the business so that it can sustain itself for the period of development until it reaches a stage where it begins to generate funds or becomes attractive enough to obtain funding from other sources.

Shareholder council or assembly provides a venue for different types of shareholders to express their perspectives and understand those of others.

Social capital refers to the benefits the entrepreneur and the venture derives from a network of relationships. It consists of bridges and bonds. Bridges are the direct and indirect links of an entrepreneur with others, while bonds are deep-set relationships between individuals.

Social competence is the ability to interact with others effectively, to make a good first impression, to be persuasive, and to be emotionally sensitive.

Sociocultural trends relate to the social and cultural forces that are influencing the markets and the level of competition. Examples include increasing diversity in workplace, smaller household sizes, higher awareness and concern for natural environment.

Stakeholder map is a technique to plot the internal stakeholders in their respective positions on the three-circle model. The aim is to understand the reasons behind different perspectives of internal stakeholders and to identify who are the most salient stakeholders now and likely to gain power in the future.

Tacit knowledge is the nonverbal, non-codified knowledge that is difficult and sometimes impossible to communicate among individuals.

Technological trends refer to new products and services derived from intellectual property, advances in transportation, communication, and so on that affect the ways we live and work.

Value creation is the ultimate aim of an enterprise for the founders through a sense of accomplishment, growth, and achievement; for the family via a sense of harmony, security, and growth of the collective; for the business through sustained profits and growth; and for the community by satisfying customer needs while generating employment and contributing to societal prosperity.

Values are broad tendencies to prefer certain states of affairs over others and determine what an individual considers to be good or bad.

INDEX